PLEDGE OF
ALLEGIANCE

LAWRENCE MARTIN

PLEDGE OF ALLEGIANCE

The Americanization of Canada in the Mulroney Years

M&S

Canadian Cataloguing in Publication Data

Martin, Lawrence, 1947–
  Pledge of allegiance

Includes index.
ISBN 0–7710–5663–X

1. Canada – Relations – United States.
2. United States – Relations – Canada.
3. Canada – Politics and government – 1984–
I. Title.

FC249.M37 1993   971.064'7   C93–093149–1
F1029.5.U6M37 1993

The publishers acknowledge the support of the Canada Council and the Ontario Arts Council for their publishing program.

Printed and bound in Canada. The paper used in this book is acid-free.

McClelland & Stewart Inc.
The Canadian Publishers
481 University Ave.
Toronto, Ontario
M5G 2E9

To Maureen

Contents

1

"Brian Understands"

As they took their places at the cabinet table for a meeting of the National Security Council, the president's men had a good sense of the favour with which Ronald Reagan looked upon Brian Mulroney. With Mulroney's election in September 1984, it had been immediately apparent to them that a great friend of the United States had come to power in Canada and that the president would be most pleased. That same September, Richard Burt, the assistant secretary of state, wrote a memorandum to be used as the basis for a Reagan briefing. "Mulroney is the frankest advocate of pro-US positions to run Canada in thirty years," Burt declared.[1]

President Reagan quickly discovered the truth of this, and he established such a warm alliance with Mulroney that some of the purebred conservatives who surrounded him objected. They thought Reagan should be tougher in his treatment of Canada on issues such as military spending. They wanted an even deeper loyalty to Republican positions from Mulroney – even though the prime minister was already being attacked at home for his lap-dog comportment.

Because of the president's fondness for Mulroney, the hawks had been hesitant – until the National Security Council (NSC) meeting – to press their case too strongly. Caspar Weinberger, the secretary of defence, led their push. A driven, hard-ass right winger, he had quarterbacked the biggest military build-up in American history. He and colleagues, men whom Pierre Trudeau once labelled "Pentagon pipsqueaks," saw Canada's contribution to the free world's defence as trifling. Here was the second largest land-mass country in the world, they snickered, but you could fit its entire military on a football field and still have room for the game.[2]

Reagan had heard that dig. He'd also laughed heartily one day when his defence secretary opened a security briefing with another broadside. "Mr. President," Weinberger began, "the good news is that Canada has now surged ahead of Luxembourg in defence spending."[3]

The Pentagon's dissatisfaction extended to officials of other departments, notably to those on the Nicaragua desk in the State Department who were appalled by Canada's tolerance of the Sandinista government. Like the Weinberger circle, these officials made their views clear to the president's close adviser on Canadian relations, Tyrus Cobb.

A distant relation of the fabled baseball star of the same name, Ty Cobb was the special assistant for Canadian affairs on the NSC. The State Department was the country's formal instrument for foreign policy, but the NSC, operating out of the White House, enjoyed the advantage of proximity to the president's office. Cobb, then in his mid-forties, was a career military man, a Vietnam war veteran, and a lousy baseball player. He brought together the administration's views on Canada, prepared briefing papers for the president, and sat in on summit meetings. Because of his boss's lack of interest in detail, Cobb's work wasn't easy. Many wondered whether the president even bothered to read his briefing materials. For the former movie actor, what counted was the pictures not the print, and, for even the most weighty gatherings of heads of state, his preparation was suspect. In Williamsburg, Virginia, in 1983, Reagan had hosted the economic summit of the Western powers. In advance of the meeting, Chief of Staff James Baker gave him a sealed briefing book containing a summary of all the crucial discussion points. Baker then dropped by Reagan's suite just before the opening session, only to find the book still in wraps. As politely as possible he asked the president what had happened. "Well Jim," the Gipper casually replied, "*The Sound of Music* was on last night."[4]

In putting together briefing papers for the president, Cobb could only assume that he would read them. The NSC meeting preceded a summit meeting between Mulroney and Reagan early in Mulroney's stewardship. Cobb, who tended to agree with the hardliners, prepared briefing papers that employed unusually aggressive language in advising what Reagan should say to the prime minister. Reagan should push Mulroney hard, give him hell, Cobb's briefing papers said, especially on defence spending.

For the NSC session, almost all of the big power players in the administration showed up. Such an august assembly wasn't unusual, but many Canadians would have been surprised to learn of the degree of attention, for it hardly fit their idea of Canada as a Washington afterthought. They were accustomed to putdowns such as that in the *New Republic* magazine which, during a particularly dry season in Washington, opined, "It's so dull around here it's positively Canadian!" Not much had changed, Canadians believed, since the day in the 1950s when Lester Pearson emerged from a meeting with Dwight Eisenhower. Dismayed that Ike, the golfing president, claimed never to have heard of a pressing Canadian issue, Pearson grumbled to an aide, "You'd think his caddie would have mentioned it to him."[5]

Taking their chairs at the rectangular table before Reagan entered the meeting were the secretaries of state, defence, the treasury, and top representatives from almost all major departments along with Ty Cobb, who had forwarded his briefing notes to the Oval Office. Most often Ronald Reagan entered the cabinet room with a California breeziness and big-sky smile. The president would pump a few hands, exchange pleasantries, and pass out his favourite candy – jelly beans. He sought to put everyone at ease, and usually succeeded.

On this day, however, there was no smile or handshakes or small talk. This time the Gipper didn't pass around the candy. Gripping the toughly worded briefing notes, he walked purposefully to his place at the table and surveyed the group. "I'm not sure who wrote this," he angrily declared, "but I want you to understand one thing. I don't talk to Brian Mulroney this way."

A pause followed while some around the table nervously shuffled their documents. Looking for a place to hide, Cobb "sucked in" the rebuke.[6] He should have known better, he told himself. He should have considered the president's special attitude to Canada and to Brian Mulroney. Cobb had heard the president too many times, at too many meetings. "Brian understands," the Gipper would say. "I don't have to bring this matter up with him. Brian understands."

2

The Gipper's Vision

Ronald Reagan became convinced that "Brian understands" following the performance of the prime minister at the 1985 meeting of the Commonwealth nations at Nassau, in the Bahamas. Before this event there had been many signals. But the prime minister's outburst in defence of America at the Commonwealth conference left no doubt.

There, in a closed-door session, Brian Mulroney listened with growing irritation while Third World leaders repeatedly denounced Washington for imperialism, the nuclear arms build-up, and the North-South income gap. As the diatribes continued, Mulroney decided he had heard enough. Grabbing the microphone and summoning the low-octave power his voice so easily commands, he declared, "Let me tell you something about the United States!" There followed a tribute to the land of the brave and the free so fulsome, so glowing that American diplomatic cables from the conference fairly smoked with reports of it. These accounts, embellished in the retelling, made it back to the Oval Office. President Reagan heard in detail about how his Canadian friend had stood up for America, how he had beaten down the ingrates, how he had let them in on the truth about the greatness of the United States of America.[1]

From that moment on, Mulroney was golden in the Gipper's eyes. Though many disagreements on policy questions arose, at the personal level the bond was set. Those around the White House cabinet table who criticized Mulroney ran square into the Ronald Reagan wall. The president who prized anecdotes always had one ready for them – that of Mulroney among the infidels in the Bahamas. Reagan would play the scene back and he'd tell the antagonists to calm down. They should know, the Gipper would say, that "Brian understands."

This rapport with Mulroney, this fraternal trust, was of unusual significance because, unlike presidents before him, Reagan had a special vision of the North American continent. It was a vision he quietly promoted throughout his stewardship and one that held serious portents for his northern neighbour. In other times the vision wouldn't have amounted to much, but, by extraordinary coincidence, Reagan's tenure paralleled that of a Canadian leader who shared in the American dream.

Although the popular image of Reagan was of a shallow man – "if you walked through his deepest thoughts," quipped a congressman, "you wouldn't get your feet wet" – this weakness did not mean he suffered from a lack of ideas or commitment to them.

Appearances were deceiving. At meetings on Canada, the Gipper often looked like he was off in his own dream world. He seldom spoke. Sometimes he reached for a jelly bean, sometimes he nodded as if trying to indicate that he understood the discussion, sometimes he visibly sagged as if about to enter into a long winter's nap.

But while details failed to move Reagan, simple notions, like his blueprint for a Star Wars defence system, held him spellbound. No matter how many scientists testified to the contrary, Reagan could not be moved from his belief in a protective anti-nuclear weapons skydome.

When it came to his vision for North America, Reagan's ideas received far less attention than his Star Wars scheme, but they enjoyed a similar unwavering commitment. In his view, Providence had prescribed a singular role for the United States. It was the world's beacon of hope and freedom, the shining city on a hill. By virtue of its geographical placement, Canada, as Reagan saw it, was also blessed by Providence. It shared in the divine American mission. It was to be embraced in what Reagan termed a North American accord, a plan that saw Canada, the United States, and Mexico as an integrated unit, a family.[2]

The North American accord advocated shared energy resources, open commerce, and co-operation so intimate that Canadian observers would be allowed into U.S. cabinet meetings. In its ideal extension, it would bring about a continental federation or commonwealth of some kind. Geographically, the continent was one. The split that came with the American Revolution saw those loyal to Britain fleeing north to take refuge in what became known as Canada. Maybe, in Reagan's thinking, the schism that had endured ever since could be ended and the continent happily unified – if not in practical terms, then surely in spirit.

To give voice to this concept of a much closer continental unity was a bold step. Even though the inevitability of continental integration seemed written in almost every statistic of Canada-U.S. relations, no one was supposed to recognize the trend enthusiastically or recommend a speeding up of the process. Canadians had always frowned on such talk. A merging of the continent was viewed as possible only by hostile, never felicitous means. Prime ministers spoke of closer ties only gingerly, and mainly in the context of economic necessity. To do otherwise was to wound Canada's national pride.

In the first decades following Confederation, Canadians were suspicious of the covetous designs of presidents Grant, Harrison, and Teddy Roosevelt, all of whom saw merit if not practicality in Manifest Destiny, the doctrine invoking the United States' right "to overspread the continent allotted by Providence for the development of our multiplying millions."[3]

To Roosevelt, the most learned among them, the adoption of Canada made perfect sense. As Americans, Canadians "would hold positions incomparably more important, grander and more dignified than they can ever hope to reach."

The Canadian imagination didn't extend to the prospect of membership in the union to the south and the great benefits that could follow. Not considered by Canadians was the attractive mix that could be fashioned if Canada, as part of an American federation, could take the best the United States had to offer while maintaining the advantages of its own system – the social programs, the sane gun laws, the more peaceful racial climate.

The difference between the two countries was such that fifty-six years passed after Confederation before an American president set foot in Canada. If the first visit, the 1923 Vancouver stopover of Warren Harding, provided any kind of lesson to the Americans, it was to keep a distance. Harding cut short a game of golf after six holes, due to what was thought to be the beginnings of a heart attack. Dinner left him in worse condition – he suffered ptomaine poisoning and an acute gastrointestinal attack. He left Vancouver that night, collapsed during a speech in Seattle the next day, and died a week later.

Calvin Coolidge, best remembered for such profound utterances as "When people are out of work, unemployment results," never made it north of the border, and neither did Herbert Hoover. Franklin Roosevelt, who took an unusual interest in Canada, changed the course of the relationship. His productive rapport with Mackenzie King created a new warmth and led to the signing of pivotal bilateral defence and economic treaties at Ogdensburg, New York, and Hyde Park, New York, in the early 1940s. But Roosevelt's idea of North America never extended to Reagan's notion of a far-reaching, peaceful integration. Nor did the musings of Truman, Kennedy, Johnson, Nixon, and the rest, all of whom had cold wars to fight and Canada to take for granted.

Reagan began toying with his accord idea in the mid-1970s, and made it public with his campaign kick-off speech for the 1980 presidential election. "A developing closeness among Canada, Mexico and the United States – a North American accord – would permit achievement of that potential in each country beyond that which I believe any of them, strong as they are, could accomplish in the absence of such co-operation."

Canada's Pierre Trudeau, who returned to power in early 1980, was forging a nationalist energy policy that was the antithesis of continentalism. Reagan's proposal was dismissed in Canada and failed to gather momentum in his own country. He dropped it from his speeches, but after his election victory he took it up again. Before he was even inaugurated, Reagan attempted to hold meetings with the Canadian and Mexican leaders. The Mexican president, Lopez Portillo, went along, but Trudeau declined to attend. Reagan did get to Ottawa two months after his inauguration, but probably wished he hadn't bothered. The National Energy Program had soured relations, as had Reagan's withdrawal of a bilateral fisheries treaty from Senate consideration. The chill extended beyond the official level to ordinary Canadians, who stood on Parliament Hill jeering the Gipper's environmental and defence policies. No American president has been given a worse reception in Canada than Reagan on that day. It became so disrespectful that as Reagan concluded his remarks to the assembled crowd, Trudeau, no great fan of the Californian, felt compelled to take to the podium and admonish the placard-waving demonstrators. "Hey guys, when I go to the United States, I'm not met with these kinds of signs." He asked that they show some respect and give the president a big cheer. Some cheered, but most in the large crowd only booed more lustily than they had before. Reagan took refuge in the Parliament Buildings behind him.

It appeared then that Reagan's vision of continental integration was all but buried, consigned with so many other ideas to the category of forgotten flirtation. But the idea had seized his imagination. Joe Joeckel, a Canada-U.S. specialist who worked in the State Department, saw Reagan turn misty-eyed when speaking of it. "When he talked about the whole continent, he had a special glow."[4] Advisers who told him to forget the accord were ignored. "Quite frankly his advisers were all against it," said Ty Cobb. "They were saying 'Well, Mr. President, I'm not sure Canadians react too well to this, and there's not much enthusiasm for it here in America.'"

But as if aware that events might conspire in his favour, as if aware that a Brian Mulroney would come along, Reagan pressed on. In public he was discreet, conscious of Canadian sensibilities. "But behind the scenes, in meetings, he would keep at it," recalled Ty Copp. "He never backed away from the idea that this was the direction we ought to be moving in, that Canada was part of the family."[5]

3

A Star-Spangled Tory

Ronald Reagan sought and lost the Republican nomination for president in 1976. In the same year, Brian Mulroney sought and lost the leadership of the Conservative Party. Reagan remained in politics after his defeat while Mulroney embarked on a new career – working for the American empire.

Following his loss to Joe Clark, Mulroney contacted the board of Hanna Mining in Cleveland to inform its executives that he was still interested in the position they had previously discussed – running the Iron Ore Company of Canada. Shortly thereafter he was climbing the steps of IOC's Sherbrooke Street headquarters in Montreal. Big business, American and Canadian, was his new world.

Although new to it, and although the leadership defeat still ate at him, Mulroney moved easily in big-money circles. His urbane smoothness, his contacts, and his outward self-confidence saw to that. The corporate perks – the big salary, choice residence, company airplanes, company retreat – soothed the pain of his plunge in political esteem. Mulroney loved the perks, and it surprised no one that, once settled in at IOC, he set about upgrading them. The former IOC president hadn't had a chauffeur. Mulroney employed a chauffeur. The old, slow company aircraft was traded in for something more slick, something more like the beauty in which Mulroney streamed through the skies with Power Corp. chairman Paul Desmarais. The old offices were small and outfitted with dental-office furniture. Soon there was space, and soon the space brimmed with the right stuff.[1]

Style was important. To be important you had to look important. To this end Hanna Mining had helped provide Mulroney with a new executive home high up on Mount Royal, and Mulroney, delighted with the status it symbolized, loved to show it off. A story made the rounds about an acquaintance coming to town and asking him where he was living. Mulroney's eyes lit up at the question. "You know the mountain?" he asked. The friend nodded. "At the top," Mulroney declared. "Right at the fucking top!"[2]

Mulroney's day featured long lunches of cocktails and fine wines and brandies, with the odd bit of food thrown in. Often he ate and did his power-drinking at the stately Mt. Royal Club, located next door to his IOC offices. There, ever the stroker, the consummate networker, Mulroney kept the political channels primed. Relations with Joe Clark, the new Tory chief, were strained, but Mulroney had a pipeline to the Opposition leader's office in the person of J. Duncan Edmonds.

J. Duncan Edmonds was Clark's articulate, strong-voiced, senior policy adviser. He was also well known as a vocal proponent of continental integration. He was perhaps the leading Americanist in Ottawa. A graduate of the London School of Economics and adviser to the Liberals' Lester Pearson when Pearson was in opposition, Edmonds had become chairman of Public Affairs International, a powerful Ottawa lobbying and consultants' organization. There, working on a blueprint for the country's future, he became convinced of the coming integration of Canada and the United States. The lesson of history, Edmonds determined, was that integration was unavoidable. The key, therefore, was to recognize the obvious and forge a continental bond, a partnership with the Americans, that would be in Canada's best interests.

Edmonds' vision was similar to Ronald Reagan's North American accord. Specifically, Edmonds was proposing a Treaty of North America. Under this treaty free trade would be one component of a broad compact that would include new legal structures and binational bodies to harmonize the interests, economic and political, of the two countries.

Like Reagan, Edmonds found that this was a difficult brief to argue. No Canadian political party or leading political figure publicly favoured such an approach. But continentalism was an obsession with Edmonds. He buttonholed everyone around him. People who otherwise regarded him as a disciplined thinker wondered why he chose to pursue such an unpopular cause with the relentlessness of a carnival barker. After Ronald Reagan proposed his North American accord, Edmonds met with Richard Allen, a close Reagan adviser, to explore common ground. He found he had more in common with the American than with his own leader in Ottawa. Clark wasn't interested in full-blown continentalism – he thought, probably correctly, that it would be too politically contentious. Disappointed but undeterred, Edmonds took his campaign to other Tory frontliners. One of the places his hobby-horse led him was to the wood-paneled grandeur of the Mt. Royal Club and to Brian Mulroney.

As a defeated leadership candidate, Mulroney wasn't the best of catches for Edmonds. He wasn't even a member of the Conservative caucus. But he was still the only thing the party had going for it in Quebec. What's more, Mulroney's ascendance to the presidency of IOC suggested something to Edmonds: it suggested that here was a friend of the United States.[3]

In fact young Brian Mulroney had been firmly stamped with the American imprint. His instincts told him that the United

States was the promised land. As early as boyhood, and as late as the day in 1983 when he became leader of the Progressive Conservative Party, Brian Mulroney's chief source of income was the United States. It was a well-known feature of his biography (primarily because Mulroney himself liked to tell the story) that as a youngster he captured the favour of the American patron of his home town. That patron was Robert McCormick, the owner of the *Chicago Tribune* and the owner of the paper mill in Baie Comeau that was its lifeblood. When McCormick came to Baie Comeau, a children's choir, which included little Brian Mulroney, sang for him. McCormick was so impressed by Mulroney that he chose him to sing solos. McCormick or one of his lackeys would slip little Brian, just seven or eight years old, a big American bill for his work.

Mulroney moved on from Baie Comeau to attend college at St. Francis Xavier in Antigonish, Nova Scotia. Americans formed a considerable portion of the student population there, and Mulroney and Sam Wakim, who became a close friend, hung out with them. "Brian thought they were great," said Wakim. "I had a roommate who was American. Great guy. They were part of the gang. It was no big deal. There was not much difference between us and them. They were the same as us."[4]

Mulroney most closely identified with Americans of Irish descent. John Kennedy was elected president while Mulroney was in university, and this development, an Irish Catholic making it all the way to the top, spurred his ambition. He was an Irish Catholic whose parents were Mulroney and O'Shea. J.F.K. was an Irish Catholic whose parents were Kennedy and Fitzgerald. "I used to muse," Mulroney reflected when he had become prime minister, "that perhaps they had all been friends one day long ago and that they had known each other in the old country, before dreams came true on a continent far away. There must have been a connection, if only a sentimental one, to explain the strong, almost tribal admiration I felt for a leader I had never met."

He came to be more and more impressed by the cut and thrust of the American way – the every-man-for-himself ethic. As his old friend, and later adversary Lucien Bouchard described it, ambition for Mulroney was "shaped by a certain romanticism which led him to see a society to conquer rather than to change; and a world whose cruelty can be avoided by those who are shrewder or luckier than the rest." The United States, survival-of-the-fittest America, was where this drama was played out in bold gestures. America was where the winners were.

The people who gave Mulroney his entrée into the corporate boardrooms of the United States first spotted him in 1969 when he was practising labour law in Montreal. Mulroney impressed them as thoroughly as he had impressed Robert McCormick. The Iron Ore Company had a strike on its hands at the time and hired Mulroney to help reach a settlement. His work mightily pleased IOC president William Bennett, who was drawn by the splendid Mulroney mix of immaculate urban polish and down-home rural charm that appealed to so many. Bennett gave Mulroney a bonus of a big TV set for his work. The two were soon friends, and Mulroney, a vigorous bachelor, was soon dating Bennett's daughter, and before long there was something more: Bennett began eyeing him as a possible successor to head the company. In Brian Mulroney he saw the makings of an American branch-plant star.[5]

The Iron Ore Company of Canada was no run-of-the-mill branch plant. None other than C. D. Howe, the grand continentalist, the *bête noir* of Canadian nationalism, had been responsible for establishing the company.

In the early post-war years, when their natural resource stocks were depleted, Americans looked to Canada to fill the void. Enough oil, copper, iron ore, and zinc to last for generations lay north of the border, and in the resolute figure of Howe, the Americans had the man who would provide them with access to the vault. Howe so dominated the King and St.

Laurent cabinets that he was labelled the Minister of Everything. His industrial policy, that of unbounded American investment, drew fire from the nationalists who saw him as a maximum continentalist. They charged that Howe, born and raised in the United States, was turning Canada into an economic satellite of America and making it the most foreign-owned country in the industrialized world.

Howe's solution to the Americans' need for iron ore was in the vast, untapped resources of the far reaches of Quebec. In order to convince a group from Cleveland to set up operations in the province, he offered major incentives: accelerated depreciation and special breaks on allocations of steel. The result was the creation of the Iron Ore Company of Canada.

In the 1970s, the legacy of Howe was still strongly represented at the company in the person of William Bennett. The William Bennett who was to pluck Brian Mulroney from his barrister's office had served as Howe's right-hand man for C. D.'s entire political career. Bennett was Howe's private secretary, executive assistant, House of Commons adviser, speechwriter, plotter. Howe biographers Robert Bothwell and William Kilbourn wrote that, as Bennett grew older, "he acquired a certain uncanny resemblance to his boss. . . . It was as if he were a slighter, smoother version of the real thing."[6]

Howe and Bennett were early and avid supporters of free trade. In the late 1940s, Howe helped negotiate a comprehensive accord with the Americans but then saw the deal fall victim to one of Prime Minister Mackenzie King's many whims: in this case, a providential visitation. In his diaries King wrote of a "quite extraordinary experience which I took to be perfect evidence of guidance from beyond." He had picked up a book that had sat on his shelf untouched for two decades. From a chapter entitled "Soul of the Empire," he concluded that "for me to be placed in the position of being the spearhead of commercial union [with the U.S.A.] as the last act of my career would be to absolutely destroy the significance of the whole of it." To Howe and Bennett's dismay, King killed the plan. With a stroke of the pen, the course of history turned. The avid pursuit of continental integration would be left to someone else: the Montreal lawyer Bill Bennett had groomed to run the IOC.

By the mid-1970s Bennett had, in fact, begun to lose confidence in Mulroney. The more he got to know of the man, the less he liked. He was distressed, among other things, by Mulroney's seeking of the Tory leadership. But these second thoughts came too late; Mulroney had already greased the path to Cleveland. When his leadership campaign failed, he was able to get the IOC position.

When J. Duncan Edmonds, his interest in Mulroney aroused by this new branch-plant, CEO status, came to see him at the Mt. Royal Club it was in the spring of 1978. Lunch began in the leathered bar, where Edmonds' and Mulroney's chatter was interrupted by the appearance of Earle McLaughlin, the chairman of the Royal Bank and a high priest of the establishment. As McLaughlin came into view, Mulroney, always looking for the better chance, was quickly on his feet and across the room, calling the chairman "Earle," and laying on the big schmooze. "Good to see ya, Earle. . . . How are ya, Earle? . . . Hope you enjoy your lunch."[7]

After drinks, Mulroney and Edmonds moved into the swanky, old-money dining lounge, where waiters passed in penguin suits and lights glanced off their silver trays. Following their meal, the two men returned to the bar where they kept the brandy flowing until 3 p.m. At that time, Duncan Edmonds departed and emerged onto Sherbrooke Street, smiling. He'd heard Mulroney out, and he had become convinced that Brian understands. The IOC president gave the impression that he wanted to go in the direction Edmonds was charting. "He gave me the idea," Edmonds recalled, "that he was totally in favour, that it fitted his own experience and that it was something we had to be moving toward."

Mulroney wanted copies of Edmonds's proposed Treaty of North America to distribute among friends. He talked about how support might be developed in big-business circles and suggested a dinner for the business élite to discuss the treaty plan. Mulroney's enthusiasm faltered only once – when the election of 1911 was mentioned. Citing the defeat of free trade in that campaign, Mulroney remarked that there could be political difficulties in the revival of such a scheme. But Edmonds found Mulroney's knowledge of that campaign skimpy. He explained why the situation in 1911 was not comparable, and Mulroney appeared to agree.

In the months following their lunch, Mulroney phoned Edmonds at his Rockcliffe home in Ottawa for follow-up talks on continentalism, the foibles of Joe Clark, and other matters. Mulroney never introduced himself. Edmonds was expected to know it was Brian from the low lilt and timbre of the voice. As Edmonds saw him then, the young Montrealer was neither a big policy guy nor intellectually stimulating, but rather an engaging, winsome political operator. He sensed from the conversations, though, that Mulroney did understand the economic reality of power on the continent – he knew where the strings were pulled. Although Mulroney had not gone public with such pro-American positions, Edmonds felt that his love for America was deep-seated and no mere flirtation. He had reason to believe, moreover, that as the Americanization of Brian Mulroney continued, as his years at IOC extended his involvement in the U.S. corporate world, his commitment to continentalism would only grow stronger.

Indeed Mulroney's American business friendships flourished, and as he spent more time in the United States he learned how the American engine worked. He developed in a way that would lead the State Department, upon his election as prime minister, to describe him in private memoranda as a "loyal Ally" and to note applaudingly that he subscribed to American values. Undersecretary of State Richard Burt noted that whereas Pierre Trudeau liked to lecture and was only interested in scoring debating points, Mulroney took a more mature, positive approach, free of traditional Canadian insecurities over sovereignty. [8]

As IOC boss, Mulroney flew into small towns deep in Quebec, dispensing his company's largesse to the locals and presiding over their economic fate. He didn't have children's choirs sing to him, but he could not help but be reminded of the scenes from his boyhood when the American patron of Baie Comeau came to town. Now Mulroney stood in McCormick's shoes. Though not American, he was acting on the Americans' behalf.

Mulroney performed many good and charitable works while at IOC, including the spearheading of a fundraising drive for St. Francis Xavier University. For a big bite of the target sum of several million dollars, he called upon his big-business friends in the United States, some of whom had attended the school. Ken Taylor, the former Canadian ambassador to Iran who had helped American diplomats escape when Iranians took them hostage in 1979, assisted Mulroney in the effort. Taylor, a hero to many Americans, had moved on to New York to become Canada's consul-general. As he developed a wide range of contacts in big business, he noticed how easily Mulroney, who became a friend, moved in that milieu. Mulroney's contacts in Cleveland and New York were particularly impressive. Taylor found they were notably stronger with the traditional establishment types who felt they could affect public policy through the clout of their companies. "He was very comfortable in their presence," said Taylor. "I don't think he offended any of his conservative friends or associates by his ideas. But I don't think he saw the world in quite their terms. I think he brought a bit more of an embattled, small-town, rural type perspective."[9]

Though Mulroney would one day denounce the wave of junk bond buy-outs that swept America, Ken Taylor and others also saw in him a fine eye for the quick deal. Mulroney would have excelled in this area of the business world, Taylor concluded. "He was a wheeler-dealer himself. It's in his character."

One of Mulroney's good friends in corporate America was the spectacular rogue Ross Johnson. A Canadian expatriate who once sold light bulbs in Winnipeg, Johnson rocketed up the corporate ladder in America's bonfire-of-the-vanities decade, matching and surpassing the Americans in the big-money, leveraged buy-out, greed game. He gained control of RJR Nabisco (annual sales $17 billion) and ran it on whims and bourbon and song until his messy fall at the close of the decade. What mattered to Johnson were the perks and the power, and the games one played to get them. He surrounded himself with sports superstars, corporate jets, and the opulence of a king. Having known Johnson when he lived in Montreal, Mulroney and his wife, Mila, became fast friends with him and his wife, Laurie. The four of them would get together to "do" Manhattan and celebrate success.

Mulroney was never so flagrant as Ross Johnson, but the big leagues, taking the leap, making the deal, were all part of the American world in which he revelled. As for Canadian humility, as for self-effacement, reticence, and distrust of success, there was little evidence of this in the circles where the IOC president ran. Mulroney was the big-game hunter. Success and excess were what it was all about. Winning, in the American tradition, was everything, and losing could not be tolerated. Mulroney had once experienced losing big when he was beaten in the Tory leadership campaign, and it had almost crushed him. He wore the pain like a cross, and his rancour poured out in booze-drenched spasms. His rage was at its height when, after the convention, he had picked up a copy of *The Globe and Mail* to see a story alleging that his campaign had paid for hotel rooms for delegates, a practice that violated convention rules. While telephoning the reporter to deny the report, his voice cracked with emotion several times. Mulroney would pause, fight back the tears, and steady himself. Then he'd pour out another torrent of invective.

"We fought long and hard and we got fucked by the caucus," he shouted. "But I've never done anything dishonest in my life. And when you would take a seventh- or eighth-ranked echelon prick that I've never heard of in my life and . . ." That the story might mar his reputation almost shattered him. "You may not owe me anything. But, by fuck, you owe me the right to clear up my reputation. I lost this election but I lost it honourably and well. I've been an honest guy all my life and, by fuck, I'm not just a . . . [voice breaks]."

He explained his position on vote-buying. "Do you think, for Christ's sake, that if I was going to buy votes or I was going to buy hotel rooms that I'd do it through somebody or my people would do it through someone I've never met in my life? I mean Christ Almighty, it makes no sense. I'd do it through [here he mentioned two names from his campaign team]. Or I'd do it through, you know, somebody who would be discreet."

The dialogue closed with Mulroney, almost Nixonian in his anguish, breaking down. "All I've got in this life, all I have in this whole world is my professional reputation for honesty." He started to weep. "Jesus Christ, you've done me great harm."[10] He began another sentence, but, unable to complete it, hung up the phone.

As he did not have an abiding ideology or policy agenda, what drove Mulroney was the prestige of influence and power. When this, the driving imperative of his life, was threatened as it was by the leadership loss, little else remained.

That this highly skilled, star-struck performer would hit it off with Ross Johnson and later with Ronald Reagan, that he would see eye to eye with Duncan Edmonds and the American way for Canada, was simply a matter of instinctive attraction. "You've got to remember," said a former Mulroney aide, "that growing up in small-town Quebec he was part of a double minority or even triple minority situation."[11] He was an Anglo in a predominantly French town in Quebec, which was a minority in Canada, which, in turn, was a minority on the continent. Mulroney was a pebble at the foot of a mountain, on top of which stood the world beaters: the leaders of the United States. Canada was one thing. The real prize, however, the apex of ego gratification, would be to make it on a continental scale; to stand in the White House shoulder to shoulder with the president of the United States and survey the continental domain and suck in the rare air.

4

Declaration of Independence

In April 1972, when Brian Mulroney, the rising star of labour law, was charming Iron Ore Company executives and preparing to marry the perfect wife, Richard Nixon came to Ottawa.

The prospect of the visit elicited no enthusiasm. Nixon had no time for Trudeau, his private descriptive for the prime minister being a seven-letter word beginning with *a* and ending with *e*. Canadians felt similarly toward Nixon, viewing him as a force of darkness. Fearing protesters would pelt him with snowballs, Ottawa's public works department dispatched a platoon to hose down the Parliament lawns with steaming water until the snow melted away.

Nixon and Secretary of State Henry Kissinger were preoccupied with getting the United States out of Vietnam, and sandwiched Vietnam crisis meetings into their Ottawa agenda. Kissinger was also cultivating his swinging bachelor image at this time. He escorted Ottawa TV personality Charlotte Gobeil to a National Arts Centre gala, where the oozing Canadiana so bored him that he pleadingly asked her if it would ever end. When it did, Kissinger escorted the comely Gobeil to her home, only to be startled upon arrival to see her steady male companion emerge from the shower stall, bare as a pumpkin.[1] Meanwhile Bob Haldeman, Nixon's arrogant henchman, was fuming over Kissinger's disappearance and ordering his Canadian hosts around like minions.

This was hardly the smoothest of summits. In a peculiar way, however, the discomfort and angst were all rather appropriate. Trudeau and Nixon were getting together, not to sing hackneyed choruses of bilateral bliss over the world's longest undefended border, but to chart different directions for their countries.

Nixon stood in Parliament and decried past speeches of presidents and prime ministers as cliché-riddled bores, the result of which was to create "the false impression that our two countries are essentially alike."

Not about to add to the dross, Richard Nixon proclaimed, "It is time for Canadians and Americans to move beyond the sentimental rhetoric of the past. It is time for us to recognize that we have very separate identities, that we have significant differences, and that nobody's interests are furthered when these realities are obscured."

Canadian nationalists cheered. "No self-respecting nation," Nixon continued, "can or should accept the proposition that it should always be economically dependent upon another nation. Let us recognize for once and for all that the only basis for a sound and healthy relationship between our two peoples is to find a pattern for economic interaction . . . which respects Canada's right to chart its own course." He put it yet more emphatically. "Mature partners must have autonomous, independent policies."

If ever there was something approaching a declaration of Canadian independence from the United States, Nixon's speech was it. From the author of *détente* with the Soviet Union and *entente* with China came *realpolitik* for Canada. Nixon was cutting his northern neighbour free of American expectations.

His declaration came less than a year after Washington moved off the gold standard and imposed a 10 per cent surcharge on imports. Often exempted from such punitive trade actions in the past, Canada received no such immediate dispensation this time. The effect was to add to the momentum towards a redefinition of the way Canada and the United States did business together. Momentum had already been building. Canadian opposition to perceived American economic and cultural dominance had become more concerted as assassinations, racial tensions, and the Vietnam war soured attitudes toward the great republic. The governing Liberals had a strong nationalist core that asserted Canada's need to gain control of its economic destiny. As for the chemistry between the leaders, there was none. One was a flippant intellectual, the other a tense and brooding plotter who strolled the beach in San Clemente in black wingtips. No one could imagine these two men climbing on stage together to sing "When Irish Eyes Are Smiling."

Trudeau had come to the office of Prime Minister with a more sceptical view of the United States than that of either his predecessors or, it would certainly turn out, his successors. Unlike Brian Mulroney's attitude, which bordered on awe, Trudeau affected neutrality and occasional condescension. During their respective stewardships, public policy toward the United States clearly reflected their contrasting personal outlooks. Shaping the attitude of each were the telling experiences of youth. While the boy Mulroney had sat in the arms of his home town's American patron, charming him with renditions of "Oh Danny Boy," the young Pierre Trudeau had been barred from crossing the U.S. border. In the height of the cold war, Washington listed Trudeau as a potential subversive. He had travelled widely, visiting Communist China and the Soviet Union. In an era when Richard Nixon was accusing Helen Gahagen Douglas, his opponent in the 1952 California senate campaign, of being "pink down to the colour of her underwear," this fraternization with the Chinese and Soviets was crime enough to land Trudeau on the CIA's suspect list.

In his background, in his style, in his instincts, Trudeau was more European than American, and his policies reflected that penchant. When Nixon, who harboured none of Ronald Reagan's visions of a continental neighbourhood, suggested Canada could go its own way, Trudeau gladly took him up on it.

What began after the Nixon visit was perhaps Canada's last great experiment in nationalism, in charting a destiny that offered an appreciable degree of independence from the United States. The conditions were right – a mandate from Washington coupled with a mandate at home. An answer could be sought to the most pertinent of Canadian questions: was there an alternative future to that of continental integration?

External Affairs Minister Mitchell Sharp laid out the possibilities for Canada in his Three Options paper. Sharp offered the status quo as the first option, intensified Americanization as the second option, and diversification, the route of less dependence on America, as the third.

The status quo option gathered some support, notably among finance and trade bureaucrats, but the overwhelming choice was for the third option. What struck Sharp was the reaction to the proposal for further American integration. "It didn't get a single vote,"[2] said the veteran government man who had mulled over questions of trade and finance since as far back as the 1940s under King. No one in the cabinet, no one in the upper ranks of the civil service, no one in the Prime Minister's Office spoke out in favour of the option that would come to be the darling of the Mulroney decade. In the 1970s the second option was presumed dead. All the momentum was toward reducing the American influence, not increasing it.

The new nationalism was born in the years following the publication of Sharp's Three Options paper. It would come in two phases, and the commitment of the Trudeau team would be sporadic. In the first phase, before the introduction of the National Energy Plan (NEP) at the start of the 1980s, the government created the Foreign Investment Review Agency (FIRA) to screen principally American takeovers. It also created Crown corporations like Petro-Canada, and removed tax breaks for American publications as a way of promoting Canadian culture. The centrepiece, though, was the trade diversification measure – the establishment of a "contractual link" commercial agreement with Europe and Japan. Trade dependency on the United States, which was roughly 70 per cent, was to be appreciably reduced. Europe would be the big new customer.

The idea had been tried before. Ostensibly appalled at the one-way track Canadian commerce found itself on following the C. D. Howe era, John Diefenbaker announced a plan to shift 15 per cent of trade back to Britain. As with many of the Chief's plans, however, Business Britannia was born of sound and fury and came to signify nothing. There was little enthusiasm for the idea, and although the prime minister was typically enamoured of his own rhetoric, he didn't follow up on the plan.

The Trudeau Liberals were aware of the precedents and the problems. They knew that the advantages of dealing with the American market next door were too obvious and too alluring. They knew it was the biggest market in the world: a market where the same language was spoken and which spread the length of its 5,000-mile border. They realized that to alter such a long-established pattern of trade would require a Herculean effort from a staid government bureaucracy and from a historically parochial Canadian business sector.

External Affairs eagerly supported the third option. The pinstripers, the Europeanists, the mandarins whom Brian Mulroney would come to suspect deeply, tended to look upon Americans from a position of superiority. As members of the internationalist school with such prestigious predecessors as O. D. Skelton and Norman Robertson and Lester Pearson, the External men believed their country deserved more than membership in a continentalist enclave. John Halstead was one of them. He had old school written all over him. He was one of the department's foremost Europeanists, and he had used Nixon's imposition of the 10 per cent surcharge as the rationale for making the break and stopping continentalism. He was excited by the third-option idea, which he had helped to develop. Nothing was more important to him than taking the Canadian destiny out of American hands.[3]

However, a different view prevailed in the Trade and Finance departments, which saw the European diversion scheme as a dead loser. They worked to torpedo the third option before it had a chance to draw breath. It didn't matter that the third option was the official policy of the government; the civil servants had power, quiet power.

One leader of the third-option resistance was John Blackwood, who oversaw western hemispheric trade in the Department of Industry, Trade and Commerce. Born and raised on the southern edge of Manitoba, Blackwood was a border boy, brought up semi-American and conditioned, as he put it, to think semi-American. In this he was typical of many who would figure prominently in Canada's turn toward the United States. "Lots of us," Blackwood says, "came from parts of the country where the United States was a vital part of our lives." They concluded early on, says Blackwood, that "we are stuck with the Americans whether we like it or not."

He and other colleagues talked to business leaders and found no enthusiasm for the Trudeau initiative. "We'd talked to the big companies in Quebec and Ontario and they said they couldn't get into the European markets, that the Europeans would screw them by citing product standards and other roadblocks which would make their products ineligible." The Europeans were only interested in Canada's raw materials, which they were already importing in sufficient quantity. As for manufactured goods, argued Blackwood, as for Ganong's chocolates or Stanfield's underwear, it was a no go; the number of Euro-buyers would fit in a phone booth.

Convinced now that they were right, the Blackwood group still had to contend with the stuffed shirts, as they saw them,

over in External Affairs. They were looking for some sophisticated argumentation and were coming up dry until the day a
twenty-year-old summer-student employee walked in the door.
Summer students seldom did more than get coffee and try to
look earnest. However, this one had a keen interest in the third-
option question. He asked Blackwood if he could have some
computer time. He explained that by statistical analysis he
could demonstrate that the trade diversion plan was unreason-
able. At first Blackwood, only half-jokingly, responded,
"What's computer time?"

"You gotta remember," he says, "no one knew much about
computers in those days, including myself. But this kid was a
whiz on the stuff and so we thought, 'Hell, anything's worth a
try.'"[4]

The student was dispatched to the department's computer
room in Montreal. He took government, United Nations, and
European Community statistics, threw them all into the
blender, and came up with exactly what his Ottawa bosses
wanted: a flurry of charts and models pointing to the non-
viability of the European option. "It was stuff that I didn't
clearly understand," Blackwood says, "but which showed that
even with a massive effort you might move about 2 per cent of
our trade to Europe over five or ten years."

Armed with the printouts, Blackwood and company met
with the smooth talkers from External Affairs. When the External men started in confidently about how trade diversification
could be accomplished, the Blackwood crew was ready. They
unveiled their charts and graphs, calmly informing their opponents that they had their heads in the sand. Here was scientific
proof!

Ed Ritchie, the estimable diplomat who had been ambassador to Washington, sat on the other side of the table. "He ripped
the charts right out of one of our guy's hands," Blackwood
recalled. "Christ, were they pissed off."

As the meeting wore on, it was apparent that speculative

assertions of the External mandarins could not hold up against the ostensibly sophisticated data. Blackwood's ITC crew left the room smiling.

The confrontation was but one episode in the backstage drama to decide whether there was any way for Canada besides the American way. But the victory for the continentalists represented the direction the drama would take. "The trouble," said External's John Halstead, "was that almost all the people in the domestic departments were convinced that the U.S. was the only partner worth paying any attention to." As for seeking a new pathway to Europe, "they didn't even try."[5]

With no push from the government, Canadian business became even less inclined to take up the new direction. Like the bureaucrats, it saw the future, and the future was in the North American backyard.

5

Ottawa vs. Bay Street

Winston Churchill, it is written, quietly subscribed to the notion that capital should be made to be more the servant of the state than its master. With varying degrees of commitment, Trudeau and other Canadian leaders subscribed to the same thought. They believed that if Canada was to survive as an entity distinct from the United States, the power of Ottawa had to be used skilfully to balance the big-money forces in the continent's economic capitals.

Corporations, or "private governments" as philosopher George Grant called them, were by nature non-national. Since profit-making was the most important activity of the economically powerful, and since nationalism in a country such as Canada was seen to lessen market potential, it was not in the interest of big business to act with the integrity of the nation in mind. The conviction was best articulated by Grant. "No small country," he wrote in *Lament for a Nation*, "can depend for its existence on the loyalty of its capitalists."[1]

By the 1980s, when the era of globalization set in, the phrase frequently heard was, "business no longer carries the flag." Grant was being made to look prescient. He had been convinced that, if left to their own devices, big-business forces in

Canada and the United States would mesh, the values of the two countries would mesh, and eventually nothing would be left of Canada but the formality of the border line.

His case against C. D. Howe and the continentalist Liberals of the 1940s and 1950s was that they had marched down this very road. They didn't use any balancing power. In the nationalist view, the American-bred Howe, insensitive to the significance of Canada's control of its own economy, had made a scorched-earth run for the big American dollar. Like any businessman the priority for the Minister of Everything was the bottom line. Progress was measured in economic growth, and the best prospects for growth were in integration with the biggest, richest market in the world, right next door. In order to grow, Canada had to Americanize.

Even the nationalists conceded that under Howe's open-floodgate investment policy, the American-spurred growth was impressive. Canada had moved from being a largely agricultural country in the 1930s to being a thriving, industrialized economy by the mid-1950s.

For the nationalists, however, if continued growth meant continued Americanization, it could only mean the end of Canada. In the global economy, with trade barriers tumbling and with an ever-deepening interdependence of economies, big-money interests would win out over national interests. The idea of creating an alternative, better society north of the forty-ninth parallel would gradually be given up, the process of surrender would be furthered with the arrival of the first post-Howe government to let Bay Street and American values predominate. The question put by the distinguished journalist and historian Bruce Hutchison would then be answered. In his book *The Struggle for the Border*, Hutchison asked: "Could a nation conceived in vague compromise and dedicated to the defiance of continental logic endure? Would Canadians permanently pay the price set by nature for their endurance? Or . . . would they admit defeat, accept the logic, liquidate the national experiment and fall piecemeal into the embrace of their rich American neighbours?"[2]

The federal governments of Canada always had to choose between the prospect of a distinct nation and the prospect of more wealth, between the national agenda and the continental agenda. Remarkably, most of them chose the former, repeatedly asserting the balancing power of government, and repeatedly defying the free-market economic logic of continentalism in order to build and maintain a distinct nation.

Over time Ottawa's activism imposed an east-west infrastructure over the continent's natural north-south economic pull. The activism came in the form of tariffs, regional development programs, east-west transportation systems, a national broadcasting network, and a social welfare system which the United States did not offer. Much of the east-west overlay did not always make economic, bottom-line sense. But the idea was that a price had to be paid to be un-American, that only a vigorous central government could give the country its form and substance and glue. A country needed symbols and tariffs and standards to hold it together and make it a unit. In a domain so vast and thinly populated as Canada, the American free-market model would dissipate any sense of national identity.

Canadian leaders suspected all along that more wealth would be accrued through quicker integration with the American economy. Even Robert Borden, the Conservative leader who toppled Wilfrid Laurier and his free trade proposals in 1911, appeared convinced of it. That he wasn't at all sure he was doing the right thing in opposing free trade was evident in a notable remark to a friend. Referring to a statement by President William Taft, who said that if Canada did not move commercially closer to the United States, it would be forever locked into a disadvantageous trading system, Borden said: "The most serious feature of Taft's utterances is their profound truth."

As early as 1854, Canada entered into a modified reciprocity arrangement with the United States, only to have it annulled by the White House twelve years later. George Brown went to Washington in 1874 to negotiate another such deal, but failed. Laurier failed in 1911, and Mackenzie King pulled away from an agreement in 1948. To a degree therefore, it was only fate and happenstance that prevented a more complete continental integration before the 1980s. But to a greater degree it was support for the belief that free-market continentalism does not a nation state make.

What gave Brian Mulroney pause in the early 1980s, when he turned away from the lessons of history, was the knowledge that among earlier prime ministers it was those from the Conservative Party who most aggressively championed the anti-continentalist course. By and large the Tories had been the Canada-first crowd, and the Grits, until the 1960s, had been the continentalists.

The fear of annexation, assimilation, and integration had been a major factor in the formation of the Canadian union in 1867. The challenge for Canada then was to wean itself off the fading superpower, Britain, and at the same time maintain its independence of the ascendant superpower, the United States.

Maintaining Ottawa's independence of Washington became a driving imperative of successive Conservative leaders. John A. Macdonald's trans-Canada railway and tariff wall kept out the American influence. While privately sceptical, Borden, the next Tory prime minister, stayed the course on nationalism. In 1921 the sonorous-voiced Arthur Meighen campaigned against Mackenzie King with a high-tariff policy. Meighen's trade policy was to match Washington "brick for brick" in building a protectionist wall.

R. B. Bennett was a Bay Street Tory, an aristocrat whose shoes, as one writer put it, "not only glisten but gloat." But his pro-business bent did not presuppose a pro-American bent. Bennett, who was very British in orientation, forged such national institutions as the CBC, maintained a great distance from the White

House, and avoided liberalized trade negotiations with Washington until undergoing a deathbed conversion.

Diefenbaker, who promoted Canadian independence with evangelical zeal, recklessly wielded Ottawa's balancing power. "We are a power, not a puppet," the Chief thundered during the controversy over the placement of American nuclear warheads in his country. "I want Canada to be in control of Canadian soil. Now if that's an offence I want the people of Canada to say so!" His thrust was east-west, also north – any direction but south. As well as advocating a trade diversion to Britain, Diefenbaker explored an Arctic option. He invoked, with great futility as it turned out, the grand vision of the North. "The North with all its vast resources of hidden wealth; the wonder and challenge of the North must become our national consciousness." His fear of American dominance provoked bitter confrontations with John Kennedy over the Cuban missile crisis, the issue of nuclear warheads on Canadian soil, and other questions. In the end his rampant nationalism alienated the entire ruling class: Bay Street, Wall Street, his civil service, and politicians from all parties, including his own. Only small-town and rural Canada supported Diefenbaker. Grant, who readily acknowledged that the Tory leader's own foolhardiness contributed to his downfall, credited the Chief with the strongest stance against satellite status ever attempted by a Canadian. This stance came with a high price, however. A harsh statement issued by the Kennedy administration contradicted Diefenbaker's positions on nuclear arms and NATO, touching off a Commons furore which led to the defeat of the Tories on a non-confidence motion. In Washington they cracked open the champagne. McGeorge Bundy, one among the best and the brightest who had had a hand in drafting the statement, wrote a memo some years later to President Lyndon Johnson. "I might add that I myself have been sensitive to the need for being extra polite to Canadians ever since George Ball and I knocked over the Diefenbaker government by one incautious press release."[3]

The one chorus that rang loudly from the Tory policy makers was No to free trade / No to integration. In what might be seen as a vindication of their approach, the Liberals altered course under Pearson and Trudeau and raised the nationalist banner. Pearson didn't share Diefenbaker's anti-American vehemence on some aspects of foreign policy, but he did enact much of the social security legislation which gave Canada a more distinct, compassionate character than its neighbour. Pearson brought in Walter Gordon, who became minister of finance in 1963 and a great champion of the balancing power. Adhering to the Churchill dictum, Gordon determined to make capital the servant of the state – not its master. Set on regaining economic sovereignty, he brought in a budget with a 30 per cent takeover tax to be levied on sales of shares in Canadian companies to foreigners. The measure caused such an uproar, led by an apoplectic Bay Street, that it had to be withdrawn within days. Gordon said that in acting to maintain its independence, Canada "was no different from the British, the French, the Swiss, or the people from other countries, including the United States. Some may call this nationalism and so it is."[4] Like Diefenbaker, Gordon drove the business barons mad. Another one of his proposals, that subsidiaries be forced to sell 25 per cent of their equity stock to Canadians, was regarded by industrialist E. P. Taylor as "absolute nonsense, contrary to good business principles, unnatural and monstrous."

The nationalists argued for a distinct English-Canadian society. That their views were seen as unnatural and monstrous was suggestive of the degree of opposition they faced. The experiences of Diefenbaker, Gordon, and Pearson demonstrated the dangers for Canadian politicians who tried to wield the balancing power. Bay Street, Wall Street, and the monied interests backed by the White House constituted a formidable force. In the end, the White House had prevailed against Diefenbaker – knocking him over, in the words of Bundy. Before long, Bay Street and Wall Street knocked over Walter Gordon, forcing his retreat. And in one of the most infamous moments in Canadian-U.S. history, Lyndon Johnson didn't exactly knock Lester Pearson over, but rather, in response to his criticism of LBJ's bombing of North Vietnam – a show of independence on foreign policy – Johnson took him by the shirt collar on the porch at Camp David and lifted, all the while roaring profanities that could be heard in the next county.

In the context of these precedents, Nixon's 1972 speech granting Canada a freedom of sorts in the exercise of nationalism was important. This latitude would endure, by and large, throughout Ford's presidency and into Carter's. But while the Grits made some use of this freedom, in the 1970s they never became excessively nationalistic or automatically antagonistic to the United States. Trudeau at first showed erratic and only moderate commitment to nationalism. He realized that, third option or not, American ties were of overwhelming importance. At the personal level, Trudeau was respectful and proper with the presidents in the pre-Reagan years. No matter what he and Nixon said behind each other's back, they were professional in their dealings. In Ford, the Canadian PM faced a distinctly unintellectual counterpart, whose questionable pronouncements included the memorable: "If Abe Lincoln were alive today, he'd probably roll over in his grave." But Trudeau developed a leisurely rapport with Ford, and they took to skiing together. For Jimmy Carter, Trudeau had an abiding respect, and though they communicated infrequently, he saw much that was honourable in the Georgian's earnest, studious approach.

By the end of the Carter presidency it was apparent that Trudeau's new trading initiative with Europe was not succeeding. The predictions of John Blackwood's summer student were coming to pass. As for the Foreign Investment Review Agency, the other main item on the third-option menu, the effects were more symbolic than real. In fact if there was any success for the nationalism of the 1970s at all, it was in the area of symbolism.

Symbolism was important. Countries endure on myths and symbols. Not many Canadians knew bilateral trade and economic statistics, but they had a sense of whether the PM was standing up for the nation. No matter if the reality was different, Canada, as Teddy Roosevelt had noticed, had to be seen to be acting the role of an independent country. "Canadians," Roosevelt remarked, "like to indulge themselves as a harmless luxury in a feeling of hostility to the United States. Practically, this does not operate at all. Practically, Canada will take an American, Van Horne, to run its railway system and America will take a Canadian, Hill, to run its."

The symbolism was fine, but after their re-election at the beginning of 1980, the Liberals wanted to do something of tangible significance. On October 28, 1980 – this so perfectly ill-timed as to be one week before the election of the president who favoured a North American accord – the Grits came forward with their most ambitious nationalist measure of all: the National Energy Program.

The goals of the program were to make Canada self-sufficient in energy, to increase Canadian ownership to 50 per cent in what was a primarily foreign-owned sector, and, very much in keeping with the balancing power, to secure federal government paramountcy over resource policy. If the third option wasn't working as a result of the measures taken in the 1970s, there were other ways for Canada to gain command of its destiny. The program was one of the most striking pieces of Canadianization ever attempted. This was a nationalist's dream, the stuff that George Grant and like-minded patriots longed for. Public support for the NEP soared. It had ego appeal. Opinion polls registered an unheard of 80 per cent approval rating. Plans called for sons of the NEP, extending the same principles to other foreign-dominated sectors of the economy. The nation would be bought back, satellite status forgotten.

But the NEP came a decade too late. Its success was predicated on a continued increase in world oil and gas prices –

something that almost every expert agreed was likely. The program also needed an understanding attitude from the Oval Office. Both conditions were present in the early 1970s. Both were absent in the early 1980s.

The 50 per cent ownership level targeted in the NEP was thoroughly modest compared to the Americans' 82 per cent control of their own petroleum sector. American officials conceded that this was so, but were still outraged at the methods Ottawa was employing to attain its goal, particularly the so-called back-in provision, which gave Petro-Canada a retroactive 25 per cent equity interest in each oil and gas development on Canadian lands. Incensed corporate American interests, especially early participants in the Hibernia oil project off the coast of Newfoundland, found a ready audience in the business-friendly Reagan administration. Unlike Nixon's approach, no recognition of Ottawa's right to pursue "autonomous independent policies" sounded from the Republican administration of the early 1980s when Trudeau ruled Canada. The new attitude in Washington was more akin to that in the times of Diefenbaker and Pearson: that is, when Canadianism gets out of line, when the balancing power is being wielded too enthusiastically, slap the Canadians around a bit until they get it right. Accordingly, on March 5, 1981, Secretary of State Alexander Haig sent Canada a formal note growling about unnecessary discrimination against American interests. It was backed by a threat. "Should the balance of concessions be disturbed, the United States would be obliged to consider how a new balance might be achieved."[5] The pressure from the White House continued to the point that Ottawa considered sending home American ambassador Paul Robinson. Enraged at the NEP, Robinson was stumping Canada like a mad elephant. Just how serious the Americans took the NEP was indicated in a cable from his embassy. It compared the NEP to France's Maginot Line of World War II. The gist of the memorandum[6] was that though the nationalist energy program had the look of a great fortress against American penetration, it would, just like the Maginot Line, crumble, fall, and be overrun. American oil interests would get their way.

The pressure mounted with loud opposition to the energy plan from the West, particularly from Alberta, which thought Ottawa was robbing it of oil windfalls. Ottawa modified the NEP so that in some instances compensation was given to American oil companies; but more importantly, movement on the sons of the NEP policy slowed and eventually halted.

Other factors came into play. One of the developments sparking the embassy's cocky Maginot-Line memorandum was the drop in world oil prices. As prices fell, interest in the development of Canadian energy sources did the same. Americans left the oil patch in droves. In a development of considerable significance for the country, the huge projected federal revenues from oil developments never materialized, leaving a giant hole in the federal treasury. This contributed to the running up of a deficit and a national debt that would hamstring the succeeding Tory government from day one. In 1991 Marc Lalonde, the author of the NEP, was still lamenting what had transpired. "We would have had no deficit today if the price of oil had gone where it was predicted to go."[7]

The deep recession compounded the energy plan's troubles. The state of the economy increased pressure on the Trudeau government to repair relations with the United States. The business community had had enough of nationalism. Michael Pitfield, Pierre Trudeau's top-gun civil servant, learned a lesson during his many years of service that he would recall as a senator watching Mulroney and the Tories. "Business thought it was bad form for us to make a calculation of our self-interest as a nation," he said. "The bulk of Canadians are easy prey to the business community in this country and to U.S. interests. They can quite easily shake a bag of gold and make it difficult."[8]

Complementing Trudeau's nationalism on energy policy was his strongly independent stance through the early 1980s on foreign affairs. Although he was under considerable pressure from the White House to fall in line like a good NATO footsoldier, Trudeau opposed the Americans on arms spending, Star Wars, Nicaragua, Soviet policy, and the invasion of Grenada. Mulroney wondered as he looked on, first from his IOC boardroom and later as Opposition leader, how anyone could treat their most important ally in this way. He was particularly appalled by the failure to support the Americans on Grenada.

Trudeau's final affront to the Reagan hardliners came with the launching of his world peace mission to pressure the White House and the Kremlin to the bargaining table. Believing the Soviets could reform their ways without being forced into a stand-off, the prime minister often took a neutral approach that shocked Republicans. In Ottawa he frequently lunched with Soviet Ambassador Alexander Yakovlev. "I liked caviar," said Trudeau, "so I went." In fact, he sensed Yakovlev had important things to say, and indeed, Yakovlev was later recalled to Moscow by Mikhail Gorbachev to become a father of *glasnost.*

The Trudeau peace mission became too much for the Reagan administration. Lawrence Eagleburger, the undersecretary of state for political affairs, decried the Trudeauvian comportment as something "akin to pot-induced behaviour by an erratic leftie." More remarkable than this slam itself, recalled Michael Pitfield, was the reaction to it by the barons of Canadian business. They cheered. "They picked it up and used it against us," said Pitfield. "It was typical."[9]

While Trudeau did maintain autonomy in foreign policy, and while his Liberals fought to keep the NEP afloat, it became obvious that this latest phase of the third option was hardly more successful than the efforts of the 1970s. Canadian ownership of its energy sector did increase, but the dive in oil prices crippled the policy and the industry, leaving the NEP without credibility. After more than a decade of third-option experimentation, the Liberals were faced with a depressing bottom line. For all their efforts they had only held the line on continental integration, and had not begun to reverse the trend. Liberalization of world trade, realized in decisions of the General Agreement on Tariffs and Trade (GATT), for example, had offset programs like FIRA and had resulted in an overall increase in trade dependence on the United States since Trudeau's arrival.

At the same time something else was at work to undermine Canada's progress toward a distinct society. For all its nationalism, the Trudeau government had brought in a measure which over the long run could very well serve to be one of the major steps in the Americanization of Canada. The Liberals' decision to include the Charter of Rights and Freedoms in a patriated constitution was a body blow to the impulse of collectivism that had helped unite the country. A hallmark of Trudeau's Canada and of his policy-making was the maintenance of a strong central government. The Charter was a strong decentralizing force. It would spawn special-interest groups, lobbyists, factionalized parties. It would make citizens more rights-hungry and wary of responsibility; citizens who embraced an individualism that was more American than Canadian.

By 1983, when Brian Mulroney was crowned leader of the Conservative Party, the nationalist will of the Grits was fading on most fronts. The country wanted economic growth. Third-option policy-making had not succeeded in providing it. A tried-and-true formula for growth was Americanization. The second option would get a second look.

6

Thunder Bay's Big Boys

"There's a real beauty for you," crooned Brian Mulroney, oozing with sarcasm on a hot, wind-whipped spring day in June 1983. "Now there's a real honey – free trade with the Americans!"

The candidates for the leadership of the Progressive Conservative Party were moving into the campaign's final days, and the mellifluous-voiced Mulroney – looking good, looking Robert Vaughan handsome – was in Thunder Bay, Ontario, poking fun at rival John Crosbie. The Newfoundlander, his support surging as the convention date approached, had staked out some highly pro-American positions. Spotting an opening, Mulroney attacked Americanization.

"Free trade with the United States is like sleeping with an elephant," Mulroney shouted, invoking the simile popularized by Pierre Trudeau. "It's terrific until the elephant twitches, and if the elephant rolls over, you are a dead man."

And, "I'll tell you when he's going to roll over. He's going to roll over in times of economic depression and they're going to crank up the plants in Georgia and North Carolina and Ohio and they're going to be shutting them down here."[1]

The highballs with J. Duncan Edmonds at the Mt. Royal Club were long forgotten. So were Mulroney's pro-American instincts. He wasn't finished: "That's why free trade was decided on in an election in 1911," said Mulroney. "It affects Canadian sovereignty, and we'll have none of it, not during leadership campaigns, nor at any other times."

The speech of the IOC boss was to delegates who would be attending the leadership convention. The business done, he travelled to the Thunder Bay airport where he stood on the tarmac, his eyes moving restlessly. His wife, Mila, came into view, and a reporter, reaching for conversation, made a complimentary remark. Mulroney instantly brightened as he looked over at Mila. "Isn't she great?" he exclaimed. "Isn't she fantastic?"

For a moment he seemed relaxed, but the anxiety of ambition that so frequently gripped him was soon apparent. Mulroney bears tension in his upper back, and when he is feeling stress his shoulders rise like a slow elevator. Now, as the conversation moved back to Crosbie and the campaign, they began their ascent.

On the plane he was seated between the reporter and Mila. "What do ya think?" he asked the journalist of his chances. "Really close," came the reply. "The candidate who performs best at the convention will win it. You'll need a real stemwinder there."

"I'll give them a stemwinder!" Mulroney said determinedly. His hands were tightly squeezing the black leather armrests. His wife placed her hand on his, and whispered to him. His shoulders lowered and he sank into his seat and he closed his eyes.

When he heard the news of Mulroney's opposition to Crosbie's continentalism, J. Duncan Edmonds was puzzled. For a time he had thought he might have two of the frontrunners for the Tory leadership aboard his all-American bus. Not now. In high-level politics it was not unusual for a candidate to change position and play to the perceived audience, but Mulroney's apparent switch-over bothered Edmonds. "It was a complete contradiction of what he said to me and what his view was, given his relationship with the Iron Ore Company."[2]

Crosbie, on the other hand, impressed Edmonds for publicly coming forward. Crosbie's American inclination had been bred in the bone. His father, Chesley A. Crosbie, campaigned for the union of Newfoundland with the United States in 1948. He was viewed as the annexation man. A union, the elder Crosbie had said, would mean "the difference between proud prosperity and a frugal livelihood." He saw it as being "only a matter of time before Canada too will be compelled to seek a similar Union with the United States."

Like the others, like the border-boy Tories who would push for the new continentalism, young John Crosbie was raised in a very pro-American environment. "Americans were far more popular in Newfoundland than Canadians," he recalled. "So I was never as hung up about the United States. There's always seemed to be a hang up with the Toronto cultural literati about the U.S. But that's never been the feeling in Newfoundland or Atlantic Canada."[3]

Aware of Crosbie's sympathies, Edmonds had set out to recruit him for his continental integration crusade. They met for dinner at the stately Royal Ottawa Golf Club, and it was soon apparent to Edmonds that this blunt, pugnacious Newfoundland MP bore some hereditary stamp. He wasn't propounding annexation, but he saw the Canadian future and the stars and stripes were writ large in it.

During Crosbie's leadership campaign, Edmonds helped him develop a policy of liberalized trade with the United States as part of his platform. Some of Crosbie's senior supporters, in particular the portly Jean Pigott, were nervous about the idea, and it received less billing than was initially planned. Jean Pigott and her sister Crete owned a bakery in Ottawa. They fretted that free trade might well signal the end of Pigott pastries.

For years it hadn't been safe to discuss free trade, but Crosbie sensed the public attitude was changing. Not one of the serious contenders, however, not Clark, not Mulroney, not Wilson, not one from the party hierarchy, agreed with him. This group, which would be singing the praises of free trade a couple of years later, now looked on Crosbie's leanings as entirely misguided. Such an embrace of the United States was not only an affront to Tory tradition, but, as Mulroney indicated in Thunder Bay, there was a sense in the party that the country wasn't ready, that the elephant would roll over and crush its bedfellow.

It was a notable coincidence that Mulroney chose Thunder Bay for his anti-free trade outburst. This was the old home of the patron of Mulroney's company, and C. D. Howe might not have been amused to hear such un-American sentiments from an IOC president. After spending his youth in New England, Howe came to Canada and taught at Dalhousie University in Halifax. He then moved west and made a fortune in the grain transportation business in Thunder Bay (then the twin cities of Port Arthur and Fort William) before taking up politics.

While he didn't know it then, Mulroney was also preaching that day on the turf of another strong continentalist, a man whose pro-American views would rock the External Affairs establishment in Ottawa and spearhead a shift in the department away from its European tradition. The metamorphosis of a country such as Canada required a consensus among the members of the ruling class – the politicians, big business, the upper echelons of the civil service. The man who brought the most resistant faction of the civil service into the fold was Derek Burney. Burney, a key Mulroney lieutenant, figured centrally in the birth of the new continentalism.

At the time of Mulroney's Thunder Bay speech, Burney was an ascendant force in External Affairs, heading up a trade policy review for the department. He hadn't shown all his cards at this time, but he had begun quietly moving away from the Pearsonian internationalist school and was developing a vision of

Canada as a nation of the Americas. He believed that if Canada was to succeed, it had to end its European flirtation and come to grips with its geographical destiny.

Not of the typical diplomatic cut, Burney was a big, craggy, heavy-footed man who projected power and a hunger for more of it. He was direct and tough. His look and style was that of a guy who ran a steel mill, not a wing of External Affairs. "The good thing about Derek," observed Michael Hart, who worked with him for many years, "is that he tells you to your face you're full of shit. I mean, most of the stabbing is done in the back around here."[4]

Burney grew up in the Fort William half of Thunder Bay, not far from the Minnesota border. C. D. Howe and the constituency he represented in Parliament were across the way in Port Arthur. Nevertheless, Howe and the American connection were never far from Burney's mind. He was very much a border boy. "I worked the pulp and paper mills and grain elevators as a kid, so I was sure as hell conscious of trade and trade links to the United States. Absolutely."[5]

Burney never sang for C. D. Howe. But the picture presented to him as an ambitious youth was not so different from the one presented at the same time to Brian Mulroney then growing up in Baie Comeau. "I saw these big paper rolls going to the *Cleveland Plain Dealer* and the Chicago papers," Burney said. He knew early that what made the Fort William/Port Arthur economy hum was what kept Baie Comeau humming as well – the American engine.

He was of Conservative stock, something that set him apart from many in his department, and was brought up with the winning-is-everything creed. His father, George, sat on the city council in Fort William and ran Burney's Taxi. George Burney, a committed Conservative, was thrilled one day when John Diefenbaker, not yet party leader, came to town and he was asked to go to the airport to meet him. George Burney died when his son was eleven, but a lasting memory for young

Derek was of his father coming home that night. He was aglow, bursting with pride at having just met the great John Diefenbaker.

Derek Burney was always a doer. At high school, Fort William Collegiate, he was president of the students' council, performed the lead role in the school play, and participated in just about everything that counted. "He runs the building," the school yearbook said. "Just ask him and he'll tell you so."

As a teenager Burney campaigned for Conservative candidates in his home town. At Queen's University in the late 1950s and early 1960s, he joined the Progressive Conservative student club. Intrigued by Diefenbaker, who was at the time being befriended by a teenage Brian Mulroney, Burney wrote one thesis on the Chief and the Conservative Party and another on the debate over placing nuclear warheads on Canadian soil. For the latter, he journeyed to Ottawa to interview Flora MacDonald, who worked at party headquarters and who was impressed by young Derek's eagerness and pragmatism.

Burney had an eye for politics, but neither the Conservative leader nor Pearson of the Liberals captured his imagination. Both appeared at campus rallies. Pearson, Burney recalls, arrived tired, could barely make it through his speech, and was more concerned about learning the score of that night's hockey playoff between Montreal and Toronto than anything else. A party official periodically walked through the crowd with a placard updating the score. Pearson interrupted his speech. "Give me a look at that, will ya?"

In contrast, Dief rolled into town full of piss and vinegar. His thunderstorm oratory rocked the auditorium. On one side he faced rows of yellow-jacketed Queen's students who heckled him mercilessly. On the other sat a large group of Dief-defenders, senior citizens who had been bussed in to provide the old warrior with some support. Dief's gambit this night was to pull out a piece of paper, a communication from Defence Secretary Robert McNamara, suggesting that Bomarc missiles stationed in Canada would make Canada the target of a Soviet attack before the United States. This sent the Chief into full flight, alleging that Canada was being used by the Americans as bait. "I have this paper!" he roared. "I have this paper! We were decoys! Decoys!"

Burney watched the seniors taking in the Chief's every word. "Yes John," came their devout response. "Yes John." Then they turned their wrath on the uppity, disrespectful students. "Get out! Get out!" the bluehairs chanted. "Get out! Get out!"

It was grand theatre, but the low level of political discourse turned Burney off the idea of a political career, and he chose instead a place where the prestige, particularly in those days, was high – the Canadian foreign service. The diplomatic route took him to New Zealand, Japan for a long stretch, and to South Korea as ambassador, before he returned home to move into trade and American affairs.

To his new beat he brought new attitudes. His Fort William youth had taught him the importance of the American market, and his long experience in Asia built upon it. "The message was that the forces of competition in the world were coming and we'd better get ready. What Japan was achieving, what Korea was about to achieve, gave a very clear message to me that the status quo was not going to satisfy Canada's stake in the international trading world."

Having tried to promote Japanese and Korean interests in Canada, Burney felt he knew how out of step some of Canada's industrial sectors had become and realized that the country's 1950s-style economy had no staying power. He also learned the importance of developing winners, of niche marketing. "You can say the Japanese are planned protectionists but they are really niche marketeers to the ultimate. They go after a market, they dominate it, they capture it."

Burney believed that Canada had to develop niches of its own. But the key question was where? In what market? This is what made Derek Burney a second option man. "We could do that within North America, within the relative confines of an even North American playing field. But we would not be able to do it in the global market on our own. There, we could not do it."

In External he found his colleagues' minds stuffed with notions of third options, NEPs, and FIRAs. "You had a lot of guys who had designed these policies who were still hanging on to strips of one form or another. And we had the traditional Canadian reserve of how close can we get to the United States without losing ourselves in the process." Michael Hart, one of Burney's few mind-mates in the department and an important ally, was struck by the degree of commitment in the department to the old ways. Hart felt that Canada suffered from a lack of direction, a feeling of drifting, and that this was directly related to Canadians' "failure to come to grips with their identity and vocation as an American nation."

Hart, too, was a Canadian with an American stamp – he was educated at Calvin College in Michigan and at the University of Virginia. Returning to Canada in 1974, he taught at the University of Prince Edward Island. Uncertain if he could keep his job, he wrote Ottawa's foreign service exams. He received a phone call from an excited official in the department who had big news: Hart was the first person from P.E.I. ever to pass the exam.

After moving to Ottawa he became an articulate and outspoken standard-bearer for continentalism. He thought the internationalists had their heads in the sand, and he was tickled one day when a senior mandarin and trade specialist gave the old thinkers a piece of his mind. "The problem with you guys," the veteran declared, "is that you spend all your time sitting on your asses talking to each other here in Ottawa without getting out there and learning how the world is changing."[6]

With Europe closing ranks and a dynamic Asian market too distant in miles and mindset for Canadian exporters to make a dint, Burney and Hart felt the only option left was the American option. In the political back rooms at this time (1982-83), a split in the Liberal ranks was opening up between the nationalists represented by Marc Lalonde, Lloyd Axworthy, Herb Gray, and the like, and the more pro-business types: Ed Lumley, Don Johnston, Gerald Regan, and others. The search for ways out of the recession, coupled with the pressure from the United States against nationalism and the third option, saw the pendulum gradually swing to the Lumleys and Regans.

When Ed Lumley took the trade portfolio from Herb Gray, Burney was heading up a trade review and there was a happy meeting of minds. The good-natured Lumley and the hard-driven Burney were on the same track. Lumley was a closet free trader and yet another whose American ties had pushed him in that direction. The quintessential border boy, Lumley had spent his life as a businessman in Windsor and Cornwall. From both towns he could look across the river to the big engine. His mother lived in Florida, his father-in-law was born in Idaho, and his grandfather lived in Detroit. He was about as Americanized as a good Canadian could get, and he saw the world differently from most Trudeau Liberals. The way the world economy was shaping up, he was convinced Canada had to have a partner. "And once you say to yourself you need a partner, there is only one partner."[7]

The Burney-Lumley chemistry resulted in an initiative to explore sectoral trade agreements with the United States. It got a further push and was made public in 1983 by Gerry Regan, the former Nova Scotia premier who drew his political inspiration from W. S. Fielding, an ardent free trader of Laurier vintage who had also served as premier of the province.[8]

The idea behind sectoral free trade was to extend the Canada-U.S. Auto Pact to other areas of the economy such as the steel, agricultural machinery, and information industries. Trudeau's attitude, Lumley said, was "Let's explore all options." "Remember," said Lumley, "we needed jobs."

The sectoral free trade approach didn't extend far enough for

Lumley and Regan. Had they sensed a will for it from their Grit colleagues, they were prepared to push for full free trade. But there wasn't enough support to bring such a proposal before cabinet. "We told them to go screw themselves," said Lloyd Axworthy, a prominent member of the nationalist wing.[9] Regan backed off but later regretted that he did. "All I'm ashamed of," he said, reflecting on his days in the Trudeau cabinet, "is that my efforts to get free trade were so tentative."

Free trade talks never got started. The sectoral talks didn't go anywhere. Nonetheless, an era was closing. Beginning with Diefenbaker in 1958, and continuing with Pearson and Trudeau, the country had been witness to a quarter-century of largely unsuccessful efforts to assert a greater economic and cultural independence. But now the Grits had moved from nationalism and NEPs to a willingness to explore liberalized trade with the Americans. Now the public service was moving from the old European tradition as exemplified by John Halstead, among others, to one of heady continentalism as preached by Derek Burney. Now Ronald Reagan, with his grand continental vision, was at his peak in the United States. And now that nationalism was passing in Canada, stepping forward to erect something in its place was a prime minister with more admiration for the American way than any in Canadian history.

7

"I Like Ron Reagan"

On the very day in September 1984 that the Progressive Conservative government of Martin Brian Mulroney was sworn into power, Derek Burney was at the door of the Prime Minister's Office. Mulroney had said that one of his first acts would be to visit President Reagan. In his role as External Affairs' point man on American relations, Burney wanted to know more. He had been working on a memorandum for Mulroney that promoted the case for the new continentalism. This fit comfortably with what Mulroney had been advocating on the hustings. In place of suspicion and confrontation, it was time, the Tory leader had said, to start giving the United States the benefit of the doubt.

Burney knew where the new prime minister stood, but he wasn't aware that Mulroney and his advisers, Bernard Roy, Fred Doucet, Charles McMillan, and others, harboured deep suspicions about the senior public service. They thought the service élite was stuffed with Trudeau-conditioned bureaucrats who would undercut their purpose. They wanted to pass them by and deal with the Americans directly.

So when Burney sat down in the PMO, the cold looks rushed at him from all sides of the table.[1] He explained he wanted to help them prepare for the Reagan-Mulroney tête-à-tête, whereupon a

Mulroney man, as Burney remembered the conversation, shot back, "What makes you think you can help us?"

Burney countered, "Well, that's my job."

What type of things could he do? he was asked. "Well, normally," Burney replied, "we'd prepare a briefing book for the prime minister."

Someone looked at him. "We do our own briefing books."

Burney was shocked. Surely these people must know, he told himself, that the External Affairs Department plays a central role in planning a prime minister's trip to Washington. He persisted. "Do you know what kind of issues the Americans are going to want to discuss?"

"How would you know?"

"Well, I've been doing this for two years and I also have been following the campaign and I have a rough idea where you guys are on these issues."

It went on, until finally one of them said, "Well, let's see what you can do."

Burney got in the last volley. "By the way," he said, "I'll want to see the prime minister before the trip."

He left, shaking his head. John Diefenbaker had been paranoid about Liberals in the civil service throughout his stewardship twenty-five years earlier. The new Tories offered more of that, and just as worrisome to Burney was that they were babes in the wood. "They were unbelievably new to government," he said. So new they didn't realize that in Derek Burney they might have one of their own – a conservative with a pro-American agenda.

The doubting, at least as it applied to Burney himself, wouldn't last long. One of the first papers to hit Mulroney's desk was Burney's analysis emphasizing the need to rethink American relations. This was solid second-option stuff, which did not necessarily represent the consensus of Burney's department. In fact, it left many of his colleagues smarting. They saw in Burney's act a haste to curry favour with his new political boss.

One who held this view was the tough veteran of trade wars, Mel Clark. Mel Clark was one of Canada's leading experts on trade. In the 1950s he had been sent to Geneva as Canada's first full-time representative on the General Agreement on Tariffs and Trade (GATT), the world-trade negotiating body. He had come to favour the GATT system of reducing trade barriers multilaterally as opposed to achieving liberalization of trade on a bilateral or continental basis. Back at home, Clark established the government's multilateral trade office, remaining in Trade and Commerce until the early 1980s when he left to set up his own consultant's shop.

Mel Clark had admired Burney's first trade review paper because, while laying out the possibilities for sectoral trade, it basically favoured the traditional, multilateral way. But the paper Burney sent to Mulroney after the election was a different matter. Now Burney was denigrating the performance of the GATT and leaning very much toward bilateralism. When Mel Clark saw it, he turned purple. "It was just bloody propaganda!"[2]

Burney, as Clark saw it, had looked about him for the right opportunity, had seen Mulroney's big American train coming down the track, and had scrambled aboard. "It was a power move on his part," said Clark. "He put his finger out in the corridor and said, 'What does the master want today?' and gave it to him."

It was bad enough for Burney that Mel Clark, with all his Ottawa contacts, felt this way. Worse was that Clark accidentally came across Burney at Ottawa's Chez Jean-Pierre restaurant. Chez Jean-Pierre was the chic, power-broker's restaurant of the day. You wanted to be seen there among the potent and the refined, looking good and appearing every bit a charter member of the ruling class.

Burney had been feasting with a party of about ten, and they all were heading for the front exit when Mel Clark walked in. Before Burney could get out a "How are ya Mel?" and ease on by, Clark was on him like a terrier in full view of the patrons. He told Burney he'd read his goddamned paper and it was an awful goddamned thing and that any self-respecting civil servant would be ashamed to put his goddamned pen to it. What he, Burney, was doing with Mulroney, Clark shouted, was perfectly transparent. He was kissing ass!

As Burney's group stood open-mouthed taking it in, the tirade wore on. What Burney said about the GATT in the memorandum was goddamned garbage, Clark said. It was impossible to defend in front of anyone knowledgeable and he goddamn well knew it. Clark was expecting a searing comeback. Burney could certainly give as well as he could take. But on this occasion Burney remained silent. Said Clark: "He just stood there with a weak smile on his face."

While Clark thought Burney had no bedrock of principles, unlike Bob Bryce or Norman Robertson or the other great names of the civil service, others in the Ottawa establishment weren't so sure. Some saw "border-boy" written all over Burney. They felt his American lean came from the heart. They saw a pure pragmatist, a hard-nosed executive, sharp and honourable. Whatever the case, whatever the motivation, Burney was soon able to convince Mulroney that he could be counted upon to help chart the new American direction. Not only did he help, Derek Burney became so impressive in Mulroney's estimation that, before Mulroney's first term was up, he was invited to become the PM's right hand man, his chief of staff.

Following his election, Mulroney wanted to register quickly his new policy toward the United States. He had read a history of relations between the presidents and the prime ministers and found their frequent acrimony disconcerting. His game plan, he remarked, was simple. "First thing", he told the media, "I've got to get the president of the United States on board."

Tradition allowed that new Canadian prime ministers put in a modest period of time, at least enough to find a place to hang their hats, before checking in with the White House. But in the same month as his election, Mulroney was *en route* to Washington in response to an invitation from Reagan. Soon thereafter he began knocking down old pillars of Canadian nationalism. He went to New York to entice American business leaders to a new, open Canada. Then he hosted the Shamrock Summit in Quebec City, where he joined the president in glorious song.

Mulroney had made a splendid impression at the White House when, as Opposition leader, he came calling on Reagan three months before the election. Both showmen, both of Irish heritage, both conservative, and both intent on speeding Canadian-American relations on a glittering new path, Reagan and Mulroney got on famously. Ty Cobb, Reagan's adviser on Canada, was struck by the instant camaraderie and rapport Mulroney was able to develop. His starting point, as Cobb saw it, was his belief that Canadians had not gained anything from Pierre Trudeau's prickly approach to American affairs. So Mulroney was saying, Why not try something different? His attitude, said Cobb, was, "I'm going to take a new tack. America is basically a force for good in the world. I like Ron Reagan. Let's approach it from that point of view."[3]

The act of having an audience with the president of the United States was itself a personal triumph for Brian Mulroney in a way that it wasn't for Trudeau, Pearson, or Laurier. This, to Brian Mulroney, was what success was all about. This was the big house at the top of the moutain. Right at the top. Stepping out of the White House for the first time in June 1984, Mulroney met with reporters. "We are at the dawn of a new generation," he told them, "and of new possibilities for our two countries."

Shortly after his election in September, Mulroney left no doubt about where he was heading when he declared to the *Wall Street Journal*, "Good relations, super relations with the United States will be the cornerstone of our foreign policy."

Never had a prime minister made such a brazen declaration on American relations.

In Washington, meanwhile, the satisfaction about the election among those who involved themselves in matters Canadian was palpable. Not since 1963, when Diefenbaker was defeated and Kennedy's men celebrated, was there such interest and relief. The genial Gipper had just about had it with Trudeau, the bad feeling boiling over at the G-7 summits. In Williamsburg, Virginia, in 1983, Reagan was affronted when, teaming up with France's François Mitterrand, Trudeau, in effect, called the American president a warmonger. The president didn't take it too well, and then a year later in London, Reagan, as he said in his biography, was "horrified" by the Canadian prime minister. Again urging more accommodation to end the cold war, Trudeau lambasted British Prime Minister Margaret Thatcher. So offended was Reagan that he rushed to the Iron Lady's side after the meeting. That man "had no business talking to you like that," Reagan said. "He was way out of line."

The president had only met Mulroney the one time three months earlier, but he knew the boy from Baie Comeau represented a complete change from Trudeau. In preparation for Mulroney's first visit as prime minister, Reagan was given memoranda with "talking points" for what he should emphasize in private sessions. The memos reflected the administration's great satisfaction with Mulroney's politics.

The memoranda instructed Reagan to applaud Mulroney's "strong defense of the free market, expanded international trade and private investment." He was to congratulate Mulroney for pledges of increased defence spending and for his refusal to join in the campaign for a freeze on spending on nuclear weapons. He was to compliment the prime minister for his views on deregulating the energy market and having a more open mind to foreign investment. In all these areas in which he warred with Trudeau, Reagan could now waltz with Mulroney.

A special emphasis in the memoranda was on the Gipper's free-market philosophy and how Mulroney shared in it. He was to make the point that he wanted Canada to join him in the mission of selling the free-enterprise approach to the developing world. It was the "clearly superior" way.[4]

If there was candour in their conversation it did not extend to the question of Iraq. At this time events were unfolding that would lead to the Iran-Contra scandal over the U.S. supply of arms to Iran in exchange for hostages. On the Iran-Iraq war, however, Reagan was to tell Mulroney that "to prevent a widening or intensifying of the conflict, we have worked and will continue to work to prevent arms resupply to both sides."

After listing all the new Canadian policies for which he was so grateful, the Gipper was instructed to tell Mulroney that there could be no deal on the one thing the prime minister wanted in return – White House action on the acid rain problem. A memorandum from Secretary of State George Shultz to Reagan written just before Mulroney's arrival suggested how the president should handle the situation. "Mulroney will feel obliged to mention acid rain," said Shultz. "You could hold to our established policy, but phrased in a manner that avoids embarrassing Mulroney with his public."

In this and other briefing documents from U.S. officials, the implication was that Mulroney was pushing hard on the acid rain issue, not so much because he wanted to, but because of the political pressure at home. The Reagan administration knew as early as Mulroney's election that the acid rain issue would be the one big sore point in relations. "After a 'honeymoon' period with the U.S., we foresee a real chance that Mulroney will pick this topic as suitable to demonstrate his independence from Washington," a State Department briefing paper said.

The Republicans' insightful analysis of Mulroney's intentions extended to trade. It was clear to them that a Canadian proposal for free trade could soon be made. Memos referred to the need for Canada to seek bilateral deals to counter threats of protectionism in the United States. An option Mulroney might move toward was a "generalized free trade agreement with safeguards or bilateral agreements on practices such as antidumping, procurement and subsidies." Reagan was advised to state his endorsement of the principle of liberalized trade and to seek more detail from Mulroney on his government's plans. Though the State Department was evidently satisfied with the Tory government's approach to trade, there was no indication from the memos for this and other meetings that the United States wished to take a lead in pushing for a free trade pact with Canada.

At the September meeting with the president, Mulroney sought to convey the impression to Canadians that Canada would now count in Washington; that the Canadian view on the great multilateral questions of the day would now receive attention. Reagan had a meeting scheduled with Andrei Gromyko, the Soviet foreign minister, after the Mulroney parley. "Clearly I think by inviting me down prior to his meeting with Mr. Gromyko," said Mulroney, "he wanted to establish the special relationship which allows us input prior to major decisions being taken." Such input hadn't been apparent in recent times. When Reagan had launched the invasion of Grenada a year earlier, Pierre Trudeau had not been informed in advance. He was nearly last on Reagan's list of leaders to call.

No overriding policy purpose attended the first Mulroney-Reagan session and no major decisions were taken, and the haste of it stirred images in Canada of a new branch-plant manager reporting promptly to head office to get his orders. It had been Diefenbaker who taunted Lester Pearson in the House of Commons with, "When are you going back for further instruction?" Mulroney did not worry about rushing into the American embrace. Shakespeare's dictum: "Wisely and slowly, they stumble that run fast," was not heeded. To the jibes of Canadian nationalists, who were already accusing him of kowtowing to Uncle Sam, he had a ready response. "I'm concerned about the 1.6 million Canadians out of jobs who are not concerned about nationalism but who are concerned about providing for their families. A healthy, strong relationship with the United States of America in no way presupposes any subservience on our part."

Economic growth, not nationalism, would be at the top of the government's agenda. Voices of the right on economic issues, Michael Wilson, John Crosbie, and Don Mazankowski, got the key cabinet posts while red Tories were shunted off to the minor portfolios. The word was soon out that two of the most prominent symbols of Canadian nationalism, FIRA and the NEP, were about to be decapitated.

In a telling sign, Mulroney stacked his government with border boys or their approximates – men who had worked for American businesses or branch plants, like the prime minister himself; or whose work created close ties, like Finance Minister Michael Wilson; or who, like John Crosbie, had it in the blood.

Besides the cabinet, the Conservative caucus, especially the Ontario group, was littered with small businessmen with *laissez-faire* mindsets. This would be a government in which you could tell the program by the players. Charlie McMillan, an academic with special expertise on Japan, was a friend of Mulroney and would work as one of his senior policy advisers for four years. He admired Mulroney but could see early where one of the big problems lay. "Mulroney's instincts were Cleveland and Palm Springs," McMillan said. "Hc had a huge comfort zone on Canada-U.S. relations. What he didn't understand were Canada-Latin America, Canada-Europe, Canada-Japan relations."[5] The problem was obvious, McMillan said. There was no counterweight to the pull of the United States.

Perhaps no one exemplified the new look better than Mulroney's choice for the post of trade minister – a position that would gain special significance. The job went to Jim Kelleher. A lawyer from Sault Ste. Marie, Kelleher was new to Ottawa, new to the cabinet, new to trade, new to pretty much everything except the United States.

The Sault was right on the U.S. border, and the closest Canadian city was Sudbury, 200 miles away. In Kelleher's youth nobody wanted to go to Sudbury, and if they did, the one road was almost unnavigable. All the action was where the good roads led – across the border.

Young Jim Kelleher played on a high school football team which played under American rules – eleven men to a field instead of twelve. The league he was in featured all American teams, except for Sudbury. For the annual Sault-Sudbury game, Canadian rules were used. This, remembered Kelleher, caused considerable consternation for his Sault coach. "He didn't know what to do with the twelfth man," said Kelleher. "So he just told him to stand in the backfield and stay the hell out of the way."[6]

Kelleher, one of the men who would spearhead the drive for free trade with the United States, grew up, in his own words, "sort of being American." He played sports American-style, he did much of his socializing across the border, and he became a lawyer whose practice was heavily dependent on American clients. He bought himself a home in Florida, and made a great many American friends. He was one of the consummate border boys, and, as he saw it, this was good preparation for joining the Mulroney government. "I guess the only thing I had going for me was that I was born, raised, grew up and practised law in a border city. So I didn't have a problem with the Americans."

When Kelleher arrived in Ottawa, the importance of free trade in Canadian history had little meaning to him. It wasn't taught in his border schools. "I'm going to be honest," said Kelleher, when asked if he had a perspective on the issue, "and tell you no. I don't know how I can tell you anything else." Kelleher was a straight shooter, so frank that he earned the epithet Honest Jim. "I had just arrived from Sault Ste. Marie," he said, "and I'll be the first to admit that my knowledge of international trade was about nil. I don't think our own people, our own government, really were aware of what we were starting to do."

Kelleher soon got help. Derek Burney became his deputy, and, to no one's surprise over at External, Honest Jim got the American gospel according to Big Derek. It wasn't long before Kelleher was a convert to the idea of free trade and the new continentalism. Alarmed at first, Burney was discovering that the fact that the PM's men and people like the trade minister were so new had its advantages. Being such a greenhorn, Kelleher was almost totally dependent on the public service professionals. Burney, whom he described as "a border boy like me," became his key man.

There were the Kellehers, the Wilsons, the Crosbies, and Mulroney himself, and there was Derek Burney and a slew of border boys. But the picture wasn't all black and white. Joe Clark, neither a business Tory nor one with any particular interest in the United States, became external affairs minister. Stephen Lewis, the eloquent NDP evangelist and a voice of nationalism, was made ambassador to the United Nations. Douglas Roche, whose views on arms control were leagues to the left of Washington's, was named disarmament ambassador.

On the same day that Reagan and Mulroney were meeting in the White House, External Affairs Minister Joe Clark, who had warred publicly with Mulroney in 1976, in 1982, and in 1983, was addressing the United Nations in New York. "I come to this podium in the tradition of Howard Green," Clark told the assembly. The mere mention of the name Howard Green was enough to rattle any State Department veterans old enough to remember him. Green, external affairs minister under Diefenbaker, was one of the most anti-American, strident nationalists to hold the position in Canadian history. A cold war dove, he challenged the Kennedy administration on almost every instance of its foreign adventurism, and he particularly enraged the new frontiersmen during the Bay of Pigs crisis. When the American-sponsored invasion of Cuba, designed to overthrow Fidel Castro, was repelled, Howard Green, in a wondrous display of small-power braggadocio, had the gall to suggest to the best and the brightest in Washington that they allow Canadian professionals to handle the problem.

The show of conceit prompted a memo to President Kennedy from Secretary of State Dean Rusk. Rusk wrote that Green "has exhibited a naive and almost parochial approach to some international problems which was first attributed to his inexperience but which is now believed to be part of his basic personality." He went on to call Green stubborn, self-righteous, and extremely sensitive "to any implied interference with Canada's independence of action." Even if all that Joe Clark meant by the "tradition of Howard Green" was the desire for a more assertive UN role in East-West relations, the implicit neutralism would still be frowned upon in all corners of the White House.

It was through Clark's recommendation that Douglas Roche, a long-time friend, got his appointment. One of the first things Roche did before formally beginning his assignment was to travel to Victoria, B.C., to seek out Howard Green's advice. Roche sat with the old man, then in his eighties, and listened carefully.[7] Howard Green hadn't changed. He told Roche that of all the countries in the world he would have to deal with as disarmament ambassador, his biggest problem would come from the one located directly to the south. Roche would find his words prophetic, too prophetic for his liking.

Roche and Joe Clark were very much aware of the new prime minister's bias. Only one month after joining the cabinet, Clark tried to rationalize the Tories' new pro-American slant in a speech and press conference in Vancouver. "There has been a dramatic maturing in Canada," Clark asserted. "If fifteen or twenty years ago we had to worry inordinately about the strength of our identity and feel ourselves threatened by the United States, we have a much stronger identity now. You find it in business, where Canadians are investing abroad, you find it in the arts, where Canadian singers and writers are finding international audiences for their work." It all meant that Canada could "go into relations with the United States with much more confidence than we had before." While Clark sometimes tried to put more distance between Canadian and American foreign policy than the PMO wanted, on economic questions his vision of Canada as a decentralized community of communities put him more in league with his free-market colleagues.

Mulroney put conservatives in business-related positions and moderates in foreign and social policy areas. This balance reflected the man. Mulroney was hardly right wing on social issues. His small-town, small-money roots, and his minority status as an Anglophone in Quebec, fuelled him with a concern for minority rights and a tolerance not found in the redneck segments of the party. On the commercial side, his business career, the influence of Michael Wilson, and the tenor of the times, pushed him further to the right than anyone would have imagined.

A pragmatic politician without any real intellectual conviction, Mulroney was moved mainly by expedience. He could be readily swayed by the trend of the time. While he would staunchly defend minority rights, any liberal tendencies on social spending were outweighed by concerns about the massive debt his government faced. Moreover, big-spending, compassionate governments were out of fashion. Reaganism, Thatcherism, and the triumph of the market were in vogue. "When we took power," says David Crombie – the former tiny perfect mayor of Toronto who became Mulroney's minister of Indian and northern affairs – "if there was any sense of an agenda at all, it was an agenda in large part determined by the resonance coming from Washington and London."[8]

Mulroney, said Crombie, was a follower of fashion. "He wears the clothes of the day, and that's not necessarily such a bad thing for a politician. There's a line from Hegel about the wind of God in the trees. You catch it and hang on. So what he saw was Thatcher and Reagan as heroes of the day. And I have a feeling if fishermen got to the head of the line tomorrow, Mulroney would have rubber boots on. And I don't mean that in a phoney way."

Crombie and the other red Tories understood to some extent how the $35 billion deficit would affect policy. Flora MacDonald, Mulroney's employment minister, had been in the short-lived Clark cabinet in 1979. "I remember how shocked we were then that the deficit was $10 billion and projected to go to $11 billion. I mean that really threw us. So we tried to do things to bring it down such as new taxes and increases in petroleum prices. Well, the Liberals really skewered us on that stuff, got back in power and continued their spending modes just like before. So then we get back in power in 1984 and the deficit was projected at $35 billion.

"You look at that, and you say, What is your major thrust going to be? A concern I had as a red Tory was that if you allowed that deficit to build and the national debt to grow further, you jeopardize the whole social underpinnings of the country."[9]

Mulroney then, as Flora MacDonald saw it, had little choice but to reduce the role of government in the economy and push the market solution. This meant – especially given the prime minister's "very real empathy with the United States" – taking the route of the American model; this by a country already considered by many to be Americanized to the brim.

While MacDonald understood the need for fiscal restraint, she also felt that social policy was getting short shrift. The most powerful cabinet committee was the one that dealt with economic development. "The social policy committee," said MacDonald, "just didn't have the clout. I could see it because I was on both. I could see the concentrations of Sinc Stevens and Bob DeCotrets and Mike Wilsons." One top Mulroney adviser put it more bluntly. Those in the cabinet fighting for funding of social programs and the arts, he said, were just looked upon as "a pain in the ass."

Given the nature of the man, given the nature of the times, what happened with the Mulroney government wasn't hard to figure, said David Crombie. "Those struggling for community values lost out to the market."[10]

8

When Irish Eyes Are Smiling

The election of Brian Mulroney excited Ken Taylor and his new boss, Nabisco emperor Ross Johnson. Mulroney, they knew, was right for Wall Street. They wanted the prime minister to have the proper Wall Street platform to get his message across. They set to work arranging the venue.

Taylor had become a convinced continentalist. "I find it remarkable," he said, "that people are reluctant to come to terms with that sort of concept, because that's the reality." He could never quite figure out the nationalist crowd back home, the one that wanted to maintain the old Canada, the inward-looking, sheltered country, apprehensive of its big neighbour. He had left Canada to get a better education, an MBA at Berkeley, California. He returned to his home in Calgary to look for a job, but could find nothing. Although he had been half-expecting it, Taylor was hit hard by this and decided that pursuing his big dream would require getting out. A job in the Canadian diplomatic service allowed him to expand his horizons and achieve fame as a diplomat during the Iranian crisis. After his stint in New York as consul-general, he turned down overtures to go into Canadian politics as a Mulroney Conservative, choosing instead a career in corporate America with Johnson.

Johnson and Taylor decided that a speech to the Economic Club of New York would be the best vehicle to market Mulroney. The message would be that Canada was open for business again. The two men made the arrangements and persuaded the prime minister to appear.[1]

His visit marked a change of season in Canadian politics. In the Trudeau era visits to Wall Street were never a top priority. John Blackwood, the trade official who helped torpedo the third option, had gone on later in the 1970s to serve as deputy consul-general in New York. He was on hand one time when Trudeau came to speak to the business barons. "They hated him," he recalled. "To them he was a leftist."[2] That neither surprised nor bothered Blackwood much. What did bother him was the reaction of Canadian businessmen who had come to New York at the invitation of Solomon Brothers, First Boston, and other Wall Streeters. "These guys sounded just like the Americans," said Blackwood. "They were just as negative. It was shocking. I mean I wasn't exactly pro-Trudeau. But I am a Canadian."

It was Blackwood's job in New York to explain Canadian policies to the business class. He appeared once in 1977 with Jake Warren, Canada's ambassador to Washington, at what was billed as an editorial board meeting of the *Wall Street Journal*. It turned out, recalled Blackwood, to be something quite different. "The bastards. We walked into a Dow Jones board meeting. They tore the hell out of us." Jake Warren was hounded by Dow Jones people about labour disputes at a newsprint mill Dow Jones was building in Quebec. Others attacked FIRA. The Wall Street CEOs, said Blackwood, couldn't come to grips with the Canadian mentality. They couldn't understand that Canadians would want to slow the flow of real American money.

Mulroney wanted the real money. He journeyed to New York in the first week of December 1984, and said the magic words – words put together with a little help from Taylor and Johnson. "Our message is clear," said the prime minister. "Canada is open for business again."

Not only was it open for business, it was going to start doing business the American way. Canadians' image in the world would be rebuilt, Mulroney asserted, "as a people committed to the entrepreneurial spirit." The prime minister noted that the federal government had traditionally played a much more activist role than the government of the United States, and that this had been sometimes necessary and good. But no more. "Today's reality, however, is that government in Canada has become much too big. It intrudes too much in the marketplace. It inhibits and distorts entrepreneurial activity. Some industries are overregulated, others are overprotected."

Canada, he was saying, would turn to the right, to market forces, to smaller government, to the American way. The $35 billion projected deficit inherited from the Liberals as well as a high unemployment rate were caused by protectionism. "Simply put, at a time when the world economy was becoming more interdependent and open, Canada turned inward and interventionist." FIRA in 1974 and the NEP in 1981 were the chief culprits, Mulroney explained, and this was all "indicative of the misguided belief that regulation by politicians and bureaucrats was superior to the decisions of individuals and firms competing in the global marketplace."

It was straight from Reagan's play book. The Gipper had made a political career of campaigning for smaller government, of his desire to "get the government off the backs of the people."

To put meat on his words, Mulroney spelled out the new red-carpet treatment for foreign investors and told of his plan to remove the discriminatory provisions of the NEP. Pierre Trudeau's goal of Canadian ownership of 50 per cent of its oil and gas resources was effectively abandoned.

An initial draft of Mulroney's speech had included a paragraph revealing that the prime minister was willing to entertain proposals for a free trade agreement.[3] Although this was deleted from the final text, it was clear that the politician who the year before had denounced John Crosbie's proposal in categorical terms was still the same man who had lunched with J. Duncan Edmonds at the Mt. Royal Club in 1978.

The speech was a smash hit. Ken Taylor talked to his friends in corporate America and found them ecstatic. "They couldn't believe it. I can't overstate it." After the dampness and the fog of Trudeau and FIRA, the skies had suddenly cleared. American business, observed Taylor, now said, "Let's do something up there." The open-for-business speech heralded the rebirth of the C. D. Howe era; its rebirth and extension. Mulroney was dismantling the nationalist walls put up after the Howe era and opening the gates again. And now, with the appearance of free trade on the agenda, Mulroney was moving to take the big step Howe had never achieved.

In a prescient analysis at the time of the New York speech, Denis Stairs, a professor at Dalhousie University, looked at the American future to which Canada was now being directed. The die was cast, he said. Talks would begin on free trade by 1986, and an agreement would be signed before the end of the decade. Outsiders would begin to assume that the two countries were speaking with one voice. A cold-shower effect would see the closure of many Canadian plants during the implementation of the agreement. The failure to escape U.S. domination by achieving trade links with other countries had led to such a fate. This could no longer be avoided and might not be so bad. "We can't beat them so we might as well join them," reasoned Stairs. "At least in the form of economic union."

Of the competing visions of the country, the continentalist model was again the one in favour. As far as the nationalists were concerned, Canada had never really been closed for business. In their view, this was simply a myth that had grown like many myths do – by dint of repetition. Canada's problem, as they saw it, was the opposite – the country was too open for business. It was one of the world's leading trading nations, dealing more with the outside world than other leading industrialized democracies. The degree of foreign ownership of its economy was higher than in all other such nations. Statistics from FIRA, the agency the Tories now renamed Investment Canada, revealed the extent: 76 per cent of Canada's chemical industry; 100 per cent of the auto industry; 100 per cent of the tobacco industry; 91 per cent of the rubber industry; 59 per cent of the electrical industry; and 63 per cent of the petroleum industry. Almost 50 per cent of Canada's manufacturing sector was controlled by foreigners. Eighty per cent of Canadian trade with the United States was already free.

At this time the world's most booming national economy, the country all economists were drooling over, was Japan, which had barriers far higher than anything Canada had ever erected. Compared to Canada, Japan was closed. Canada's FIRA was regarded as heavily protectionist, yet European countries had FIRAs of their own to protect investment, and their central governments had as much or more influence over their economies as did Ottawa. Foreign ownership levels in Europe weren't nearly as high. The wealthy, healthy Scandinavian countries had economies that were more planned and protected than Canada's. The new Asian tigers in the Far East – Taiwan, Singapore, Indonesia, and South Korea – were significantly dirigiste.

Ed Lumley, the pro-business Liberal, saw a lot of hypocrisy in the criticism of a Canada under so much foreign control trying to do its little bit, through FIRAs and third options, to protect what it had left. When he appeared as trade minister in New York, he trotted out the old line about not throwing stones when you live in glass houses. "I would recite their own protective legislation back to them. What about your Jones Act and your mining act and tell me about your Buy America laws, about how you just paid so many more dollars for transit cars because of those laws?"[4]

Still, while Canada had one of the world's most porous borders, a large body of opinion in Canada and in American business quarters suggested that the protection that remained, including FIRA and non-tariff barriers, was producing an environment that stifled the development of companies that could be competitive on an international scale – the very type of companies that were the key to success in the new global economy.

At the moment, for example, when Mulroney spoke in New York, Donald Macdonald, a former charter member of Walter Gordon's school of nationalism, was coming round to the view that his earlier beliefs had been mistaken. Macdonald, who held many portfolios in the Trudeau cabinets, including finance, had been appointed by Trudeau in 1982 to head a royal commission to probe Canada's economic future. He found that in fact there was too much protection and that only through competing head-on with the United States could Canada develop global winners. "I had a feeling our policies hadn't succeeded," Macdonald said later, reflecting on his days in the Liberal government. "FIRA had created a less competitive economy. When you looked at our big companies, Bronfmans, Power, and others, FIRA was making it too easy for these guys."[5]

Macdonald felt that the believers in the old Canadian way were forgetting a development that had undercut the old Canada – the decline of the resource industry. Increased competition from the developing countries and an abundance of supply meant that international resource prices were declining. Canada could no longer get rich off its seemingly infinite supplies of ores and lumber and oil. Like Sweden, Canada would have to begin shifting out of the resource economy, and this would mean seeking competitive advantage in other areas. The way to achieve that was to open Canadian business to the continental marketplace. Open competition would produce winners who could then compete globally.

It wasn't that there was anything wrong with the old Canadian way. It was just that the world was changing and forcing the country's hand. No one was selling out the country. The tides of history were washing Canada closer to the United States, as they had been doing since the day the country was born.

*   *   *

Partly through the work of historians of British bias, such as Donald Creighton and W. L. Morton, the notion developed that misguided public policy had turned Canada from the path of an essentially British-European nation to an American one.

But another school of thought, espoused by historian Jack Granatstein and others, suggested that while the nation's leadership on the nationalist-continentalist question was important, the process of the integration of North America was an inevitable development.

The outcome was not due to public policy, but to circumstances beyond Ottawa's control – such as geography and two world wars that had ended British supremacy as a world power and vaulted the United States into unchallenged paramountcy. Given its location on the continent, Canada had little choice but to follow the new market reality.

To some it was obvious as early as the turn of the century that geography alone had sealed Canada's fate. In 1908 Samuel E. Moffett wrote a thesis at the University of Columbia entitled "The Americanization of Canada." Summing up, Moffett wrote: "The conclusion to which all the converging lines of evidence unmistakably point is that the Americans and the English-speaking Canadians have been welded into one people."[6]

The assimilative process, as Moffett called it, could be traced in infinite detail even in those days. The American system by which automobiles keep to the right instead of the left as in Britain already prevailed in Canada. American baseball had already taken over from lacrosse as the leading Canadian summer sport. The Royal Military College, created in 1874, was copied from America's West Point. American holidays, Labor Day and Thanksgiving, had been adopted in Canada. The legal profession had been Americanized by dropping the English distinction between barristers and solicitors. As for the certainty of economic integration, Moffett chose the words of the Liberal Sir Richard Cartwright. Cartwright said in 1894 that the success of the country would not be achieved without it. "That fact is written by the finger of God in every mile of the frontier between that country and Canada."

While integration was already well advanced as the century turned, the broad change in Canada's orientation began taking shape at the time of World War I. The financial strain of the war became so burdensome that Britain could no longer pay for its Canadian imports. A pooling of resources in North America to help the British led to a Canada-U.S. understanding that their border should effectively cease to exist for the duration of the war. As a result of this co-operation, economic ties greatly increased. Before 1914 foreign investment in Canada was 23 per cent American and 72 per cent British. Four years later it was 36 per cent American and 60 per cent British. In pre-war days Canadian exports to the United States were less than half those going to the mother country. By 1918 the United States had virtually caught up with England as the Dominion's number-one export market. Before the war Canada imported twice as much from America as it did from Britain. After the war, the margin was ten to one.

This trade and investment swing toward the Americans became less pronounced a few years later, but the overall change in business patterns was permanent. "The defeat of reciprocity in the 1911 election," wrote Granatstein, "seemed only a temporary check, one virtually nullified by the greater necessity of wartime integration and cooperation."

The Dirty Thirties' depression, and the big American tariff wall that went up as a result, reduced the north-south flow of trade. But reason commanded that the trade barriers be reduced, and Mackenzie King and Franklin Roosevelt oversaw this process later in the decade. As World War II began (before C. D. Howe took control) the United States was the number-one investor in Canada, providing some 60 per cent of investment capital. America was Canada's largest trading partner, and imports from the United States were four times those of second-place Britain.

During the war, the ties that bound Canada and the United States were extended to areas such as defence. As it became all too apparent early in the war that Britain might not be able to withstand the German power, King brooded upon the vulnerability of his country's own negligible forces. If Britain fell, who could defend the Dominion? Who but the Americans? King had built a personal rapport with Roosevelt. In 1940 the two men had drafted a joint declaration of defence in FDR's railway car in Ogdensburg, New York. Done in a matter of minutes, it created the Permanent Joint Board on Defence. An economic partnership in defence production was begun.

Britain's beleaguered economy during the war caused another balance of payments crisis for Ottawa. The Canadian deficit with the United States had been balanced by a surplus from Canada's trade with Britain. Since Britain could no longer afford to buy from Canada, King again had to turn to Roosevelt to work out a deal. The two leaders agreed that the United States would purchase more supplies and munitions from Canada – enough to keep the trade in balance. Washington would forward the supplies to Britain under the lend-lease formula, which waived payment until after the war. The Canada-U.S. deal, known as the Hyde Park Agreement, was hardly a forsaking of the Empire as some Canadian nationalists later suggested. Rather it meant that Canada could continue to supply Britain with desperately needed war materials.

The resultant surge in Canada-U.S. economic activity saw American investment in Canada jump to 70 per cent. Exports to the United States tripled. By 1945, as Granatstein concluded, "Canada was part and parcel of the continental economy."[7]

The question that loomed in the post-war years was whether anything could be done to restore Canadian accounts to a more diversified, less dependent position. But with so many countries ravaged and broke, there were few markets to which trade could be redirected. The Marshall Plan, which provided giant sums of aid to Europe, meant that some trade with Britain could be restored. But the demand created by the Marshall Plan funds also generated enormous economic activity in the United States. It was hardly surprising that Canada took advantage.

Meanwhile the birth of the GATT in the early post-war years began a trend that later frustrated the maintenance of an east-west infrastructure in Canada. By reducing tariffs the GATT encouraged north-south trade flows on the continent at the expense of east-west ones. Trade barriers between Canadian provinces grew over time, while barriers to the United States diminished. By 1990 Ontario was trading three times as much with the United States as with Quebec. Despite Canadian public policy, the natural north-south pull was prevailing. Another blow to the east-west psychology came in the mid-1960s with adoption of Canada's own flag, a move which symbolically severed the bond with Britain. Third-option efforts then failed to re-establish a strong European link.

The march of time was taking Canada south, and viewed from this perspective Brian Mulroney's continentalism could well be defended as a recognition of the obvious. But recognizing this fact did not provide a response to the cardinal concern: Where would it end? If further integration with the United States was the only route to economic growth, how could a country of such satellite nature to begin with ever hope to sustain itself? How could it ever hope to realize a dream of its own and create something unique, something better than what the United States offered?

These were questions that were not pondered by the new government. Peter White, Conrad Black's close associate, who worked in the Prime Minister's Office and later became Mulroney's principal secretary, saw no evidence of a long-range game plan.[8] Rather it was a pragmatic government which responded on the basis of its strongly American free-enterprise instincts to the exigencies of the day. After only a few months in power, these instincts had produced a complete turnaround in Canada-U.S. relations. Preparing for the Quebec City summit between Reagan and Mulroney in the early spring of 1985, State Department officials wrote that the meeting "comes at a time when relations are as good as they have been in decades." Their suppositions about Mulroney in September of the previous year had proved correct.

In planning for what became known as the Shamrock Summit, the Americans showed both self-satisfaction with what had already been accomplished and a will to push Mulroney further on defence spending and the removal of restrictions on energy trade, and generally toward an even wider embrace of the free-market philosophy. The word "partnership" figured prominently in State Department memoranda to the president advising him what to say to Mulroney in private sessions in Quebec.[9]

The memoranda revealed the mindset of the Republicans toward Canada on a number of fronts. Reagan was told:

— that "Mulroney supports freer trade. You may wish to encourage him on this";
— that the Canadian economy was "beset by structural inefficiencies, over-regulation of industry, and barriers to free markets. . . . Canada needs to take major steps towards a market-oriented system";
— that he might wish to say to Mulroney, "We believe a policy based on market-oriented growth without government interference holds out the best opportunities for our two countries to prosper as economic partners";
— that the proposed creation of Investment Canada to replace FIRA represented "a significant political departure for Canada" from economic nationalism, and that it was

an important "first step" towards liberalization of investment, but that significant barriers remained which "we
believe must be addressed";
— that he should congratulate Mulroney on his removal of
the retroactive back-in provisions of the NEP, but that
other restrictions on petroleum imports and exports
should be removed.

On questions of defence and policies on East-West relations,
it was clear the administration appreciated the track Mulroney
was on. Memoranda told Reagan:

— that Mulroney had refused Opposition demands to distance himself from Washington's stand on arms control;
— that Mulroney would "not engage in Trudeau-style public
disarmament initiatives that could undermine U.S.-
Soviet negotiations";
— that despite Liberal leader John Turner's "centrist
instincts, [the] party has moved left," and both the Grits
and the NDP were attacking Mulroney "for his refusal to
take [an] 'independent Canadian position' on arms
control."

The president was given a summary statement to relay to the
prime minister on arms spending:

We have been impressed with the frankness of your government's assessment of Canada's defence posture following
years of neglect. We too let our military fall behind the
needed modernizations schedule. It has taken and will continue to take major investments to correct these mistakes. I
am sure it will also require a major political effort to push
through the essential military enhancements in Canada.

Another memo to Reagan was more blunt. "You may wish to
push him on increasing Canada's defence spending."

Reagan was also instructed to press Mulroney to co-operate more on Washington policy toward Nicaragua, and to take greater steps to prevent leakage of strategic military technology through Canada to the east bloc.

Well aware that Mulroney was under pressure to make progress on negotiations to curb acid rain, U.S. officials decided – despite all the co-operation they were getting from the Canadian prime minister – to stonewall. The position paper given to Reagan said, "Lacking clear evidence of an 'emergency,' we decline to be rushed into an expensive clean-up." The policy, as Mulroney well knew, was chiefly at the president's bidding.

The environment was never regarded as an area in which the Gipper's expertise was rich. He had first made headlines on this subject during the 1980 campaign when, having read something about the interaction of tree leaves and atmospheric vapours, he deduced publicly that "trees cause more pollution than automobiles." The declaration startled many, among them students at a college in California who, blessed with a sense of humour, prepared for Reagan's campaign stop at their campus by slinging a banner across a big, beautiful oak. "Chop Me Down," it read, "Before I Kill Again!" In the same campaign, Reagan had told mortified environmentalists, "A tree's a tree. How many do you need to look at?"

In the mid-1980s, Reagan still clung to his radical theory of foliage. Bill Merkin, a top American trade official who later negotiated free trade with Canada, sat in on an NSC meeting to observe the president first hand. Merkin had heard the Reagan pinbrain jokes and the stories of him dozing off in meetings. Now, positioned right behind the Gipper, he had a ringside seat.[10]

For the longest time the president didn't speak. He ate jelly beans and occasionally nodded and looked bored. But finally, when someone mentioned Canadian complaints about acid rain, Ronald Reagan drew to attention. "Well, you know," he said, in what would constitute his only remark for the entire meeting, "trees pollute more than people do. So I don't know what all this fuss over acid rain is about."

As Merkin's jaw dropped he glanced around the table to gauge the reaction of others, but couldn't see any faces. They were all buried in their papers. No one wanted to challenge the Gipper on that one.

On the specifics of acid rain, the president had read another article and formed another abstruse theory – that success in preventing forest fires was a major cause of acid rain. In the old days when large forest fires were more prevalent, the fires apparently left a deep cover of ash through which acid rain was washed. The acid was thereby leached out of the rain. In modern times fewer forest fires meant more acid rain seepage. The president fastened onto this theory. Suddenly acid rain was not the fault of American industry – it was due to the good work of modern-day fire fighters.[11]

For the Shamrock Summit in Quebec city, the White House temporarily sidelined the acid-rain problem by agreeing to appoint a U.S. envoy to explore the matter jointly with a Mulroney appointee, former Ontario premier William Davis. "It was an attempt to be responsive," said the State Department's Carroll Brown. "But it also was an attempt to buy some time – although that was never said." As modest as this compromise was, it still met stern opposition in Reagan's Office of Management and Budget. It took a last minute, long-distance phone call to the president from Secretary of State George Shultz, who was in Central America at the time, to overrule the dissenters and give Mulroney the face saver.[12]

At the Shamrock Summit, the Americans' arrogance was not limited to discussions on acid rain. The Canadian government and some American officials themselves were angered by Caspar Weinberger's gratuitous intimation in a TV interview that Washington would station missile launchers on Canadian soil if it felt the need. "It was rude and disrespectful," said the State Department's Joe Joeckel. "It was outrageous what Weinberger said." Joeckel had prepared what he felt was an eloquent speech for the president on the theme of the new partnership, but once the White House got hold of the script, bilateral clichés and standard cold war rhetoric were inserted. One of the added lines praised Canada's ability to produce good beer. Joeckel fought hard to get the reference withdrawn, and succeeded.

As well as the temporary acid rain compromise, the Quebec meeting produced an agreement to appoint Jim Kelleher and an American counterpart, Bill Brock, to examine ways of reducing or eliminating trade barriers. The significance of the summit, however, lay not in the modest agreements or the hitches along the way. Of greater note was the atmosphere. Since coming to power, Mulroney had been busy appropriating American policies. For the Shamrock Summit, he took on the American style. The glitz, the glamour, the practice of politics-as-picture-show took over. The summit was Hollywood brought north. Mulroney was a natural at the big schmooze, at show-biz corn, and he was much in awe of the way the Reagan presidency was selling in the United States. He wanted some of the magic for his own "administration," as he sometimes referred to it.

Bill Fox, his press secretary, had observed the Reagan style while working as a newspaper correspondent in Washington, and on Mulroney's instruction had immediately set about trying to import some White House glamour to Ottawa. In one effort Fox arranged for the prime minister to speak from a lectern complete with the Canadian coat of arms. Ottawa reporters responded by bursting mockingly into "Hail to the Chief" at its first unveiling. On another occasion Fox tried formally announcing the prime minister's entrance, as they do for the president in the United States. "Ladies and Gentlemen," intoned Fox in a drumroll voice as Mulroney entered, "the Prime Minister of Canada!" By the time the snickering and hooting from the assembled scribes abated, the press secretary had decided to take a break from making a president out of a prime minister.[13]

For the Shamrock Summit, the PMO prepared like a White House advance team. Pictures were the name of the game, and so teams were sent to scout out the best angles and backdrops for the cameras. To make sure there could be no upstaging of Brian Mulroney, Governor General Jeanne Sauvé, who would normally, as head of state, welcome the president, was not invited. By dubbing it a "working visit" as opposed to a state visit, the governor general could be left out. Cabinet ministers were relegated to the wings as bit players.

Although the PMO had a dozen or so in its advance group, it was no match for the Reagan storm troopers – about sixty in number who set upon Quebec City like a whirlwind. They entirely refurbished the floor of the hotel where the president would be staying. Every possible backdrop for the president was studied and, if necessary, redecorated. It was all in keeping with tradition. For a visit in 1979, which had to be cancelled, an advance man for Jimmy Carter pulled out a fleet of toy limos from his briefcase, set them on a table, and with everything but accompanying *vrooms* showed his Canadian hosts who would be driving where and when. For Nixon's visit in 1972, Bob Haldeman's advance group wanted a new paint job in one of Trudeau's offices. The tan-colour background wasn't suitable for TV. They wanted a high-gloss indigo, which they never got.

The strategy worked. The Shamrock Summit went off as gloriously scripted. It was picture magic, a memorable triumph of spectacular backdrops and high-office glitter revealing the soothing rapport between president and prime minister and the renewal of the special relationship between the countries. In what one writer termed "the political equivalent of Entertainment Tonight," Mulroney and Reagan joined voice in a rendition of "When Irish Eyes Are Smiling." Mulroney was in full song, while the Gipper's accompaniment was closer to half-hearted. The president hadn't been forewarned that he would be expected to join in a duet. The instruction in his briefing papers said, "You are seen side by side with Mulroney, enjoying an evening of Canadian culture. This media spectacular helps build a favourable public response to the Summit." As a symbol, the sing-song was fraught with pitfalls for Mulroney, given how he used to serenade another big American, Robert McCormick, while sitting on his lap as a boy in Baie Comeau. But the prime minister wasn't bashful about making a political show of joyfully embracing America. This was how he wanted it. These were his instincts taking over, shouting out, laying it on, and when it was over, he fairly glowed with pride.

Mulroney would regard the Shamrock Summit as one of the finest memories of his stewardship.[14] When he returned to the House of Commons in Ottawa, he floated on a wave of euphoria above the scorn of opposition critics. John Turner mocked the smiling PM for the songfest, saying that he hadn't changed much since his boyhood days. "He's still singing for the Americans – except now we're the ones who have to pick up the tab." NDP leader Ed Broadbent accused Mulroney of acting like Reagan's kid brother. "Canadians do want to be good neighbours," Broadbent said. "However we recognize seriously that while our destinies are indeed connected we must continue the struggle of our ancestors in this nation to build on this part of the continent." Canada's history, Broadbent continued, could be seen as "one long struggle against assimilation." Don't, he pleaded, give up that struggle.

9

True Believers

After the triumph of the Shamrock Summit in 1985, the Canadian economy, benefiting from an American-led world boom, was beginning to hum. It would go on a long expansionary roll. The country was in a relatively positive frame of mind. In the West, unburdened of "sell-your-own-wheat" Pierre Trudeau, and encouraged by Mulroney's pledges of reconciliation, a greater sense of belonging prevailed. A first ministers' conference in Regina had been a noteworthy success. Canadians, as Joe Clark kept telling audiences, were feeling confident. Clark had been moved at the Quebec City summit, not so much by the Mulroney-Reagan duet as by the unusually fervent singing of the national anthem in French and in English. "Some say not everything in Quebec was spontaneous," asserted Clark. "Well, that was."

National unity was not especially imperilled at this time. There was no urgency to begin a risk-ridden search for a reworking of the Constitution that would mollify Quebec. With a sunny economy, there was no urgency to move toward a radical restructuring by way of free trade with the Americans. Threats of protectionist trade measures blossomed in Washington, but these had been commonplace throughout the history of the bilateral relationship. To attempt an economic overhaul of

American relations would be to disregard the lesson learned by Mackenzie King. After the Liberals had been defeated in the 1911 election over the free trade gamble, King, noting that his party had attempted a parting of the ways when times were prosperous, wrote in his diary: "The moral is to make no appeal in good times for something better. It is only when people are hard up that they see the advantage of change."

For the Canadian psyche, no issues were bigger or potentially more bruising than a recasting of the United States' role from without and of Quebec's role from within. To attempt either would be a grave business. To tackle both at the same time – when the country was at relative peace – was to embark on a mission of exceptional magnitude and risk.

Brian Mulroney, big game hunter, took the plunge. Quebec and the United States were always bright lights in his thinking on Canada. Now they would shine brighter. On American relations there had been no campaign promise for free trade. Once in office, however, a series of coincidental developments pushed the government toward it. Free trade suddenly fit the philosophy of the times. And it fit the philosophy of the men at work.

With the formal go-ahead at the Shamrock Summit to explore liberalized trade, Jim Kelleher, Mulroney's wide-eyed man on the trade beat, began testing public opinion. The trade minister had been getting a crash course on the ways of the world. He'd been sent off to Europe to inform governments there of the demise of FIRA and the dilution of the NEP. The trip helped unburden him of his breathtaking credulity. "I began gradually to become – I hesitate to use the word – a world person. I began to fully realize what Marshall McLuhan had said about the world being a global village. It slowly began to dawn on me that this [free trade] was going to be something of significance."[1]

Kelleher liked and understood Americans; not so the Europeans. "You've got to understand I had a couple of bad experiences with the Europeans," he explained. Shortly after taking his post, Norway and Sweden became members of the European Free Trade Association (EFTA). These were big lumber-producing countries, and their membership meant Canada would no longer be able to export so much timber to EFTA countries. Kelleher was called to Brussels where all this was explained to him. He was angry. This was upsetting. The Europeans weren't being nice. "They didn't give a hoot about Canada," he recalled. "They just cut off a big chunk of our access." The experience helped convince Kelleher of what his mentor and spoonfeeder, Derek Burney, had been telling him: a new, secured relationship with the Americans was necessary.

To forge such a relationship, the government would require support from the ruling class. In the key power centres, leading figures would emerge to carry the ball. Derek Burney would steer the bureaucracy, Tom d'Aquino of the Business Council on National Issues (BCNI) would take care of business, and Michael Wilson, the finance minister, would be the Americanizing political force below the prime minister. Two were border boys while the third, Wilson, was stamped Republican from the cradle. With Brian Mulroney taking the lead, they formed a formidable continentalist quartet.

In the public service, the initial reaction to free trade was hostile. "Not another soul in the bureaucracy," recalled Kelleher, "would speak to us or help us. They thought we were out to lunch. They thought this was the most cockamamie idea they'd ever heard of." But then the trade minister noticed a shift. "Suddenly it began to dawn on the bureaucrats that 'Christ, it looks like this free trade thing might go ahead. It looks like the PM is very supportive.'" Then, noted Kelleher, the sliming began. "It was unseemly. Unseemly. All of a sudden every deputy minister in the goddamned place wanted in on this. All of a sudden we could hardly fit in the meeting room, Derek and I."

The one exception was the Finance Department. Finance,

gung-ho on free trade since day one, wouldn't let Kelleher out of its sight. Finance under Michael Wilson, said Kelleher, was "with me everywhere but the lavatory."

In the foreign affairs sector of the public service, Mulroney was discovering that his fears of a Trudeau-inspired Liberal bias were largely unfounded. In Finance he was getting the same message. The senior mandarins there were about as far left as Caspar Weinberger. They were as hard-headed as the blue Tory who presided over the department itself, Michael Wilson.

Of all the semi-Americans who came to power in Canada in 1984, the "Moose," as Wilson was known to some, was the closest thing the senior Tories would have to a five-star Reagan Republican. Wilson would have fit just as comfortably in the Gipper's cabinet as in Mulroney's; perhaps more comfortably. A blue-blood from cradle to Bay Street, Wilson was a diehard free enterpriser and a champion of trickle-down economics. He was anti-abortion and, in some cases, pro capital punishment. Paul Robinson, the American ambassador in Ottawa, had antagonized Canadians by parading around the country saying that Ottawa should devote less money to social spending and more to the military. Michael Wilson had barely settled into his cabinet office before he was advocating the same measures.

Politically, Wilson was regarded (wrongly as it turned out) as one of the least dexterous ministers imaginable. Stubborn, stolid, sartorially inept, a hulking grey mass without a lick of style, the Moose was charisma's antithesis. But he had an inexorable quality about him. He would plough his way through swamp and roadblocks and minefields and arrive, expression unchanged – the survivor, the terminator – at his destination.

It was with a good bit of help from Wilson that the more moderate "jobs, jobs, jobs" Mulroney of the 1984 campaign was led over to the far right of the political spectrum. Mulroney became a heavy corporate-tax cutter, a champion of low inflation over low unemployment, a prime minister whom the average Canadian viewed as Gucci-boardroom. Although, as David

Crombie said, Mulroney understood poverty more than most in his party, and although the way the Kennedys reached out to the poor had once impressed him, Mulroney would follow a Republican economic path, losing touch with the common man and losing in the process the precious political centre.

His economic mentor came by his crusty conservatism honestly. Michael Wilson's life was privileged, sheltered, and thoroughly tied to the interests of business, commerce, and capital markets. The other side of the tracks was completely foreign to him. Never having seen poverty, he couldn't hope to understand it. His father, Harry, was president of National Trust and brought Michael up to follow in his steps and look after big money. Born in 1937, Michael went the private school route: Selwyn House in Montreal, Upper Canada College in Toronto. The Wilsons lived in Rosedale, were strongly Anglican, and strolled the fairways of the plush Toronto Golf Club. At the University of Toronto, young Michael studied banking, accounting, and finance. His father's contacts landed him a job in a merchant bank in London where he spent eighteen months. Back in Toronto, he sold commercial paper and did other transactions for corporate clients at Harris and Partners, which later became Dominion Securities. He also put in two years in the Finance Department in Ottawa in its capital markets section.

William Harris, his first Toronto boss, a Liberal, saw Wilson then as a businessman who was very enamoured of the American model.[2] As a corporate underwriter, Wilson often had to look south to balance and stabilize stock portfolios. Many clients at Harris and Partners and at Dominion were American companies seeking to invest in Canada. The nationalism of the Liberal government frustrated his clients' ambitions, and gave Wilson an early distaste for protectionism.

A formative experience came in 1977 when Wilson visited Hong Kong to sell bonds and other investments. A potential investor there lambasted Canada, comparing what his tiny island had been able to do with no resources, no fresh water, and red China for a neighbour, with the achievements of king-sized Canada, which had a magnificent abundance of natural resources and the biggest economy in the world right next door. Canada, the investor said, was blowing its potential.[3]

For Wilson, who had been thinking of going into politics, moments like this clinched it. He left Dominion Securities, where he had been passed over for chairman anyway, won election in Etobicoke Centre, and became a right wing star in the party. J. Duncan Edmonds lobbied Joe Clark on his behalf, and Clark included Wilson in his 1979 cabinet as trade minister.

Edmonds had attended university with Wilson and now lived in his Ottawa neighbourhood. They frequently golfed together and, of course, Edmonds lobbied Wilson on the need for North American economic integration – something Wilson warmed to. Like others, Edmonds had no problem categorizing Wilson. On the one hand, a man of integrity, an excellent executive, enormously dedicated. On the other, a hidebound creature of the Toronto business establishment, narrow-minded and boring.

"I always had the impression that Mike was a little thin in terms of broader perspectives," said Edmonds. "We didn't have a lot of intellectual discussion, and when we tried it, I just found him – I think the word would be 'dull.' Dull as hell as a matter of fact."[4]

Jim Gillies, a Tory insider and Wilson's friend, saw him as a dedicated true-believer. "Michael has more of a free-enterprise orientation than anyone I know up there."[5] Ed Lumley found him a decent man but disturbingly ideological. The trouble starts in politics, said Lumley, when the ideological replaces the practical. "Mike's much more dogmatic than most. I don't think Mazankowski is, and I don't think Brian is."[6]

Almost everyone found Wilson decent, well-meaning. If, with his anti-inflation mania, he seemed to care little for the unemployed, if in his yen to deregulate and to strip away universality he was removing the social underpinnings that distinguished the country, it wasn't out of malice or greed. The truth was simply that he only knew one side of the country, the big-business, Bay Street side.

Failing to understand that Canada was built on and operated on different principles, Wilson brought to Canadian governance an American philosophy. The ramifications of this were profound.

Wilson was clobbered in the 1983 Tory leadership campaign, but by transferring his small band of backers to Mulroney, he helped secure himself a path to the finance portfolio. Like Mulroney, he was on record as being opposed to free trade. "I think it's not very likely we're going to see that," said Wilson. "There's an awful lot of jobs at stake. . . . Clearly there would be a tremendous adjustment process involved in moving to a full free trade agreement. Some smaller companies which are very efficient, very well managed, just would not be able to compete."

Once in office, Wilson not only became a free trade convert, but also took to pursuing an integrationist policy line more avidly than Mulroney. He prepared An Agenda for Economic Renewal – a heavily conservative document (prepared with the help of a variety of sources) that would serve as the government's blueprint for years to come.[7] All the main features of the Reagan agenda – deregulation, decentralization, privatization, tax reform, trade reform – would be adopted by the Canadian government. Everything possible would be done to clear away hurdles for big business. It was in part what non-conservatives liked to deride as trickle-down economics – the idea that if you gave tax breaks and free scope to the wealthy capitalist élite, the wealth created would make its way down to the little guy. The United States, clinging to this type of thinking, had the widest gap between rich and poor of any nation in the Western world. But Wilson had little difficulty in selling the approach to Mulroney. As for concerns about surrendering what Canada stood for, this was seen as leftist paranoia, the stuff of old Canada.

The agenda was propelled as much by the massive debt faced by the Mulroney government as by any Tory philosophy. But Wilson was a true believer, who would have pursued the American option in good times or in bad. In Mulroney's early years, there was wisdom in his push for deeper spending cuts to trim the deficit. With the economy surging, such measures seemed appropriate. But partly because of his own clumsy political manoeuvring, Wilson could not secure the prime minister's approval for a "Mike the knife" approach. Wilson's declaration that "upper and middle income social programs cannot be afforded today" was hardly misguided. It was hardly wrong-headed to suggest that, given the deficit, families with $80,000 incomes and the like should no longer receive baby bonuses. But Brian Mulroney had declared universality a sacred trust. Universality was part of the Canadian social contract that made the country unique on the continent. More maladroit was Wilson's decision to reduce old age pensions by partially de-indexing them from inflation. The move sparked old age outrage. Family allowance cuts could be afforded by the wealthy. Pension cuts could not be afforded by the elderly. Mulroney, badly wounded by the surge of grey power that greeted Wilson's plan, was eventually forced to back off the measure. As the controversy continued to register pain through the summer of 1985, the government was looking for refuge – a distraction to get the public focus off pensions. As Flora Mac-Donald explained, it made the prospect of moving quickly on free trade all the more attractive.[8]

Many other encouraging signs pushed forward the case for reciprocity. Ronald Reagan was highly supportive, the Tory caucus was behind the idea, the premiers, most importantly Alberta's Peter Lougheed, pledged strong support. Moreover, Donald Macdonald's report endorsing free trade appeared in September. Macdonald had been under pressure throughout the course of his expensive study to come up with something innovative. His endorsement of free trade, only reluctantly agreed to by several of his commissioners, gave the prime minister an important bipartisan edge in taking the initiative forward.

Without the support of big business, however, a free trade proposal would get nowhere. During previous attempts to secure reciprocity pacts, business had been cool. Tariff protection was seen to work in its favour. In the 1980s, however, a variety of forces led to a change in attitude, one of which was Tom d'Aquino.

D'Aquino was a neighbour of Michael Wilson and J. Duncan Edmonds in the select Ottawa area of Rockcliffe. The three men were philosophically compatible in many ways. All saw the need for a major reshaping of Canada's relationship with the United States. Wilson and Edmonds were good friends, but it was the Wilson-d'Aquino alliance that would change Canada. J. Duncan Edmonds, the one who had been first to the public starting line with a new plan for North America, would also become the first to fall.

A man with a boyish grin, receding hair, and a canned laugh track, d'Aquino was Canada's evangelist for big business. As head of the Business Council on National Issues (BCNI), he represented no less than 160 Canadian corporations. Full of surface smarts and eagerness, d'Aquino, the CEO of CEOs, was their government lobbyist, public relations honcho, and big-time strategist. While some saw him as supercilious, it was generally conceded that d'Aquino was effective. Smooth, multilingual, articulate, he had more dimensions than the usual big-buck business executive. He had taught law, acted as legal representative to corporations in North America and in Europe, worked in Pierre Trudeau's communications office, run his own consulting firm, and become knowledgeable on trade.

D'Aquino was raised in a small British Columbia town near the state of Washington. Like Burney and Kelleher, this ambitious border boy attended Queen's University before moving on in the mid-1960s to study in Britain at the London School of Economics and at King's College. There he developed views on political economy that placed him squarely in the continentalist camp. D'Aquino had no doubt that Canada's future lay in economic integration with the United States. "Through economic integration we'll gain economic strength," he reasoned. "And only through economic strength can we maintain our independence."[9]

The European Common Market was just a few years old when d'Aquino studied in England. Thoughts of expanding its breadth were far in the future. "But I was in a class with a few dreamers, students who dreamt that all these countries, which had once upon a time fought one another, would all come together in one great union of Europe." By the late 1980s, when a union of Europe was looking quite possible, d'Aquino and the rest were looking less like dreamers. As he saw the situation, it was primarily the big-business community in the form of the European Round Table that made economic union possible. "They're the people," noted d'Aquino, "who a few years ago said, 'Look at the major challenge from Japan and North America to our competitiveness. They have enormous advantages that we do not have, unless we can break down the barriers and truly integrate our markets.'" So big business in Europe started pushing to change the continent's mentality, the idea being that "if you happened to be in the Netherlands or in Milan, you start thinking, not of your own market, but of a European market that is 300 million plus strong, and if you can compete in that then you can compete with the Americans and the Japanese." For Canada to succeed, d'Aquino reasoned, Canadians had to think in the same way about North America.

In the autumn of 1981, d'Aquino called a meeting of big-business executives to discuss the recession and the ominous trend he saw in the North American economy. This was not just an ordinary recession, d'Aquino told the Canadian business élite, it was symptomatic of North America's entry into a period of competitive decline. The North America they had grown up in – the giant land with a rich natural resource base, healthy and unravaged by the war, with a big bite of global trade, and which ensured its people a good standard of living – was now under siege. The European and Asian nations once flattened by World War II had long been back on their feet, competing for and securing their rightful slices of the pie. New technologies were taking over, natural resource prices were slumping, and the communications revolution meant a new world.

In this environment the Americans were going to get tougher with their trading partners, d'Aquino argued, and if they got tougher, the country that stood to lose the most was not Japan or any of the European nations but America's biggest trading partner – Canada. American protectionism would knock Canada to its knees.

Protectionist barriers had risen and fallen throughout Canadian-U.S. history, and Canada had always survived them – with varying degrees of pain. Among others there had been the McKinley Tariff of 1890, the Smoot-Hawley Tariff during the Great Depression of the 1930s, and the latest shot had been Nixon's 10 per cent import surcharge. Despite the record, despite the fact that the GATT regulations limited American protectionist possibilities, and Canada did have the power to retaliate, d'Aquino was convinced that the new threat was dire. To ensure economic prosperity, he told the meeting, the new turn in the world economy meant that Canada now required secure access to the American market under a free trade agreement.

At that time the lone parliamentarian advocating free trade was Senator George van Roggen, who authored a report on its advisability. Van Roggen, an unsung hero in d'Aquino's opinion, was invited to a subsequent meeting, and while no concensus on free trade was reached by the captains of Canadian industry, the idea had been planted and, says d'Aquino, "we started conceptually pushing the idea."

D'Aquino pleaded the case, claiming that secure access was a matter of national security. Gradually, his arguments gained support. Feeding into the continental spirit was the free-market mood of the times, stoked by Reagan's and Thatcher's success. Socialism was in retreat. Debt, piling up everywhere, meant reduced capacity for national governments. The telecommunications revolution meant diminished importance of national boundaries and the surge of global, non-national corporations.

From his perch in the Privy Council office, Dalton Camp saw businessmen assuming a pre-eminence in Canada like never before. "Businessmen were becoming the new heroes, replacing politicians, replacing sports figures even. They had been given a leadership role in the world."[10] Business books took over the best-seller lists, business pages and reports multiplied in the media, conservative commentators gained high profile and credibility. All of this attested to a new faith in the private sector.

Opinion polls told the prime minister that the words of the CEOs carried more weight with the electorate than those of the politicians. This fact, and Mulroney's background as a company president, didn't mean that big business had an open line to the PMO. Number one on his list of priorities was the media. Conrad Black, the industrialist-turned-media-satrap, joked that the only reason he bought *Saturday Night* magazine was so that Mulroney would start returning his phone calls. By and large, though, the government-business relationship was tight, much closer than it was under the Trudeau, Pearson, or Diefenbaker governments. Bay Street had a powerful voice on the Rideau in the person of its own Michael Wilson. Many of the ideas in Wilson's economic agenda paper echoed positions put forward by d'Aquino's BCNI. As the government was preparing for the free trade negotiations, d'Aquino provided it with several black binders outlining what the BCNI wanted. The BCNI binders became a major reference point for Simon Reisman's negotiating team.[11]

Nationalists looked gloomily upon the Tory-Bay Street bonding. They saw the balancing power that Ottawa traditionally exercised against continental corporate interests as being forsaken. They disputed the new conventional wisdom that held first that the GATT could no longer adequately govern Canada's trading interests, and second, that in order to compete successfully with the rest of the world, Canada had to open itself as an initial step to full competition with the United States.

The long-respected GATT was suddenly under attack by Burney and others in the early 1980s for being too slow in its deliberations, too toothless in enforcement, and too feeble to provide Canada with anything resembling secure access to the U.S. market. This type of reasoning drove trade veterans like Mel Clark apoplectic. Clark produced reams of statistics that, he was convinced, showed that the GATT dispute-settlement mechanism did work, that in all but one case the United States adhered to GATT tribunal verdicts, and that Burney, Kelleher, and Wilson had it all wrong.[12]

The old nationalist guard was just as incensed by the other newly fashionable idea: that Canada had to go out on an even continental playing field where the strong would be sorted from the weak. Opening yourself to competition without first preparing to do so, said John Halstead, a third-option architect, made no sense. "It's like saying the only way to make yourself impervious to the cold is to go outside and take your coat off!"[13]

Japan and many other countries had built up a competitive economy in good measure by protection, by keeping key segments closed. Why couldn't Canada do the same? "Opening up a market doesn't necessarily produce more healthy competition," Halstead asserted. "It may produce closed factories."

History told Halstead, a former ambassador to Germany, that doing more business with America hadn't opened the door to the rest of the world for Canada. It had closed it. Since Canada had begun concentrating on the American market during World War I, trade with the United States had increased exponentially, while trade with the rest of the world had dramatically fallen off. To Halstead the reverse of the Tory line was therefore true. Integration with the United States would inevitably bring more integration with the United States.

Fortunately for the Halsteads and the Mel Clarks, J. Duncan Edmonds was sidelined. Edmonds had wanted to move even further than Mulroney into the American orbit. He was reasonably contented with the free trade agreement, but felt many more integrational steps were needed if Canada and the United States were to maximize their potential.

But Edmonds, the weaver of the early plots, the player regarded by Jim Gillies and other senior Tories as the trailblazer, suffered a stinging personal reversal that left him out in the cold, less a prophet than a pariah.

Following the Conservative victory in 1984, he'd joined the Mulroney government, becoming chief of staff to Defence Minister Bob Coates. It wasn't Edmonds' favourite area, but he thought that at least it was a way in and might lead to other things. He didn't know, however, what Coatesian intrigue awaited him. Coates, whom he found to be a hopelessly shallow and incompetent minister, had a soft spot for girly bars, a penchant that became evident on a visit to the Canadian Forces Base in Lahr, Germany. It was there that the defence minister decided he would expand his inspection of the troops to include the local fräuleins.

Well before the scandal became public, the word got back to Edmonds and others through intelligence services. The chief of Canada's defence staff then went to Coates to tell him such behaviour was inappropriate for a man in his position. In short order, as Duncan Edmonds recalled it, the defence chief was back in Edmonds' office with a report on the conversation. "Coates told me to fuck off."[14] Edmonds now decided that he'd better go and see Coates himself. He did so, to similar results. Coates told him to fuck off.

Given what he considered an intolerable situation in the department, Edmonds thought he should warn the prime minister as well as the clerk of the privy council. It was a move less than wise. Mulroney told Edmonds essentially what Coates had told him – only in more polite terms. Coates was a long-time supporter of Mulroney, and the prime minister viewed Edmonds' action as whistle-blowing disloyalty.

The word was soon out that Edmonds was to be severed from all Tory connections. It became too dark on the inside for him to survive. Despite his being proved right once again when the girly-bar scandal broke publicly, forcing Coates' resignation, he remained an undesirable.

Duncan Edmonds left government and moved to Morrisburg on the St. Lawrence, where he ran a book store and dabbled in real-estate projects in Arizona. Being the quintessential continental man, he wasn't about to give up his dream of an intimate union of Canada and the United States. From Morrisburg he could see across the river to the great neighbour to the south, but there was no ferry service linking his community to the American mainland. Edmonds determinedly set to work. Soon he had made all the arrangements to begin a ferry service. He awaited only government permission to set up a customs post. It would be needed to handle all the increased traffic free trade was creating.

10

"I Don't Want Any Surprises, Derek"

Derek Burney was the man most intimately involved in the free trade story from beginning to end – in its formative stages as a member of the civil service, in its introduction as Mulroney's chief of staff, and in its execution as ambassador in Washington. As he worked his way through the thicket, Burney observed a telling distinction between how the Tory politicians saw the process and how the mandarins in the bureaucratic establishment saw it. The politicians cared about the political and economic bottom line. Their chief interests were material well-being and votes. The two went hand in hand. As for the long-term interests of the country, as to the question of how a distinct country could be maintained when almost every thrust was toward Americanizing it, Burney sensed little interest.

Among the mandarins, however, the faceless Ottawa group that wielded the quiet power, developments were viewed in the broader perspective. "At the bureaucratic level," Burney said, "it was almost a psychological debate: Can you get closer to the United States in an agreement and not lose yourself in the process?"[1]

The grey men who had spent their careers stewing over the Canadian-U.S. chemistry were sensitive to the impact of a significant change in the mix. Washington ambassador Allan Gotlieb told the prime minister on more than one occasion that if he was planning to change the delicate historic balance of commerce on the continent, he might consider counterbalancing measures, such as ways to strengthen the central government.

Nationalism was not, however, part of Mulroney's vocabulary. National unity was a question of making Quebec and the other provinces happy. It wasn't a matter of building something to sustain the country against continentalism, globalization, and the other forces that preyed upon it. Burney noticed a curious repetition in his many discussions with the prime minister on the trade agreement. Mulroney's question was always the same: Would the agreement make an appreciable difference to the economy? Nothing else concerned Mulroney, only the bottom line

"It was almost like a code-word discussion," noted Burney. "He would say, 'Well, Derek, what's the answer to the number-onequestion?' His interest was in a balance sheet. 'Give me the pluses and give me the minuses. Tell these guys [cabinet] what we're going to get and where it's going to hurt.'"

After getting repeated assurances from Burney, Mulroney usually ended the conversations with the same line. "I don't want any surprises, Derek."

John Crosbie had a different approach. Free trade was part of natural evolution, so why not get on with it? "Some day we're going to have a North American continent that's an economic union," said Crosbie. "That's inevitable. These economic forces are there, and government policy can't stop them. It's only a question of, How do you get into a more secure position?" Canada had no choice. "They're next door and geography dictates. Whether we like it or not, we're going up or down with the U.S."[2]

Crosbie feared that Canada's abundant resources had made the nation lazy. Now, he said, it could live off its resources no longer. The country needed a wake-up call. Crosbie, like Michael Wilson, had travelled to Hong Kong, and he, too, had come back shocked. "What the hell has Hong Kong got? It's got nothing except geographical position and a bunch of people prepared to work their asses off. And Taiwan is much the same thing."

When the government formally decided to pursue free trade negotiations in the fall of 1985, Brian Mulroney never did sidle over to Crosbie and tell him he had been right all along. "And it wouldn't have been terribly diplomatic of me to remind him," said Crosbie. Nor did anyone recall that the Newfoundlander was the one who identified the deficit as the big problem in 1979 and wanted to tackle it then as minister of finance. "Ah well," said Crosbie with a lilt, "a prophet is always shat upon in his own country."

Crosbie's views on continental fusion were shared by the successor to Bill Brock as head of the U.S. Trade Office, Clayton Yeutter. Brash at the best of times, Yeutter hadn't been in the position long before making the classic blunder of calling Japan his country's most important economic partner "by far." Canada, in fact, far outstripped Japan in trade volumes with the United States. Richard Nixon had once made the same mistake as Yeutter but corrected himself.

For Yeutter, free trade was only one step on the road to economic union and Reagan's North American accord. "I have felt for a long time the ultimate objective we have to have here is something like a North American common market," he said, just as free trade negotiations got going. No one in Canada at this time was looking beyond free trade. The government said it wasn't interested in extending the concept to Mexico. But Yeutter was direct. "I would rather proceed on this exercise with Canada and then bring the U.S.-Mexico relationship along with it as quickly as possible. Then we would tie the three together whenever it seems timely and propitious to do so."

With Yeutter doing his bidding, President Reagan remained low-key, leaving the impression among outsiders that on this, as on other issues, he was typically disengaged. In fact he was keenly interested. Myer Rashish, a veteran of the Kennedy administration who helped Reagan develop the North American accord and who served as his undersecretary of state for economic affairs, said the subtle approach was simply a matter of good politics. "For the U.S. government to take the lead in the initiative [accord] would have made it look like we were trying to force something down somebody's throat."[3]

Like Ty Cobb, Rashish was struck by Reagan's commitment. "Ronald Reagan didn't waste his time on things he wasn't interested in. He was selective." But on free trade and the accord, "he had a very sincere and deep involvement."

Congress was another matter. Free trade with Canada was but one in a morass of issues faced by the legislators. The Canadians got a true sense of their worth in Washington as they tried to secure the Congressional go-ahead for the trade plan. Charlie McMillan and others in the prime minister's ensemble discovered that the senators, having passed new trade laws, didn't understand how they worked. It was up to Ottawa to explain them. At one point McMillan was chasing down Senator Al Gore and another senator in Hong Kong to tell them that, unless they got back to Washington for a crucial vote, the free trade process was dead. Members of the prime minister's staff, cabinet ministers, and diplomats became Washington lobbyists. "It was a full court press," said McMillan. "We were educating them about their own goddamn process."[4]

Ambassador Allan Gotlieb worked the Senate full time, but was repeatedly left standing in an outer office as a senator dashed by him on the way to another appointment. When his term was over, Gotlieb wrote a small book bearing testament to the frequency with which this occurred. He titled it, *I'll Be With You in a Minute, Mr. Ambassador.*

Getting several senators together for a meeting on Canada was little short of impossible. Once, however, a power team from Ottawa, including Burney, Kelleher, and McMillan, got seven in the same room for a session. "It was like this was

Canada day," recalled McMillan. "Their attitude was 'Okay, here's your two hours. Tell us what you have to say then screw off, because we've got bigger problems.'"

Having finally brought together the important senators, the Canadian side botched the moment. On a matter as important as free trade, places in history were at stake. Egos – as Honest Jim Kelleher was to find out in full view of the American legislators – could be easily pricked.

Kelleher thought he was doing the right thing at the meeting when, having made a few points, he concluded with the message that, if the senators had any difficulties, they were to just phone him for a one-on-one chat. He would fill them in. To Kelleher, these were Americans, his friends, and this seemed like a normal procedure between politicians.

But it was *not*, emphatically *not* normal in the view of Ambassador Gotlieb. He took it as a signal the minister was encroaching on his territory. With everyone looking on, he started in at Kelleher with a how-dare-you style attack. He, Gotlieb, was "the ambassador!" Communications had to go through him. Didn't Kelleher know this! How could he stand there and announce he was short-circuiting diplomatic channels?

McMillan looked on in amazement. "It was a fit of pique, a tantrum like you wouldn't believe." Kelleher was shaken. Most people in the room appeared to sympathize with him. Honest Jim perhaps wasn't the most knowledgeable or sophisticated guy, but he was a straightshooter and trying his darndest. After the meeting a blanched Kelleher had a press conference to give. A long walk separated the Canadian contingent from its limousines, and this gave Derek Burney an opening. Undeterred by Gotlieb's high rank, Burney came at him full bore. "You're way out of line," he told Gotlieb. "Way out of line." There are a number of direct channels between politicians, Burney said pointedly, and Kelleher was perfectly within his rights to suggest them to the senators. McMillan was watching. "Derek just chewed the hell out of him."

Kelleher survived the press conference held at the Canadian embassy. As he prepared to leave for the plane trip home, an embassy official asked him if there was anything he needed. Kelleher looked at him. "Yeh, after this visit, I could use a martini. Make it a goddamn double."

As there were no reporters at the meeting, Gotlieb's tantrum was safely hidden from public view. Instead it was left to his wife, Sondra, to gain the reputation of being the testy one in the family. She was caught in the act of cuffing her social secretary across the cheek at a reception during the Reagan-Mulroney summit in Washington in March 1986.

This, the follow-up meeting to the Shamrock Summit, was not a summit that the Gotliebs or Mulroney would remember with great fondness. By this time the prime minister's American policy was meeting with increasing criticism at home. Scoreboard diplomacy became the parlour game of Canadian political pundits, and the way they saw it the prime minister was losing badly. For all his fawning, the critics said, for all his favours to America, he was getting nothing in return. The U.S. side had won an end to FIRA and the dismantling of the NEP. Washington had won a commitment that Canada would align its economic policy to that of the United States. It had won a pledge that super relations with Washington would be the cornerstone of Canadian foreign policy, which resulted in Ottawa's support for U.S. Soviet policy and arms policy. In response to Reagan's call in early 1985 for allied support to isolate and punish Libya for allegedly providing support to terrorists, Canada was quick off the mark in imposing sanctions. The response from most other allies was tepid. Three months later, when American forces bombed the presidential palace in Tripoli in an attempt to liquidate Moammar Gadhafi, the Canadian prime minister was one of the few American allies to support the raid. No one in the West supported Gadhafi, but many wondered whether the bombing of Libyan civilians was the proper response.

Despite all the co-operation, including the readiness to break with more than a century of tradition and enter into a free trade pact, Canada had not been able to get any concessions on the acid rain problem in return. It was clearly, the critics said, a one-way street.

All was not so clear in Washington, however. In some quarters a different view prevailed, as was seen the day Reagan rebuked hardliners at the NSC meeting by telling them he wouldn't talk to Mulroney in the manner they wanted. The administration's right wing purists didn't believe Canada was getting a raw deal at the bargaining table. Rather, they thought the president was being too soft with Mulroney. They viewed such issues as the passage of the *Polar Sea* through Arctic waters and the question of support for the Strategic Defence Initiative from an entirely different perspective.

There were White House scenes that Canadians hadn't been witness to – one being a meeting on the *Polar Sea* affair. During the drawn-out controversy, the administration had argued that the waters of Canada's Northwest Passage were international, while Ottawa said they were national and subject to its sovereignty claims. Critics wanted Brian Mulroney to press the matter in international courts to forestall the voyage of the *Polar Sea* through the passage. They liked New Zealand's approach. New Zealand, with a population of only four million people and nine million sheep, had recently ordered American nuclear ships out of its ports, gaining a measure of respect internationally for having the guts to do so. Mulroney wasn't prepared to go that far, and was again scorned for his bended-knee attitude. He and Reagan couldn't reach a ready compromise on the jurisdiction line, but to assert Canadian sovereignty more effectively in the North, the Mulroney government decided to purchase nuclear-powered submarines. Diesel-powered subs couldn't remain under water long enough to monitor traffic. Very expensive atomic ones could.

Given all the other defence needs of NATO, and given

Canada's weak contribution, the American defence establishment did not feel that Ottawa's sub program was a wise investment. The plan would also require the transfer of highly secret nuclear sub technology. For three decades Washington had resisted requests for such transfers from other NATO allies. Led by Frank Carlucci, the director of the NSC, opposition mounted against making Canada an exception.

At the meeting to decide the issue, Carlucci put the case to the president with some confidence. Everybody in the room supported Carlucci. The chairman of the joint chiefs of staff was against the technology transfer. The director of the nuclear sub program was against it, as was the secretary of defence. The Gipper listened as Carlucci closed his case with the assertion that "to accept Canada's request, Mr. President, would be to reject the advice of every single one of your experts on this issue." Reagan, as paraphrased by a participant at the meeting, weighed in with his verdict. "Frank, we've been up and down this issue several times, and I understand it fully. I'm going to tell Brian that I'm going to go to Congress with a request to amend the Atomic Secrets Act so the technology can be transferred to Canada."[5]

The hardliners made their exit, shaking their heads again. Mulroney had won another one. They'd been annoyed before by Canada's refusal to participate officially in the Strategic Defence Initiative (SDI). Unlike Trudeau, Mulroney supported the American plan for a major strategic defence build-up, believing the White House claim that the Soviets had undertaken vast amounts of research of their own in this area. He decided that the Canadian private sector should involve itself in SDI, but that there should be no government-to-government assistance. At home this was viewed as a compromise position. But at the Pentagon, Caspar Weinberger thought Canada was weaseling its way out, getting the best of both worlds: contracts for the project and no political heat. The United States had plenty of its own domestic manufacturers who were capable of filling private contracts. What Washington wanted was an allied commitment to a new theory of deterrence.

There was more. Ottawa wasn't supporting the United States on Nicaragua or El Salvador, or backing its line on South Africa. Ottawa wasn't increasing its defence spending enough. The president was devoting more time to Canada – when there were so many other pressing matters – than anyone could remember another president doing.

Most of the issues were ones in which Canadian opposition to U.S. policy had long been taken for granted, and Mulroney's continuation of this stance earned him no credit back home for bravely standing up to the superpower. Nicaragua was such a case. Reagan adviser Ty Cobb sat in on a meeting of the president and the prime minister one day as the two men exchanged views on support for the Contra rebels in Nicaragua. Summoning up every soft-on-communism reproach he could imagine, Reagan put the case strongly that it was time for Ottawa to fall in behind him in his effort to topple the Sandinista government. But Mulroney firmly rebutted him at every point. In the end the president was left squirming, and the prime minister hadn't budged an inch. The next day Cobb expected to see headlines in the Canadian press shouting, "MULRONEY SLAM DUNKS REAGAN ON NICARAGUA!" But there was nothing of the kind. Cobb concluded that the facts did not meet the Canadian media's preconceptions and were therefore ignored.[6]

To the hardline faction in Reagan's Washington, the notion in Canada that Mulroney was jumping through hoops to please his new American head office did not square with the facts. According to the State Department's Carroll Brown and others, the only direct capitulation from Mulroney was his gutting of the NEP. Many in the U.S. administration, including trade negotiators, and many in the Canadian government, including Derek Burney, thought Ottawa could have used the NEP as a valuable bargaining chip in free trade negotiations or in dealing with other bilateral issues.

Mulroney, who was three decades younger than Reagan, was initially overawed at sitting down with a president of the United States, and wasn't put off by any of the "amiable dunce" talk about Ronald Reagan. Following an early meeting between the two, he declared, to the barely concealed guffaws of the media, that he thought the president was extremely well-informed. The reverence diminished somewhat with time. Eventually Mulroney wasn't above cracking a joke or two among friends about the Gipper's legendary mind. Many stories went round at the time, one featuring Ron and Nancy in the act of placing their orders at a restaurant. When the waiter asked Nancy for her selection, she requested the *fettucine alfredo.* "Excellent choice, Madame," the waiter responded. "And what about the vegetable?"

"Oh," replied Nancy, "he'll have the same."

As the White House circle saw it, Reagan, jokes aside, was usually able to get up to speed on the general points of Canadian issues, with some last-minute cramming. Secretary of State George Shultz had some background familiarity with Canadian issues, but had to do the same thing. "Shultz was not much different," said Carroll Brown. "He'd spend sixty days running dealing with Soviet matters, and then on the sixty-first it was time to get together with Joe Clark and he immediately was a quick study. Before every meeting there was a lot of very intense briefing and reading on his part."[7]

Whatever the pressures of time, Shultz, like Reagan, had an abiding interest in the bilateral relationship. He established a close rapport with Liberal foreign minister Allan MacEachen, and subsequently with Clark of the Tories. His approach complemented Reagan's. "Instead of just the traditional focus on Europe and the Soviets, Reagan wanted a new emphasis on our neighbours," said Richard Burt, the assistant secretary of state. "But it took someone like Shultz to carry it forward. Personal relationships count for a lot. Shultz and MacEachen, Shultz and Clark. I think Mulroney's closeness to the presidents was a tremendous asset for Canada."

In the spring of 1986, the personal rapport between Reagan and Mulroney continued to be splendid, but the glow in Canada-U.S. relations that had been kindled at the Shamrock Summit a year earlier had dimmed a bit. The U.S. administration decided to downplay the second Reagan-Mulroney summit, believing that the Shamrock love-in had gone too far, and that for this one, to be held in Washington, they should lower their expectations. There would be no sing-along this time. The Irish-background angle would not be played up this time either, and for good reason. The prime minister of Ireland, Garret FitzGerald, was in Washington on this St. Patrick's day for a Shamrock Summit of his own. Reagan was also preoccupied with a high-profile fight with Congress to obtain more financial support for the Contra rebels in Nicaragua. The president had gone on TV to cast the Sandinistas in the role of potential destabilizers of the United States. As the Sandinistas spread their Communist doctrine through Central America, millions of anguished and frightened men and women, the Gipper warned in ominous tones, would pour across the U.S. border for sanctuary. The Nicaraguans, their population only 1 per cent of that of the United States, posed "a mortal threat to the entire New World." Canada had long separated itself from this hyperbole and paranoia, which would result in a judgement in the International Court of Justice against the United States for mining Nicaraguan harbours. But while maintaining Canada's position, Mulroney was less ostentatious in his opposition to the United States than the Liberals had been.

The second summit took on a special irony for Mulroney. Long miffed by the lack of media attention his country received in the American press, Mulroney complained publicly about it. He said before the Reagan meeting took place that a great ally like Canada simply couldn't compete for publicity against the American obsession with tinpot dictators. "Canadians seem to get attention in the United States only if you're Wayne Gretzky or a good snowstorm."

As if orchestrated to illustrate the prime minister's reproach, the fear-mongering campaign against Nicaraguan President Daniel Ortega, certainly a tinpotter in Mulroney's book, hit full throttle as Mulroney arrived in Washington. Remarkably apropos also was Senator Claiborne Pell's *faux pas*. Pell, a veteran of the U.S. Senate and its foreign relations committee, got Mulroney's name wrong. He called the prime minister "Muldoon."

The gaffe was but another in Washington's long history of gaffes. Polls of Americans habitually showed that three-quarters of them couldn't properly identify the prime minister of Canada. The custodians of the White House sometimes fared only marginally better. Harry Truman stumbled hopelessly over the name St. Laurent, confusing it with the river, and finally had to ask someone in the press to help him out. John Kennedy enraged the proud Diefenbaker by pronouncing his name "Diefenbawker." When Prime Minister Lester Pearson arrived at LBJ's Texas ranch, the president, in full view of TV cameras, looked him up and down and said he'd like to welcome Mr. Wilson to Texas. Nixon's most publicized name for Trudeau was captured on the Watergate tapes, but in another slight he announced on an early Trudeau visit that he'd like to welcome the PM and his beautiful wife to the United States. Trudeau was a bachelor at the time.

Even though he flubbed "Mulroney," Senator Pell was at least attempting to compliment him. "You know," the senator blurted, "we're very lucky to have Muldoon as prime minister, because he got into office not by America-bashing but by saying kind words about us."

"Muldoon's" craving for more respect from the big neighbour went unsatisfied in many respects. The PMO was annoyed, for example, by the appointment of a no-name ambassador to Canada to succeed Paul Robinson. Robinson's replacement,

Tom Niles, was a bright, low-key state department professional, but his office-boy demeanour and lack of reputation disappointed Mulroney's entourage. Similarly, the appointment of Peter O. Murphy, a thirty-seven-year-old textile trade negotiator, to head the American free trade negotiating team, was taken as a symbol of underestimation. Simon Reisman, the quick-tempered Canadian head negotiator, was especially appalled. Reisman felt that Carrot-Top, as Murphy was soon nicknamed, was not up to his own glorious standards. The year Murphy was born, Simon Reisman was attending negotiations on the birth of the GATT.

George Shultz's response to suggestions that Canada was not getting enough attention came on the summit's second day. "No administration in the history of the United States," he said, "has devoted more attention to Canada-U.S. relations than the Reagan administration." Evidence supported his assertion. Quarterly meetings between the foreign ministers of both countries were being held, an arrangement that Washington did not have with other nations. Annual summits between the president and the prime minister had been initiated. The importance of Canadian affairs in the State Department had been upgraded so that a deputy secretary presided over the Canada portfolio.

Results from the second summit were negligible. On acid rain, the United States acknowledged the legitimacy of their envoys' report demanding action, but there was nothing to indicate that Reagan was really prepared to move on it. The president and the prime minister signed a new North American Air Defence (NORAD) agreement, which was not, as some critics maintained, a side-door entry into the Star Wars program. And on the rhetorical front, there was some vigorous promotion of the free trade process.

However, any news was eclipsed, if not by Nicaragua, then by the monumentally incidental. This was the slap, heard around the world, that was administered by Sondra Gotlieb to her social secretary, who had allegedly fouled up on her guest-list duties. By the time the chandeliers stopped rattling, Canada was in every American newspaper, rivalling tinpot dictators for the news of the day.

In the months following the summit, the Canada-U.S. relationship worsened. The two countries had agreed at the Shamrock Summit to do their utmost while exploring free trade possibilities to reduce trade friction. But after the Washington parley, the White House announced a 35 per cent tariff on Canadian exports of shakes and shingles. The PM wasn't notified in advance. For all the goodwill he had shown, the levy itself, the timing of it, and the lack of notification, were all seen in Canadian eyes to be rather astonishing. At the same time American lumber interests put forward a countervailing duty petition for a 27 per cent tariff on imports of Canadian softwood lumber. Such a tax would devastate the important B.C. lumber industry. While it wasn't certain the duty would be imposed, the odds didn't look good for British Columbia.

Ronald Reagan, as Ty Cobb said, "didn't sit there and say to everyone in government, 'Phone me each time we're going to do something on softwood lumber.'"[8] Many trade decisions were made without him. The White House officials were annoyed, however, whenever the news broke, as it did in the shakes and shingles incident, before the president could phone the prime minister to explain.

Responding to the manifest Canadian anger, Vice-President George Bush came north to deliver homilies and try to soothe feelings. "I am here," he said in Vancouver, "because there is no relationship more important to the United States than our relationship with Canada." He took time to praise Mulroney as his type of leader, and to laud the Canadian Tories as having the same values as the Republican Party of the United States. Already regarded as suspect by a large proportion of Canadians for being too pro-American, Mulroney didn't need the compliment of being compared to a Republican.

Nor did he need the words of Congresswoman Marcy Kaptor of Toledo, Ohio. Kaptor, in remarks well publicized at the time, said that because of massive U.S. dominance of key Canadian economic sectors, Canada could only be considered a "trust territory" of the United States. The declaration was made out of sympathy, not malice. "I think Canada should be a nation state," she said. "I think the Canadian people should own the majority of their industries. I feel the same way about the United States." Statistics, made public at the time, showed that the level of Canadian trade with the United States (over 75 per cent) made Canada more dependent on trade with a single country than any other nation in the world. It outdid Cuba, which was in second place with its huge dependence on the Soviet Union. In third position was Mexico, with its dependence on the United States. With plans for a North American accord to further that dependency, Mexico's American future, like Canada's, looked sealed.

11

A Continent of Many Nations

The border dividing the United States from its trust territory, as Congresswoman Marcy Kaptor called it, was drawn without regard for ethnicity, patterns of commerce, social mores, or, for much of its length, geographical formations. As is the case for most boundaries separating nation states, the forty-ninth parallel was an arbitrary, artificial divide set for political reasons. If borders developed from the imperatives of the land and demographics and free-enterprise economics, there is little doubt there would be a dramatically different boundary between Canada and the United States.

One theorist on the subject, Joel Garreau of the *Washington Post*, set about trying to discern what the map of North America would be like if politicians were evicted to faraway islands and the logic of the market and natural forces determined the territories. Garreau came up with not two hulking nations but nine region-states. He turned his map and the thinking behind it into a best-selling book called *The Nine Nations of North America*. In Garreau's model, all that was left of Canada was Quebec. The country's other parts seeped southward and grafted themselves onto compatible American territories. Nothing of today's border survived, but for the St. Lawrence River.

The cartography of Garreau emphatically buttressed the belief that the logical economic flow on the continent ran north-south, not east-west, as in the case of Canada. His book outlined five new transborder countries falling on a vertical axis from Canada. Atlantic Canada, as constituted today, would be defunct, portioned instead into a New England nation. Southern Ontario would droop into the northeast industrial heartland of the United States to form a new smoke-stack entity called The Foundry. Southern Manitoba and Sas-katchewan, Canada's granary, would combine with their wheaty American brethren to produce The Breadbasket. The great white Canadian North and resource-rich Alberta would ally with Colorado and resource America in one big vacant land mass. Garreau could come up with no better moniker for this region than The Empty Quarter. On the West Coast the bound-ary would extend along B.C.'s Pacific Rim far down into Califor-nia to mould one long, green state called Ecotopia.

Initially Garreau's work, while interestingly presented and thickly detailed, was looked upon as a fun model, a curiosity piece that would find its way quickly onto oblivion's scrap heap. There followed, however, a decade of international eco-nomic and political turmoil. Nations faced punishing debts, globalization reduced the importance of borders, economies regionalized, and out of the considerable chaos came the para-dox of simultaneous integration and disintegration. Political space no longer jibed with economic space. Power both devolved to subnational units and evolved into supra-national ones. Ethnic nationalism became a fractious and potent force. Speculation was prompted on the decline of the nation-state era.

Not all of these trends manifested themselves in North America, but a goodly number did, and Garreau's work became more and more plausible. Companies began basing their mar-keting strategies on his map of the continent. By 1990 data bases could be purchased in which marketing strategies for every consumer product imaginable were dumped into his nine-nation model. The author watched with contentment and surprise. He had not written the book to be viewed as a harbinger of a new continental order. But no one had predicted that the Soviet Union would collapse into a multitude of nations, that Eastern Europe would be liberated, and that Western Europe would take such great strides toward economic and political unification. With Canada embarking on a new *laissez-faire* era while simultaneously imperilled by unity crises, much was possible.

Garreau read about the urban sprawl from Vancouver to Portland, Oregon. He read about U.S. states and western Canadian provinces entering into joint trade missions. He heard about cross-border regions seeking economic autonomy. He heard of plans to model the Canadian Senate on the U.S. Senate, so that regions would have a louder voice. He saw regional political parties sprout, and he witnessed a devolution of power in Canada presided over by a government with American instincts. He saw the Conservatives increasingly turn the country over to free-market forces, the natural forces from which his very model had sprung.

By the early 1990s, as Garreau saw it, English Canada was undergoing its own quiet revolution.[1] As had happened in the United States, power, money, transportation networks, and education in Canada had been dispersed widely enough to regions to the point where some felt they no longer needed the centre. In both countries leaders in these regions began to feel they could manage on their own quite nicely, particularly if they were to join hands with their natural partners on either side of the border. Said Garreau: "FDR created a super government in Washington in the 1930s and 1940s because it was perceived with good reason that states like Mississippi could not solve their own problems. Now they can. Education, information, is evenly distributed. That's why the nine nations can evolve."

Some cities, Garreau observed, were becoming world players in their own right. They think they can solve their own problems. They proudly exhibit regional and in some cases ethnic identities. "Back in the 1950s the idea was that you shouldn't celebrate your ethnic diversity, that you should be as anglo as possible," Garreau said. "You hid it, if anything. Now it's different."

Canada's Marshall McLuhan had effectively forecast the power dispersal described by Garreau. Technology, according to McLuhan, would make it possible. "We are heading," he said, "for cottage economies where the most important industrial activities can be carried on in any individual little shack anywhere on the globe."[2]

The strength of regionalism, the eventual emergence of region-states of the kind envisioned by Garreau, would depend largely on how Canada's federal governments reacted to existing trends: whether they acquiesced to them and thereby accelerated them, or set about to stymie them with countercurrent public policy. The Mulroney Tories not only acquiesced, they embellished. Until their arrival, the Canadian tradition saw an assertive central government acting to restrain the north-south economic flows and reinforce the unnatural east-west infrastructure that ensured the survival of the country. The idea was to defend against America's manifest influence, not welcome it. The intervention of the state – with railways, cultural programs, communications, and economic protection – made the survival of Canada possible. The country's huge size, skimpy population, and regional disparities, made it highly vulnerable to disintegrative tendencies at the best of times. It had on its doorstep a mammoth power of ten to one preponderance. Without a strong standard-bearer and standard-setter at the centre, there could be little glue to hold Canada together. It could be argued that in Europe, where the jurisdictions were smaller, more populated, and where different languages fostered different cultures, there was less need for a strong centre. Yet governments there were generally more interventionist than in Canada. Canada's social spending at 21 per cent of GDP was, for example, less than the average of all OECD countries, which was at 25 per cent. The history of other nations of gargantuan proportion like Canada offered no comfort for those viewing decentralization as a way to unity. Only the strongest of central governments had been able to hold such countries together. In Russia and China, autocracies and dictatorships had been necessary. In the recent case of the Soviet Union, when the dictatorship was removed, the destabilized federation dissolved.

If intervention had made Canada possible, the question was whether disintervention would make it impossible, inviting a Garreau-style scenario?

No less than three major initiatives of the Mulroney government were decentralizing steps of significant proportion. They were free trade, Wilson's agenda for economic renewal, and constitutional reform. Two were realized, while constitutional reform didn't succeed – though not for want of trying. The free trade story captured all the media attention, although, in altering the essence of Canada, Michael Wilson's quiet revolution was arguably just as meaningful.

Like free trade, Wilson's program aimed at clearing away hurdles for business and harmonizing the Canadian system with the American one. Free trade would do the same by reducing tariffs, removing investment barriers, and integrating banking and financial services. Wilson's less heralded *démarche* targeted other areas for harmonization; most of them the very things that had defined Canada on the continent. Crown corporations were sold off, social programs were cut, cultural nationalism was sidelined, and national institutions were downsized. The corporations got the biggest tax breaks. Deregulation was a key theme. Universality was out. The decades-old social contract that Canadians had lived by was torn up and replaced by a new continental contract based more on the principle of survival of the fittest.

Canadians had, in the past, been prepared to pay more for their more humane country – for better social welfare, a better medicare system, cleaner and safer streets, and generally a more ordered society. Now the idea was that, given the debt and the new world economy, such a Canadian model could no longer be afforded. Ottawa would pull back under Wilson's plan, and the private sector would generate and distribute more of the wealth, just as it did in America, where, nationalist critics were quick to point out, the top 1 per cent of the population had come to possess 90 per cent of the wealth.

While many saw this radical restructuring as the only way to address the base problems facing the country, others, continentalists including the likes of free trade negotiator Gordon Ritchie, saw it as pure folly. They saw it as a surrender to the market and the American way. It was, said Ritchie, a replacement of national political power with national corporate power by "people whose intellectual apparatus was too weak" to realize what they were doing to the country.[3]

In 1987 Mulroney and Wilson brought in a tax reform package in which they unabashedly copied the Reagan model. A year earlier Reagan had slashed the top corporate tax rate. Various graduated tax levels were dropped in favour of a simplified system of three levels. Those with low incomes would pay 15 per cent, while the highest wage earners saw their taxes plummet from 50 per cent to 28 per cent. Once the Americans had set about reforming their tax system, Wilson felt that Canada had no choice but to do the same. He slashed corporate tax rates with the ringing endorsement of Bay Street. Canada had to keep pace. Keeping pace meant accepting the fiscal philosophy that was dominant in the 1980s – trickle-down economics.

Paul Reichmann, the real-estate king of the period, warned that if the country didn't move ahead with the advances of capitalism and technology on the continent, business would pack up and leave Canada. To ignore the economic trends set in motion by Ronald Reagan was not only impossible but "suicide," Reichmann said. To claim it was "suicide," to claim it was impossible not to follow the American lead was, by all appearances, to say it was impossible for Canada to have a distinct future of its own. The argument appeared to affirm the nationalist warning – once Canada got too firmly bound to the American economy there could be no exit. The vortex of integration could not be escaped. It was all in George Grant's book.

Experts like Stephen Blank, the head of the Americas Society and a leading authority on regional ties between the two economies, believed the Canadian and American economies had become so welded together that even to term their commerce a trading relationship was a misnomer. "Something is made on one side of the border and sent up across for a part, then sent back to be packaged or whatever, then shipped across again to be sold," Blank said. Because of the presence of so many multinational subsidiaries in Canada, nearly 50 per cent of bilateral trade was intercorporate; that is, between parent companies and their subsidiaries. Rather than a trading relationship, Blank said, "we are effectively a single economy. That's point one." Point two, he said, was that some of Joel Garreau's arguments had merit. "The single economy is becoming highly regionalized."[4]

During the free trade debate, Tom d'Aquino of the BCNI liked to refer to himself and the business leaders he represented as the "real patriots" of the country. He acknowledged that corporate Canada had been doing well under the Tory tax policies. "I know the argument is made that the personal tax burden has become much heavier than the corporate tax burden." But it had been mainly a case of catching up, he said, explaining that in relation to the United States and other OECD countries, corporate taxation in Canada was about average. Of those who objected to the Mulroney policies, of the "nationalists and the Linda McQuaigs of the world," d'Aquino asked, "What are you saying? Are you saying that our corporate tax rates would be increased five or ten per cent? What social benefit is that going to have? What is that going to do for investment, for jobs?" The leader of the real patriots, as he called them, went on to say that "the more heavily corporations are taxed, the more they will pass it on to the consumer."[5] But could such an attitude stem from patriotism? Or was it a rationale that so easily brought to mind George Grant's warning that "no small country can depend for its existence on the loyalty of its capitalists"?

Though it was reasonable to assume that big business would invest less if its marginal tax rates were too high, Canada had in fact prospered with much higher corporate rates, as had many European countries. With a more progressive tax system than the United States, Japan had become the world's leading economic performer.

In d'Aquino's opinion, the advent of the global economy meant that every country was losing sovereignty. Everything had become interdependent, and interdependence carried with it a loss of distinctiveness. There would be a new kind of Canadian nation, said the voice of money in Canada, one with many cultural pockets and a reduced role for the centre. More blunt than the politicians about the changing face of the country, d'Aquino stated that the goal was nothing less than the economic union of the continent. After free trade, the next likely step, he said one day over lunch in a posh Washington hotel, would be monetary union. This would constitute another major step on the road to integration, but corporate Canada's main man brought up the idea with a degree of nonchalance. His attitude was surprising, because free traders built their case on the idea that one form of integration would not lead to another, that there should be no fear of a domino effect leading to dramatic loss of sovereignty and increased pressure for union.

But with free trade, as d'Aquino understood, a common currency would make doing business so much easier. No one would have to go to the trouble of looking up exchange rates or of changing currencies when they crossed the border. Americans wouldn't have to wonder about strange faces on Canadian bills, and the life of the loonie would be unexpectedly short. Traders wouldn't have to compare daily the value of their Canadian dollar to the American dollar, and wonder what the Bank of Canada was doing.

If monetary union came about as d'Aquino predicted, logic would then suggest a customs union by which Canada and the United States, having eliminated almost all of their bilateral tariffs, would charge the same external tariffs to the outside world.

With such commonalities in place, the question would then be, Who sets the bank rate? Or, who sets the external tariffs? On such important issues, each side would naturally demand input. Decisions would have to be made by politicians on both sides in a joint forum. The result would be a serious loss of political sovereignty. The United States would naturally argue that its ten-to-one population advantage be reflected in its number of voting representatives. With a one-tenth voting share, Canadians would be virtually powerless on questions significantly affecting the economic health of their country – a country that could no longer, by any stretch of the imagination, call itself sovereign.

D'Aquino, however, rejected outright the widely held belief that economic integration would inevitably lead to political integration. The global village meant interdependence, but it also meant that Canadians would know one another better and have stronger, shared values, he said. Economic borders could be removed without affecting other boundaries. "You can still have national or subnational units that have a clear identity, one from another," d'Aquino claimed. His subnational units wouldn't fit Garreau's nine nations of North America model, because they would be retained by the border. There was too much in the United States, d'Aquino said, pausing to reflect on the nature of the society outside the hotel dining room, into which Canadians simply were not prepared to buy. "The average Canadian associates the United States with disparities between rich and poor which he is uncomfortable with, a society in which only in very few of the major cities can one walk safely, a society becoming more violent than less violent. You're told about a country that doesn't believe in the common wealth of its citizens like we do. Add to that a country whose political system is virtually paralysed, a political system that doesn't work anymore, and a country with deeply rooted social problems that are only going to get worse. In a debate these differences would be articulated, and Canadians would say, 'We don't want that.'"

Free trade was a cornerstone of d'Aquino's BCNI program. So were the slashes in the tax rates, and so would be most of the other reforms that Michael Wilson set about achieving. In the same year as the 1987 tax reform, Wilson agreed to a deregulation of the Canadian banking industry, allowing Canadian chartered banks to trade in securities and opening Canadian investment firms and banks to foreign ownership. While limitations remained on Canadian banks operating in the United States, U.S. banks got *carte blanche* to operate in Canada. This newly deregulated environment, very much in keeping with the trend of globalization, meant that within a few years the centre of Canadian corporate banking would shift to New York; there would be, as Ann Shortell wrote in *Money Has No Country*, "an evisceration of Canada's native financial core." While invisible to the average citizen, Shortell said, the move was "an integral part of the country's changing definition of sovereignty."

Mulroney picked up quickly on the deregulation trend of the Reagan Republicans, and Ottawa moved to deregulate the telecommunications, rail, trucking, and airline industries, among others. Privatized or partially privatized were Air Canada, Petro-Canada, and Canada Post.

Being under the influence of the United States as much as the border boys were meant, not only the denationalization of

Air Canada, but the gradual loss of Canada's control of its airline system. The Tories helped Canadian Airlines International secure a merger with American Airlines – this, rather than push for a merger of Air Canada and Canadian Airlines, which would have been a bold nationalist stroke. The government preferred to let continental market forces hold sway, which meant more control from the United States.

Being under the influence of the United States as much as the Tories were meant yielding to pressure to open the Canadian drug market to multinationals, primarily U.S. multinationals. It meant that Canada would even copy the way the Americans went about preparing for the free trade negotiations.

The government's move to change the drug laws began as a sideshow to FTA negotiations and ended as a full-blown controversy still churning at the end of 1992. Generic drugs or drugs produced by Canadian companies had saved Canadians, a commission showed, about $200 million a year. The old legislation limited the number of years foreign companies could have patent rights on Canadian soil. New legislation, pressed upon the Tories by Ed Pratt, chairman of Pfizer, the giant American pharmaceuticals company, would take away the advantage that kept the price of drugs 32 per cent lower in Canada than in the United States. Canadian healthcare prices, as part of the new free trading mentality, were on the road to harmonization with those in the U.S. Canadians, as the *New York Times* said, with a note of surprise, on its front page, would start paying the same amount for drugs as Americans.

Pratt served as head of President Reagan's trade advisory group, which was enormously influential on free trade and other issues. His pressure was such, as American free trade negotiator Bill Merkin explained, that the Tories feared he could derail the entire free trade negotiations if he didn't get a compromise on drugs,[6] and this fear, said Merkin, contributed to Canada's acquiescence. It was an example of what Canadian nationalists worried about. In a bilateral deal, the players with the clout, those from the country with ten times the weight of the other, end up the winners.

Pratt had become a friend of Jim Kelleher. By coincidence the two men had homes close to each other in Florida. They became doubles partners in tennis, they became hunting partners, and Pratt did not hesitate to inform Kelleher of his strong opposition to the pharmaceutical policies. "I think it's fair to say," Kelleher recalled, "that Eddie told me he didn't think Canada was acting in a very appropriate manner."[7]

Kelleher, who said he never lost a moment's sleep over nationalist concerns, had liked Ed Pratt ever since the American made some suggestions on how Kelleher should manage his trade portfolio.

Kelleher had been introduced to Pratt by Bill Brock, head of the U.S. trade office before Clayton Yeutter took over. Pratt explained to Kelleher how he could get the Canadian private sector on board the free trade train. Kelleher was excited. "Pratt's people came up to Ottawa and explained how their system worked. Based on that, we then Canadianized the American system and set up ours."

The Americanization caused Kelleher some problems. Some, like union leader Bob White, strongly rejected the Kelleher-Pratt solution, which involved setting up private-sector committees to liaise with the trade negotiating hierarchy. To White, it reeked of showcasing. "Bob White heard about it," Kelleher remembered, "and went absolutely apeshit." With respect to a cultural committee, there was a similar response from Canada's leading female novelist. "I'll never forget," said Kelleher, "the meeting when we got them all together in a room and we had our novelist friend there – the Woman." When asked if he meant Margaret Atwood, Kelleher, rolling his eyes skyward, said, "Yeh, Atwood. Suffice it to say, it didn't work out too well."

Although "the Woman" and Bob White were both opposed,

the committee system was generally well received, and Kelleher was proud of it and grateful to his American friend.

As Kelleher, who would soon be moved off to the solicitor-general's portfolio, and Mulroney, Wilson, and the rest began pushing the new American agenda, they did so before an ambivalent public. Polls, public and private, consistently told the prime minister that the electorate thought he was too close to the United States. But anti-Americanism and fears of U.S. domination were not as strong as they had been in the 1960s when America was at war abroad and in the throes of a civil-rights war at home. By the 1980s the mood had swung. As the command economies showed signs of collapsing in the East, and the *laissez-faire* roll of Reagan and Thatcher continued in the West, sympathies were not with big government activism and anything that smacked of socialism. If the mood was ever right for free trade, it was at this time – even if in 1986-87 Mulroney found his friends the Americans recalcitrant over a series of bilateral trade issues.

The Americans pushed ahead with an import duty on softwood lumber, provoking Canadian retaliation on corn imports and a most curious compromise settlement on the lumber issue. So that U.S. lumber interests could no longer claim unfair competition, Canada imposed a 15 per cent tax on its own lumber exports. Better this, Ottawa reasoned, than pay duty to Washington. But it was a mark of who had the upper hand in the relationship. It still hurt the B.C. lumber industry, and the whole affair violated the spirit of the Shamrock Summit.

Reagan had initially accepted his envoys' report on acid rain in terms firm enough for Prime Minister Mulroney to say that it marked a step "very significant in the long and difficult road toward purifying our two environments." Now, in his trillion dollar budget for 1987, Reagan ignored the report, committing only a trickle of cash to environmental protection. Canada's environment minister suggested mildly that Ottawa would have to "revisit its assumption" that Reagan cares about acid rain.

With Washington riveted by the Iran-Contra scandal and Reagan's popularity in free fall, Canadian issues slipped farther and farther from the spotlight. Mulroney candidly admitted that he didn't think he was getting a good return on his investment. "Canadians quite properly expect my government to deliver more than that of my predecessors, and if I can't then I've got trouble, and I acknowledge that I may be in the wrong, and that is what elections are all about." The prime minister was not, however, about to be moved from his strategy of ingratiation. His position was unequivocal: "I am a friend of the United States of America; I make no bones about it. I don't believe like the Liberals and NDP in throwing verbal hand grenades at Washington every other day and then trying to pretend hypocritically that you are really a friend and neighbour." Of those who feared for Canadian sovereignty, he said, "this is only the preoccupation of a small group of timid souls."

To demonstrate that there truly was concern in Washington, George Bush was sent back up to Canada to say the same things he had said six months earlier in Vancouver. When Bush arrived, the PM gave him "an earful," as the vice-president put it, about all the broken promises and neglect of Canada. With Bush at his side, Mulroney told the press outside Rideau Hall that "the government of Canada doesn't want to be on anyone's backburner or taken for granted at any time."

Bush suggested that the president and the prime minister might go the extra mile in their April 1987 summit and solve some of the outstanding problems. But summit number three in Ottawa came and went with hardly anything to mark it – no sing-song, no slap. Mulroney tried to take the offensive. Having sustained some criticism on the sovereignty issue with the voyage of the *Polar Sea*, he hauled out maps to demonstrate to the president why the Canadian claims were just, and threatened to take the matter to the International Court. Mulroney was feisty and tough. But Reagan, who was well-briefed on this issue, would not bend. On acid rain, Mulroney had proposed that the two sides draw up a treaty. With Kennedy-like eloquence, he said, "In this matter time is not our ally but our enemy. . . . What would be said of a generation that sought the stars but permitted its lakes and streams to languish and die?" Again the response was non-committal.

In his speech to Parliament, Reagan couldn't pass up another plug for his cherished Star Wars plan, saying he would plunge ahead and spend billions of dollars despite Moscow's disarmament overtures. At this MP Svend Robinson of the NDP interjected, shouting, "No way . . . Stop Star Wars now." When the Gipper then made reference to the system of nuclear deterrence known as MAD, or Mutually Assured Destruction, another NDPer, Les Benjamin, barked out, "He's mad!"

During his week in Canada, the president did give a much-needed rhetorical push to the free trade negotiations. The talks were proceeding erratically, not aided in the least by the temperamental divide between the bargaining teams. American negotiator Peter Murphy spoke in an incomprehensible grey fuzz. Simon Reisman, the man on the other side, externally combusted at the drop of a paperclip. Of the wretched lack of rapport it was said: "One couldn't talk, the other couldn't listen."

The Americans found Reisman's fiery temperament laughable and sometimes useful. At one point Peter Murphy wanted to avoid discussing a certain topic until the next phase of the negotiations. Bill Merkin, his deputy, told him he'd have to find a way to kill three hours. Murphy knew that would be no problem. He opened the meeting with incendiary comments on the need to bring culture and autos into the free trade bartering. Reisman erupted, flying into a rage that the Americans, chuckling beneath their serious demeanours, kept stoking for the required three hours. Murphy achieved his goal.[8]

When Treasury Secretary James Baker joined the discussions

for the final sessions, he, too, was treated to a show of Reisman's temper. After the lead Canadian negotiator finally concluded a fifteen-minute rant about autos, Baker slipped a note to Merkin. "My sympathies. Now I know what you guys have had to put up with."

As the Americans saw it, these negotiations were stacked in their favour. "Canada came into the negotiations at a real disadvantage," said Merkin. "They were viewed in Washington as the petitioner. We always sit back in any negotiation, whether it's with Canada or anybody else, and we have the luxury of having this huge market that the other guy wants access to and we leverage that." Despite Reagan's personal interest, there was little interference from the White House, especially after the Gipper fell into the Iran-Contra sinkhole.

From day one the American negotiators saw Canada's goal of gaining a secure access to their market as a pipedream. Increased access with some insurance coverage, yes, but secure? Never. There was no chance that Washington politicians would relinquish their own jurisdiction over something as important as trade. Only when Canada got to vote in U.S. elections, said Merkin, would it have that much influence on the American process.

If the verdict on many issues in the free trade bargaining was moot, there was no contesting the big American victory on the one issue that would make free trade tick – the value of the respective currencies.

On the question of the value of the Canadian dollar, controversy brewed over an alleged side deal. The Americans wanted a higher Canadian dollar to make any trade agreement more appetizing to them. The matter was unquestionably a sore point in the Reagan administration. With the country looking at a $175 billion trade deficit, and with Canada holding a huge surplus in bilateral trade, Canada was viewed as a major source of the problem. Treasury Secretary James Baker, whose words carried enormous weight, complained that Canada's dollar was too low when he appeared before the Senate Foreign Relations Committee in 1986. Peter Murphy made the same point several months later. Meanwhile, Commerce Secretary Malcolm Baldrige was being categorical on the subject – a higher Canadian dollar or no trade pact. Canada's minister of industry, trade and commerce at the time was Sinclair Stevens. Stevens asked Baldrige at a meeting, What will make a free trade agreement fly? As Stevens recalled the conversation, Baldrige replied, "The level of your dollar." The commerce secretary added that it would have to be close to the ninety-cent level, more than ten cents higher than the level of the dollar at the time.

Stevens remembered the conversation because Baldrige was so blunt. "He said to me, 'Do you think we would let California into our Union with a seventy-five-cent dollar? Well then why do you assume we'd get in an agreement with Canada if you could have a seventy-five-cent dollar?'"[9]

No secret deal on the dollar was made during the actual trade talks. But there is evidence that the Americans achieved their goal through other channels. While Stevens acknowledges that there was no formal agreement to get the currency higher, the former minister, forced to resign after being implicated in an influence-peddling scandal, is among many who believe that Ottawa appeased currency concerns in Washington with pledges at the G-7 summits and meetings of foreign finance ministers. In State Department briefing papers prepared for George Bush at the beginning of 1989, it was pointed out with evident satisfaction that Canada usually toed the U.S. line at the G-7 meetings. In these Canada agreed to set lower inflation-rate targets. By doing so Ottawa was effectively agreeing to a higher dollar, since the higher interest rates required to reduce inflation would have this effect on the currency.

The outcome was as the Americans would have wished it. In the early years of free trade, the United States would be granted its wish for a ninety-cent Canadian dollar. Those Canadians trying to get a start under the new trade rules were up in arms over the disadvantage they faced. Bank of Canada governor John Crow, responsible for the high interest rates, would be excoriated across the land for his absolutist crusade against inflation, leaving unemployment to soar. Of his few supporters, one would be Michael Wilson.

The story of the free trade negotiations and the various forces that entered into play has been written about most thoroughly in *Faith and Fear*, by Bruce Doern and Brian Tomlin. That the influence of the business sector in Canada and the United States was substantial in determining the content of the agreement, there is little doubt. Since business would be the sector most directly affected by free trade, it was only natural that its opinion carried significant weight. It was the BCNI that had handed Reisman the two black books stating what an eventual agreement should look like. Reisman stuck close to the blueprint. It was d'Aquino and Laurent Thibault, the president of the Canadian Manufacturers' Association, who were in almost daily contact with Reisman or his deputy, Gordon Ritchie, and who had frequent discussions with the prime minister. When the trade negotiations were derailed in September 1987, it was Canadian business leaders who called in American Express chairman Jim Robinson and got him to lobby Reagan and James Baker so that the talks could be restarted.

Whatever the pros and cons of free trade, the consequences were indisputable: decentralization and integration. Ottawa's power over cross-border flows was diminished. Barriers came down between Canada and the United States. Business was less encumbered. The agreement made the movement of goods and people between Canada and the United States easier. Goods moving from one country to the other were accorded the honour of "national treatment." It meant that the other country's goods received the same treatment as domestic goods in regard to regulations, taxes, and so on. The agreement further reduced the Canadian government's power over energy policy. Energy became continental. Trade dispute mechanisms were established, thereby institutionalizing the bilateral relationship, sealing it more than ever before. Bilateral arbitration bodies took over territory formerly claimed by multilateral ones through the GATT. The agreement integrated banking and financial services. Protection was removed from investment as well as from parts of the sprawling service economies.

It was more than a trade agreement. It was arguably the biggest step the two countries had taken together toward integration in their history. With it, and with Wilson's quiet revolution, the countries were gelling, the border becoming less and less meaningful in real terms, and unseen borders of the type imagined by Joel Garreau starting to take form.

12

One Giant Beehive

The big economic buzzword of the 1980s was the unwieldy term "globalization." Globalization meant the invasion of the outer world. It meant interdependence, interconnectedness, integration. Rather than separate entities, the world's two-hundred-plus countries were becoming part of one giant beehive.

To nation states, globalization meant reduced control of their destinies. Trade borders were coming down, communications borders were coming down, the economies of nation states were being denationalized and thrown into an international blender.

For Canada, the border-erasing trend had particular meaning. Because Canada has only one neighbour, globalization first and foremost meant Americanization. Lumped in with the other trends of the Mulroney government – free trade and Reaganomics – globalization stepped up the pace of integration way beyond anything Canada had seen. Globalization was a splendid ideological fit for the Mulroney government. Through tax breaks and deregulatory measures, the government played to the corporate agenda. Globalization did the same. The downsizing of economic borders meant that the transnationals met with less interference. They had more room to roam.

Globalization meant competition, marching out on the level playing field and meeting the other guy head on.

The cold war was over, but as Edward Ney, the U.S Ambassador to Canada, put it, "The hot war is on. The competition is just going to be plain brutal. The dynamics of international trade and competition will be harrowing. Maybe a lot tougher than the cold war with the Soviet Union."[1]

Ney, a slender, wealthy man with a raspy voice that rushed and subsided in great dramatic timbre, was the past chairman of Young and Rubicam Inc., the world's largest advertising company. He was a close friend of George Bush. With Ney's help Bush's image evolved from that of wimp – from the "Incredible Sulk" as he was known in 1980 – to the mean slugger who shredded Michael Dukakis in the 1988 presidential election.

Ney had thought long and hard about the overwhelming dependence of Canada on the United States. If Ney was a Canadian he wouldn't have liked it, he said. "I'd think what I guess most Canadians think. 'We get along with the Americans, but I wish I didn't have all my baskets in one place.' I guess you go back to Trudeau and option three and building some other ties."

Sitting in the grandeur of his wood-panelled, old-money office overlooking Parliament Hill, the ambassador put the Canadian problem in the context of his business experience. "I was in a service business. If we had a client that was over five per cent of our total business relationship we were just terribly concerned. But someone with seventy-five per cent? You'd say, 'Wowww!'"

The existing Canadian dependence was one thing, he said, but with globalization, it could only get worse. Canadian businesspeople would go where the buck was. They'd go south. "Everything is north-south," said Ney. "There's so much going back and forth that twenty-five years from now, it will be one integrated hemispheric economy." Globalization meant there was little choice. "You are in it," said the ambassador, his voice booming. "You can't hide. It's survival of the fittest!"

In some respects, globalization wasn't new. The process had been accelerating since the late 1940s, when an organization with the aim of opening up world trade, the General Agreement on Tariffs and Trade, was founded. A series of GATT negotiations achieved significant success in taking trade barriers down and creating a world environment in which the movement of goods was less encumbered. In 1948 the value of world trade amounted to $57 billion. In 1986 it was worth more than $2,100 billion.

From one perspective the development looked like craziness. Why expose one's self to competition from almost every nation on the globe? What had once caused Nietzsche concern was now being taken to the limit. "Look," wrote the German philosopher in the last century, "at the present madness of nations, which desire above all to produce as much as possible. . . . They live in ambush for one another; they obtain things from each other by lying in wait. It is called by them good neighbourliness."

The sheltered life was much more secure. Compete in one's own little market, keep the foreign influences out, nourish one's own culture. But the other side of the argument prevailed. Trade produced wealth, enhanced standards of living, enhanced progress. If better and cheaper products were being produced outside one's country but were not allowed in, progress was being stifled. Backwardness in comparison to others would follow. Argentina and Canada provided examples. Argentina chose relative economic isolation in the post-war era and lagged behind Canada, which by comparison had an open economy.

The GATT was a springboard for globalization, but what gave it its modern currency and impact was the onset of the computer and communications revolutions. Now corporations could take advantage of the more open borders created by the GATT. For the business world, these global-village revolutions meant speed, more mobile capital, mobile technology, mobile labour, mobile information. While the GATT allowed goods to move more freely among nations, these technological changes also allowed them to be *produced* among nations – transnationally. One component here, one there, one wherever conditions were right to maximize innovation and profit.

The big agents of globalization became the transnational corporations. They spread their operations through dozens of countries and were beholden to none. By the late 1980s, Visa Inc. was owned by 21,000 financial institutions in 187 countries and territories. No one nation had a majority on Visa's board. It had become, for all intents and purposes, an independent agent, controlled by no flag, just out there, largely unregulated, with control over great amounts of capital and labour. Huge transnationals like Visa, GM, and Matsushita Electric became so powerful that their GDPs were greater than those of many nations. The heads of these private empires were becoming as powerful as prime ministers, kings, parliaments. With their multiplication, the global corporations began to control an increasingly large slice of the globe's economic pie. No one was regulating them. The day could be contemplated, said author Alvin Toffler, when these companies would have their own militias and their own seats at the United Nations.

In business, country of origin meant less and less. Canada's high-tech giant Northern Telecom had spread its operations to forty countries by 1990. Two-thirds of its 60,000 employees were non-Canadian. Three of its four-member executive were Americans. Washington was viewed as Northern Telecom's real centre of power, with London and Tokyo substations gaining ground. To Nortel chairman Paul Stern, nationality considerations had to be set aside. "I think that national companies, in any business, if they maintain that mindset, will atrophy."

The more borders opened, the faster capital flowed, and the less control nation states enjoyed. The powers of national banks were significantly reduced by the vast volumes of currency being traded by currency speculators. In earlier times the central banks could affect their exchange rates by buying or selling a moderate amount of their country's currency. That moderate amount no longer made a dent, given the volumes being exchanged by the late 1980s.

"Globalization has proceeded to the point," said Roy Culpepper of Canada's North-South Institute, "where higher taxes and lower interest rates are vetoed, not by executives and legislatures, but by the telephone calls of money brokers, able to transfer billions across boundaries at the push of a button." Estimates put the amount changing hands in currency markets at fifty times the volume of transactions by trade. Thus, said Culpepper, the fundamentals of the world economy, nations' productivity and competitiveness, were being thrown out by artificial flows. "The modern-day money changers have taken over the temples of economic policy, and they must be expelled."[2]

At the same time that nations' autonomy in monetary policy was being curbed, their traditional Keynesian fiscal levers were becoming harder to pull. Big business could respond to higher levels of taxation or other forms of government intervention by shifting operations to a more favourable economic climate. Success stories like Northern Telecom placed yet another co-nundrum before governments: Why go to the cost and trouble of developing national champions if, as soon as they become successful, they start to de-nationalize and move jobs out of the country? Governments were faced with not only the challenge of building competitive industries but also, in the world of the stateless, nomadic corporation, of keeping them at home. The role of the policy-maker had once been to maximize internal levels of economic activity. Now the challenge became to adapt the nation-state economy to the demands of the world economy.

Canada was highly vulnerable to globalization because it was a major trading economy with, at least in the late 1980s, few checks on foreign investment. The country was highly porous in every economic respect. The popular notion that, in comparison to other countries, Canada was sheltered could not stand scrutiny. Even the United States, as economic consultant Paul Stothart pointed out, was a closed economy compared to Canada. "In reality [Canada] may have the world's highest levels of foreign investment but in perception we're 'closed to business,'" Stothart wrote. "We may have the world's second highest trade levels but we're 'hiding behind a shell.' The United States, with one-tenth our foreign ownership levels and one half our trade levels – now there's an open and dynamic country! – just ask Brian."

Jim Gillies, the public policy specialist and former adviser to Joe Clark, felt that the march of globalization meant that a single world market was inevitable. He had been reading about a London law firm that had its secretarial work done in Hong Kong. Such was the way of the future – a future, he said, that thrust Canada further into the arms of the United States. Canada, as Gillies reminded, did not have the crucial advantage of European nations.[3] Their cultures were distinguished by different languages, and in the new global economy, languages would be about all that was left to define cultures and nations. Bordered by America, English Canada, notwithstanding the policy of official bilingualism, did not have the natural border of language to protect it. In the past, Canada had found self-definition in its national economy. Its east-west economy had been created and sustained by government to resist the north-south pull. However, the forces pulling Canada and the United States together in the global economy were likely too strong to withstand, said Gillies. "It is very difficult to resist them because you resist at the price of lowering your standard of living. If you do that, people will vote with their feet."

The effects of globalization could be shaped and harnessed by governments whose antennae were delicately attuned to the implications of the trend. In the multilateral arena, it was possible that a new world regulatory body could be set up to keep the world from being overrun by corporate values. Harvard's Robert Reich, who later became a key economic adviser and labour secretary to President Bill Clinton, was among those calling for a general agreement on direct investment to perform such a function. He argued that the arrival of the global economy and the ending of the cold war had shaken the world's foundations so much that a new set of international institutions were necessary to maintain control. Reich and others, among them Lloyd Axworthy of the Liberal Party, wanted a re-enactment of the Bretton Woods process, a process that, on the ash heap of World War II, built organizations to sustain a new world order: the International Monetary Fund, the World Bank, and other institutions, that were now unable to address the new exigencies.

It was the fate of Canada under a Tory government not to be moving to control globalization but to be swept along in the rush. By virtue of the politics of Mulroney and Wilson, Canada was de-nationalizing from within and, by virtue of globalization, from without.

"What you had before we came to power," said Charlie McMillan, who was at the centre of Tory policy-making, "was a mindset that the national economy was central and that you subordinated global economic issues to the national interest."[4] The Tories decided, said McMillan, that all that had to change. It had to be flip-flopped. The national economy would now be opened up and subordinated to the global economy. Given the prime minister's predilections, however, opening up meant primarily going American – the second option. The de-nationalizing would be done at the feet of the United States. It was dangerous in McMillan's opinion because, contrary to the Tom d'Aquino analysis, in the global economy "political structures follow the economic lead."

In his post-power days, Pierre Trudeau was preoccupied mainly with the Constitution, but he put aside that concern to address the rise of corporate power in a speech at Stanford

University in California. In Europe, Trudeau said, "big business has taken the lead in the march toward integration by 1992, just as in the Canada-U.S.A. trade accord it was big business that decided what was good for the people of Canada. As things now stand it is also big business who will decide whether competitive forces will oblige the Canadian government to trim down its social legislation." The challenge of the future, observed the Northern Magus, would be to redress the balance. "The art of government will entail a different kind of planning than that presently practised on the people's behalf by transnational corporations. It will certainly necessitate a return to a more regulated economy where the public interest would have priority over private profit."

Trudeau's former chief lieutenant, Marc Lalonde, an architect of the NEP and an architect of national policy throughout the Trudeau years, had a view of globalization from up close. After leaving politics in 1984 he had moved on to practise trade law, and in so doing he travelled the world as the globalization whirl set in. He found that the trend was worldwide, inescapable. But rather than feed it, governments with any interest in keeping their nations together were trying to provide some solid counterweights. Canada, he said, was doing the opposite. Canada had spent a lifetime warding off continental integration but now, when nation states were so vulnerable, it was actively seeking it. "You have a concept which says leave it to the market and it will take care of everything and governments don't matter any more. I don't share this view. It's a rather primitive view of capitalism." To Lalonde, it all went back to the upbringing of the man in charge. "Whatever money Mulroney made, he made it out of the Hanna family of Cleveland. His business experience was running a store-front for the people in Cleveland."[5]

Corporation-bashing had seen its heyday in Canada in the 1960s and early 1970s, and as with nationalism generally, it was a harder sell in the late 1980s. Some of the disadvantages of foreign corporations dominating much of the economy hadn't changed. It was still generally agreed that foreign-owned companies did less research and development in Canada, that they purchased most of their supplies from outside Canada, that they didn't compete for export opportunities, that their key decisions were made outside Canada. But, in a globalized world, this litany of disadvantages stacked up less convincingly against the advantages. Investment meant jobs. It meant, particularly if the Japanese were moving in, higher productivity. It meant the introduction of new technologies. More economists were coming to the view that failure to roll out the red carpet for foreign investment, in a world where this was increasingly necessary, would stunt growth.

Globalization struck fear in the hearts of nationalists because, as well as further opening the economy to continentalism, it reinforced regionalism. Canada neatly divided itself into four regional economies: British Columbia, the Prairies, Central Canada, and the Maritimes. The economic interests of one region sometimes contradicted those of the others. The Prairies, heavily resource-dependent, were in frequent rivalry with the manufacturing interest of the centre. When resource prices soared, the West cheered and Ontario limped. When resource prices dropped, it was the other way round. Left to their own devices, with a federal government opting out of its role as regulator, provinces with such conflicting interests were moving further apart. Globalization and the free trade agreement, wrote Queen's University's Richard Simeon, served as "straitjackets limiting the ability of government to intervene in the pursuit of social or economic goals." Simeon noted a portentous development. Cross-border trade with the United States was on the increase at the same time that Canada's internal, east-west trade was on the slide. Canadians were losing their stake in one another while gaining stakes in neighbouring U.S. regions.

Regionalism was on the rise across Canada – in the form of

new political parties, in the demands for a new federal senate to empower the regions, in the demands for autonomy coming from Native people and Quebeckers, and in the visions of regional unions advocated by political leaders. The idea of a Maritimes economic union was much discussed. Premiers met to fashion a plan. In the West no less a Canadian nationalist than Lloyd Axworthy advocated a Prairie economic union, which could function more efficiently in a global economy.

Though it was rarely stated bluntly, many Canadians had given up on any Canadian dream and were prepared for membership in an American community – not in the sense of hooking on as new states of the union, but in terms of economic and psychological affinity. For archetype Tory David McFadden, globalization meant Canadians were no longer beholden to one another. It was time to admit it and move on to the next stage of development – that of becoming good corporate global citizens. Blue from top to bottom, a former member of the Ontario legislature and later a trade lawyer, McFadden sat fifty floors up in a Toronto office tower one day, looking across a skyline that suggested to him that he could be in Chicago or Atlanta. It was clear, he observed, that "people in Ohio will soon have more in common with people in Ontario than Ontarians with Maritimers."[6] The business community in Toronto already identified more with Chicago and London, he said, than with Quebec City or Regina or other Canadian centres. It was obvious to him that urban cultures were the same everywhere. So what was the fuss all about? All that was left to define Canada were rural pockets, and they weren't enough. "We no longer have a national psyche," said McFadden. "It's globalization. Let's get on with it."

He had travelled through the Far East, heard the roar of the so-called Asian Tigers, and had been incredibly impressed. Then he returned home to hear once again the dated opinions of those who still worried about U.S. domination. He liked John Crosbie's view of these people. "Nationalists want rowing as our national sport," cracked Crosbie, "so Canadians can sit on their butts and forever look backward."

McFadden had formed a Canada-U.S. businesspersons' association to foster co-operation and integration. Didn't the nationalists realize, he wondered, that in the new globalized world the threat was not from within the continent, but from without; that what was needed was partnership with the United States to take on the others – the newly unifying Europe and the Asian bloc?

One hundred years ago, McFadden said, the Ontario economy consisted of agricultural communities. The industrialization hit and the mill towns died. They're now tourist attractions. Now the era of the global village had arrived and the smokestack towns would soon be the tourist attractions. "The pioneer village era was nice in its time. But that era has gone. We can no more go back to the 1950s now than we can to Black Creek Pioneer Village."

The Canadian economy was built "on resources, on goods the world absolutely had to have." The world didn't need the resources any more, not in the same proportion or at the same price. McFadden, who sat on binational panels governing Canadian trade relations, was convinced a new economy had to be built and that it would come through open competition in partnership with the United States. His position was close to that of Michael Wilson. In the new economy, national economic growth would be externally driven by trade. Trade was formerly but one component in a nation state's economic strategy. Now it would become the priority force. Economists and political scientists divided over the advisability of this trade focus. To Daniel Drache of York University and Meric Gertler of the University of Toronto, the pursuit of insatiable markets based on a country having a competitive price advantage was a dangerous folly. "When trade sets the economic agenda for a society, a society is also letting market forces set the social and political agenda.

Employment standards, union viability and wage levels will necessarily follow a downward curve."[7]

Eric Kierans, whose experience as a politician, economist, and stock exchange executive had provided him with an informed view of corporate behaviour, found the prospect of caving in to the corporate agenda frightening. "To pursue its single goal of growth and expansion, the corporation must cross national boundaries. As it does so, it uses the surpluses drained from its home economy to finance its expansion abroad, leaving behind a weakened nation and escaping at the same time political, social and economic responsibilities. Corporations have no interest in people, in the value of politics, in the social and cultural dimensions of living. The corporate goal is accumulation and nothing else."

The gulf between the political right and left was as wide on trade and globalization as most other things. Mel Hurtig, the leader of Canada's newly formed National Party, produced a battery of statistics demonstrating that in the three previous decades when world trade volumes fantastically increased, the spread between the rich and poor only widened. "The poorest 80 per cent of the world's population saw its share of world GNP decline from 30 per cent to only 17 per cent."

Left unregulated, nationalists argued, mobile corporations would seek out the areas where it was most economical to function. "The lowest standards rule the world of globalization," said Hurtig. "In other words, if your taxes are too high because you have widely admired social programs, or your environmental standards are tougher than those in Mexico, or if your laws relating to working conditions are more civilized than in Taiwan, we'll move. It's community against community to see who capitulates first in the race to the bottom. If Oshawa doesn't make concessions we'll move to Michigan. . . . If Michigan doesn't make concessions we'll move to Mexico."[8]

The Mulroney government spurned the critics. A strong economy, it asserted, would mean a confident, proud nation, and hence a sovereign nation. A national policy, a reinvigoration of central powers, went against the Tories' expressed pro-business philosophy. The idea of a national policy reeked too much of the protectionism advocated by leftists. Just as the world was opening itself up, how could any government bury its head in the sand and put up walls? A national policy may have been necessary in John A. Macdonald's time, when the trans-Canada railway was built and when he encouraged east-west interprovincial trade by building a tariff wall along the border. It may also have been necessary in John Diefenbaker's day, when Canada was feeling particularly vulnerable after the open-border policies of C. D. Howe and could use some of the Chief's northern vision, pushing the country toward the Arctic instead of Alabama.

But Mulroney was convinced that market policies would rid Canada of this inward-looking defensiveness and make a confident global competitor out of a country too long reliant on its resource bounty.

Derek Burney, who had moved on to become Brian Mulroney's chief of staff, argued that continentalism, much as he disliked the connotation of the word, was the way of the future. "I determined that we had to go that route." As a specialist on American relations close to the prime minister, Burney could get his opinions heard. The Canadian "neuralgia," as he called it, about free trade reducing sovereignty never made sense to him because Canada was already so dependent. "If Canadians were really worried about their sovereignty and their ability to take economic decisions independent of those in the United States, what in hell do they think the Bank of Canada does every week of the year? And what do they think the finance minister in Canada does? . . . What do they think his room for manoeuvring is in preparing a budget in a given year? It was for that reason that I kept trying to expunge the phobia about free trade." The attitude he brought to the prime minister's side was that "we're in this hemisphere whether we like it or not. We either try to make use of it or we continue to try and run away from it with third options and nationalism." Canadians had spent too much time trying to be something else, trying to be "just-a-minute Europeans or quasi-Pacific," said Burney. "We're so anxious to assert our credentials as a three ocean country that we forget about the one that isn't divided by any oceans."[9]

Brian Mulroney had his last formal annual summit with Ronald Reagan in April 1988. It was billed as a no-news get-together and it lived up to the billing. Before the summit the prime minister appeared in New York to receive the Gold Insigne award from the Pan American Society, presented annually to the government leader considered to have contributed the most to bilateral relations in the Western hemisphere.

Mulroney reminded his audience at the award ceremony that one of his most urgent priorities when elected prime minister was the refurbishment of relations with the United States. Barriers to trade and investment with the Americans and reluctance to co-operate with a Washington-led NATO had been problems. Both, Mulroney told his American audience, had been overcome. His economy had been made compatible with that of Canada's neighbour because he shared the belief, as he stated that day, that "the driving force behind growth and job creation is a dynamic private sector." He proudly listed his government's accomplishments: the deregulation of the transportation and energy sectors; the dismantling of the NEP with its detrimental intervention in the marketplace; the sale of Crown corporations to private enterprises; the reform of the tax system; and the opening of financial markets and the stimulation of greater competition in financial services.

Canada had done its part, the prime minister said, and now the only problem that remained on the ledger was acid rain. With angry words, to keep in step with the mounting criticism of the United States on this issue at home, Mulroney made one last appeal. "If this relationship is to remain in sound condition, it will take further effort. You as a country are a major part of our problem and a vital part of the solution. . . . Friendship has inevitable costs. One of them is bearing whatever burdens are required to avoid polluting your neighbour's property with destructive wastes."

The summit came and went with the Gipper still not moving an inch on what he regarded as a problem of polluting trees and a lack of forest fires. The prime minister returned home empty-handed and prepared to fight an election on the prize item of his American policy – free trade.

This would be the fourth Canadian election campaign fought primarily over relations with the United States. In 1891 and 1911 free trade was the issue and the nationalist forces triumphed. Free trade was defeated. In the 1963 campaign, defence issues were more important and Diefenbaker's nationalism was rejected by the voters. With free trade again at the forefront in 1988, it meant a repeat of all the domino-theory arguments that had each time been tossed into the ring. Would one step on the path to integration inevitably lead to another? Would free trade eventually lead to a monetary union, a common market, a customs union, and some form of political union? In Canada the pro and con forces held forth gravely on the matter. Free traders argued that only the paranoid talked of such domino effects. They were playing a risky game, though, because if they had looked back they would have found that not just Canadian nationalists held the view that free trade was a step toward total absorption. The Americans themselves, those who campaigned for free trade in past elections, held the same suspicions.

In 1891 a State Department memo outlined the position of Benjamin Harrison's administration. The major tenet of U.S. foreign policy, the memo said, should be "to unite the continent, secure its independence and prevent the northern part of it from being turned into an outpost of European reaction." The memorandum went on to state a union of Canada and the United States was "likely to be promoted by everything which asserts the commercial autonomy of the continent and helps to make Canada feel that to enjoy her full measure of prosperity she must be economically a community of this hemisphere, not an outlying dependency of a European power."[10]

The words: "to enjoy her full measure of prosperity she must be economically a community of this hemisphere" had a peculiar resonance a century later. While in Harrison's day this was considered the rationale for the annexation of Canada, during Mulroney's stewardship it would get a radically different twist. The hemispheric strategy, Canada as a nation of the Americas, was at the centre of the Mulroney government's thinking – not as a formula for union, but as the key to a stronger, Canadian sovereignty.

Again, in 1911, the United States looked quietly upon reciprocity as the path to future union. Months before the election campaign, President William Howard Taft wrote to former president Teddy Roosevelt. With reciprocity, Taft declared, "the amount of Canadian products we would take would produce a current of business between Western Canada and the United States that would make Canada only an adjunct of the United States."

In 1988 John Turner, the Liberal leader, embraced Harrison's and Taft's line of thought. Free trade would lead on to other nefarious entwinements. In the course of his tirade, Turner described Mulroney as "a prime minister who signed over the sovereignty and independence of our nation, that will make us nothing more than a junior partner and even a colony of the United States of America." Regional development programs, social programs, and workers in many sectors would be endangered, "all to satisfy Brian Mulroney's unholy desire to fulfill the American dream." A trade package had been signed which "ignores our history and denies us the right as Canadians to choose an independent Canadian future."

Turner had enjoyed a long break from politics, an eight-year split from the Trudeau regime. He sat on boards of branch plants of companies like Bechtel, the arms maker once presided over by George Shultz and Caspar Weinberger, and dined with Toronto's Bay Street barons. He moved comfortably in those circles and was often looked upon as a Liberal who could well be a Tory. Having once favoured a closer relationship with the United States, he became an unlikely candidate to carry the nationalist torch. But he was able to do so with conviction after Mulroney signed a trade agreement he thought terribly one-sided, and he expected many of his Toronto business friends would share his view. To his astonishment he found out differently when he vacationed with a few of them on Georgian Bay and discussed the future of the nation. Turner met with Lloyd Axworthy afterward and said something Axworthy would not forget. "Jesus, Lloyd," Turner told him. "I've just come back from Collingwood. They don't believe in Canada anymore!"[11]

Turner had wanted to talk to them about the history of a country, not about first-quarter profits. What big business cared about, however, was first-quarter profits.

That John Turner, in the era of globalization, would have expected businessmen's patriotism to take precedence over the bottom line was perhaps naive. Even in America they seldom went that far. Bob McNamara, who went from the Ford Motor Company executive suite to the job of secretary of defence under John F. Kennedy, told the story once about how, before leaving for Washington, he was to deliver a university commencement address. In the advanced text he had included the assertion that there had to be a higher calling for businessmen than simply making money. The remark so offended the Ford executives, McNamara recalled, that they had him remove it from the text. McNamara did so, but in the live performance he pronounced the words loudly.[12]

The premier of Alberta, Peter Lougheed, a key ally of Mulroney in the push for free trade, echoed the business line that John

Turner had encountered. There was perhaps no better example of the provincialist view of Canada than Lougheed's rejoicing at Ottawa's loss of power through free trade. "The biggest plus of this agreement," crowed Lougheed, "is that it would preclude a federal government from bringing in a national energy program ever again. The key – the real win-win in the agreement – is energy."

A response to the quick-buck view came from Jean Chrétien. "What sovereign country, what self-respecting government would surrender its ability to use its natural resources in the best interests of its citizens?"

On the same subject, Lloyd Axworthy confronted Simon Reisman one night during the free trade negotiations at a reception at the Swedish embassy. He told Reisman, "You're not negotiating an agreement, you're negotiating a straitjacket." Reisman came back at him saying that Axworthy was a Liberal and Liberals had historically supported free trade. "What's your problem now?" The difficulty, said the Liberal MP, was that the agreement meant Canada would never be able to fashion a protective national resource policy again. To Axworthy's considerable surprise, Reisman agreed. The discussion ended.[13]

In the election campaign, Turner caught a wave of support following a stirring exchange with Mulroney in a televised debate, but the turnaround proved ephemeral. In the closing days, the electorate swung back strongly enough behind the Conservatives to give them a good majority in the House, though their share of the total vote (42 per cent) could hardly be said to represent majority support – either for them or for free trade. Nationalists argued that with a late rush of cash to sponsor a clamorous advertising campaign, big business had virtually bought the election. It wasn't a strong argument. The Tories would likely have won on their own. They were riding a strong economy, and seldom in politics will voters turn out a governing party during good times. Polls had indicated all along that the Grits were being hurt badly by the extraordinarily low confidence voters had in their leader. Only 10 to 12 per cent of Canadians had faith in John Turner. Realizing this, members of his party tried unsuccessfully to bring him down. He had led them to a dismal embarrassment – forty seats in the 1984 election – and following that had failed to rebuild the party, overseeing its plunge into deep debt, its collapse in Quebec, organizational dissent at headquarters, and only minimal improvement in the West. His patriotic cry in the English-language debate made the world forget – but only for a week – the record of ineptitude. His approval ratings by the end of the campaign were back almost where they had begun – far behind Brian Mulroney and NDP leader Ed Broadbent.

While the cost of corporate Canada's media blitz during the campaign totalled several million dollars, the effort on the nationalist side had also been expensive and vigorous. And no one could say the national media gave Brian Mulroney an easy go of it. During the campaign, in fact throughout his stewardship, he was frequently the subject of attacks based less on fact than on animosity.

Thomas d'Aquino could sit several years after the big vote and declare with a straight face that rather than helping the free trade cause, the infusion of cash by big business more than likely hurt it. Its brash support, he said, could very well have polarized the issue, created resentment, and pushed the nationalist forces to work harder.

Whatever its effect on the vote, Bay Street's mobilization only added to the impression that Brian Mulroney was its tool. Following the election, pressure was put on corporations to disclose their contributions. Many declined at the time, but among those who did declare their support was a goodly number of American branch plants, including Imperial Oil, Texaco Canada, and IBM. In 1891 John A. Macdonald talked about his certitude that "a large amount of Yankee money will be expended to corrupt our people" in the campaign. In 1911, and certainly in 1963, there were American efforts to influence the outcome. In 1988 the dollars came pouring in again from U.S. affiliates.

At the time of the disclosures of corporate funding, it was also revealed that on the day of the election the Mulroney cabinet had awarded preliminary approval for a foreign bank licence to the American Express corporation. Amex chairman Jim Robinson, who had met with Mulroney, had led the American campaign to gain support for free trade on Wall Street and in Washington. The suggestion, never proved, was that with the banking licence the prime minister was rewarding Robinson for his effort. That it was done so quietly on election day contributed to the air of suspicion. Toronto-Dominion bank chairman Richard Thomson accused the prime minister of making a deal but quickly withdrew the allegation.

The election won, the free trade agreement took effect on January 1, 1989, with no one on the government side, at least according to Trade Minister John Crosbie, having read it. Always one who could be counted on to liven up proceedings, Crosbie did so with a remarkable admission in the House of Commons that he hadn't bothered to read the text. It was too boring.

Seldom had opposition critics been handed such ammunition. The jibes continued for months. For his part Crosbie remained unrepentant. By 1992 he was still happy to admit that he hadn't read the document. "No, and I'm goddamned well not going to either," he said, dragging out the seven-hundred-page text from the bookshelf behind him. "I'll tell you that, and I'm telling you that there isn't one person in the whole goddamn government who's read it. I'm the only one who's honest enough to say so."[14]

A few decades of politics had numbed his senses somewhat. "At this stage of my life I don't have to kiss anybody's ass," said Crosbie. "I can say what I goddamn well like."

13

Brian and George

As George Bush prepared for his February 1989 visit to Ottawa, his first trip outside his country as president, he was given a memo. "Encourage as close a relationship as possible, without publicly crowding Mulroney," it said.[1]

A background paper prepared by the State Department for Bush warned that Mulroney's staunch pro-American policies were jeopardizing the Canadian leader's support base. Mulroney's pending approval of advanced cruise missile testing over Canada would result, Bush was told, in yet more criticism of the prime minister "for kowtowing to the U.S." And coming off the free trade election campaign, bitter nationalists would "probably focus on the painful economic adjustments that the FTA will cause in some sectors of Canadian industry."

The Bush administration was feeling pressure to help its close friend. "Mulroney's entire pro-U.S. foreign policy is likely to come under attack if he can make no progress on acid rain, the litmus test of the wisdom of that policy to many Canadians," a State Department memo said. "With their secure Parliamentary majority, the Tories will be able to fend off all opposition challenges; but Mulroney may decide that there is domestic mileage to be made by 'standing up to the U.S.' on certain issues if his pro-U.S. policy does not produce easily demonstrable benefits for Canada."

On economic issues, Bush was told to be careful not to stoke the continentalist-nationalist rivalry in Canada. "We need to stress our unique relationship with Canada, but not give the impression we seek to control their economic policy," his briefing papers cautioned. "That would play into the hands of nationalist opponents of the FTA and complicate future progress in the FTA or in other fora."

Under Reagan, as economic undersecretary Myer Rashish had pointed out, the administration had been very careful not to be seen to be pushing Canada toward a North American accord. Going back to Reagan's first meeting with Mulroney in 1984, when George Shultz had advised Reagan to phrase things "in a manner which avoids embarrassing him with his public," the sensitivity to Mulroney's position had been evident. Now Bush was being advised to pursue a similar course. Any implication that the United States was out to control the Canadian economy would be disastrous.

Quiet persuasion would suffice to achieve a quiet integration. On the issue of military and defence production and procurement, for example, Washington wanted intimate co-operation with Canada so as to make the United States less reliant on more distant powers. For his first summit meeting with the prime minister, Bush was advised: "We should continue to seek ways [with Canada] to unify our approach to both the national and world defense markets." A briefing paper cited the little-known North American Defence Industrial Base organization, set up as a result of the Shamrock Summit, as assisting in achieving the goal. "It is helping to combine our industrial capabilities and reduce our collective offshore dependencies."

Remarkably, neither Bush nor Reagan ever felt he had to make strong public criticism of positions taken by the Mulroney government. It was an indication of their degree of satisfaction.

Unlike Reagan, Bush was prepared to move on the one big issue on which Mulroney needed help – the environment. Bush wanted to be known as the foreign policy president and the education president, the environmental president, and many other presidents. Memos show that he had decided upon his election to bring forward a clean air act that would address the acid rain problem.

But the White House strategy for Bush's Ottawa stopover fell short of providing any guarantee. Briefing papers advised Bush to get Mulroney's agreement to avoid a public confrontation over the issue while the president worked on a solution. In the last line of a memo, Bush was also reminded not to give away anything for nothing. Mulroney had been fighting for four years to get some action on acid rain, and had done far more than meet the other side half-way in the process. But now Bush was being told to go for a quid pro quo. "It is likely that we can come to terms on acid rain," the State Department said. "But we should see if we can get something for it."

Canadians, including some of Mulroney's own supporters, wondered, as Mulroney went about providing unilateral concessions to the United States on the NEP, FIRA, and other issues, why he didn't require in return that the White House yield some ground on trade or on other issues that were important to Canada. But Mulroney's starting point as such a strong American advocate left him in a weak position. "If you set out as a policy goal to have superb relations with a country," said John Halstead, "what happens to your leverage?"

Whether Bush ever heeded his advisors and asked for something in return is unknown; the fact that he had an acid rain solution in the offing was probably incentive enough to render the prime minister co-operative on Bush's major concerns. Indeed, as it turned out, Canada co-operated fully on all the president's big-ticket items – his foreign ventures in Panama, the Gulf, and elsewhere.

It was the multilateral arena that captured Bush's imagination, and it was here, much more than in matters affecting the direct bilateral relationship, that the Bush-Mulroney rapport developed.

The election of George Bush in 1988 had done nothing to alter the pals diplomacy that Brian Mulroney began with Ronald Reagan. Though the world had changed more in Bush's first two years in power than at any time since World War II, and though Canada had gained, with the close of the cold war, a freedom in the exercise of foreign policy it had not known before, the American instincts of the Mulroney government remained determinedly the same.

For the first seven decades of Canadian confederation, Ottawa's foreign policy was set in Britain. Just as it gained autonomy in external affairs, World War II and the ensuing cold war circumscribed this liberty as Canada was compelled to follow the line of the American-led NATO alliance. With the end of East-West enmity, however, NATO lost its main reason for being. Canada no longer had to mould its approach to the world so as to keep Washington content. After 120 years of subordination, freedom had arrived.

Rather than exercise Canada's sovereignty, however, Mulroney did the opposite, establishing even tighter ties to the American foreign policy line under Bush than under Reagan. Mulroney was closer in age to Bush, had already known him for four years, and practised politics the same way. Both were phone-aholics who prized loyalty and had little time for the "vision thing" as the street-talking Bush termed it. The mix was right. "Mulroney and Bush," said Ambassador Edward Ney, "were a hundred per cent good friends."

If, under Reagan and Mulroney, the Canada-U.S. relationship had reached a harmony comparable to that under Franklin Roosevelt and Mackenzie King, the 100 per cent friendship described by Ney would take it a step further. Though noisy trade disputes sometimes lent a querulous tone to the proceedings, at base the bilateral bliss, reflective of the understanding between the men at the top, was unprecedented. The compatibility brought its rewards. Benefiting from his intimacy with this president, Brian Mulroney would have meaningful input on the great multilateral questions of the day, perhaps more of this than any other prime minister. Mulroney would be at Bush's side at the president's retreat in Kennebunkport, Maine, when Bush was plotting strategy for the Gulf War. He would receive calls from Bush on multilateral matters that had little to do with Canada. He would be Bush's pick as the new secretary general of the United Nations.

At the same time, pals diplomacy exacted a fee. It necessitated a degree of sycophancy unholy to Canadian tradition and rather at odds with the opportunity for Canada to signal that, with the cold war over, its foreign policy was free of American influence. The prime minister still criticized Washington often enough. But on big questions the rules were clear. Loyalty prevailed. You didn't cross your friend.

Bush had innumerable international contacts, but those whose friendship and opinion he valued were few. Mulroney gained membership in the club, not just by virtue of his skill as a stroker, but also by demonstrating on several occasions to the president that he was a sharp, well-informed interlocutor. One such time was November 1989. Mulroney had travelled to Moscow to meet with Soviet leader Mikhail Gorbachev, who was then in the process of relinquishing control of Eastern Europe. One of Mulroney's first duties back home, given his ties to Bush, was to brief the president on the Soviet leader's thoughts. The telephone wouldn't do, and the president of the United States was not about to fly all the way to Canada for a briefing. So Mulroney gladly went to Washington.

With him went Joe Clark, principal secretary Stanley Hartt, and Washington ambassador Derek Burney. Arriving at the White House at 6 p.m., they found a group that included President Bush, Secretary of State James Baker, NSC director Brent Scowcroft, and CIA director Bob Gates. After cocktails

Mulroney, who had a large black binder in front of him, began the briefing. In the three hours that followed, he held the floor alone for two. The black binder remained shut. Occasionally he would look over to Clark for confirmation. But for the most part it was Mulroney alone, working from an encyclopedic memory, speaking in clear, articulate patterns, holding his audience riveted. Baker, a man who rarely dropped his guard, interrupted a couple of times to express his fascination at what Mulroney was reporting. The president rarely interjected. At the end, according to an American participant, Bush looked over at Mulroney and told him he no longer needed his briefing books. "You've given me more help tonight on this subject than I have ever had." Many times thereafter the prime minister was a source for Bush, delivering, particularly after his meetings with other heads of state, what Edward Ney termed "tremendously important stuff."

Following Iraq's invasion of Kuwait in 1990, Bush was attempting to gather allies to his side for counteraction. The degree of co-operation was encouraging but for François Mitterrand. Bush was frustrated by the French president's hesitance and spoke to Mulroney about it. The Canadian prime minister offered a solution. With Mitterrand, he told Bush, it was all in the way the game was played, and the game had to be played with a degree of flattery. In a manner consistent with their buddy-buddy rapport, Mulroney, according to American officials, told Bush, "Here's what you do. You set your alarm clock for two o'clock in the morning and you call Mitterrand in Paris. It's seven or eight in the morning their time but François knows it's the middle of the night in Washington and that this thing is so important that you're up half the night. You tell François that he is the key, that the whole thing depends on France's co-operation. Then watch him come around."

As confirmed by a Bush confidant, the president followed Mulroney's advice almost to the letter, and Mitterrand soon joined the allied effort against Iraq.

This degree of kinship was unusual for presidents and prime ministers and for the Canada-U.S. relationship itself. Also unusual were other trademarks of Mulroney's approach, features that reflected his commitment to the United States. One such trademark was his decidedly hawkish streak; another was his wish to carve out a more active role for Canada in the American hemisphere.

Until Mulroney came to power, Canadian tradition prescribed a role for Ottawa as an agent of restraint against Washington's more aggressive tendencies. Ottawa was the peace-broker, the bridge-builder, the cool eye on the hot rhetoric. The post-war era saw Pierre Trudeau's world peace mission, his cutbacks in NATO, his attempts to lower the temperature of Soviet-American confrontations; it saw Pearson's honest-broker role in the resolution of the Suez crisis and his opposition to Lyndon Johnson's bombing in Vietnam; it saw Diefenbaker's fulminating against what he felt was needless adventurism on the part of the Kennedy adminstration.

Mulroney's guiding principle, his give-them-the-benefit-of-the-doubt approach, effectively abandoned this tradition. In siding with the Reagan and Bush Republicans on foreign aggression, and in making aggressive noises of its own, his government became arguably the most hawkish Canada has seen. The Mulroney Tories loudly backed the invasion of Panama and supported the bombing of Libya; they led the allied charge in support of the United States in the Gulf war, breaking the custom that Canadian troops serve only as peace-keepers; they were among the last of the cold warriors to recognize historic change in the Soviet Union; they threatened to be in the vanguard of a military invasion of Haiti; they increased defence spending following the disappearance of the Soviet threat; and they cut back on foreign aid and began tying it to economic structural adjustment toward a free-market base. They could rationalize their right-wing economic policies by pointing to the nation's debt and world trends, but on foreign affairs there was no such rationale or imperative. Instinct did the talking.

Instinct also moved the Mulroney Conservatives to assume more formal status in the orbit of the Americas. In keeping with Mulroney's declaration that "our international vocation will be turned more and more to our own hemisphere," Canada at long last joined the Organization of American States.

On the economic side, the prime minister had moved to secure Canada's place in the American firmament. With the free trade agreement, a new continental relationship was institutionalized. Now, in becoming a member of the OAS, step two in making Canada a true nation of the Americas was realized.

Throughout the century, Ottawa had turned down overtures to join the OAS. Since the organization was in the immediate hemisphere the shunning was all the more strange. Canada, after all, was the great mixer. It belonged to almost every other major international organization: NATO, the OECD, la Francophonie, the Commonwealth, the G-7, the GATT, the CSCE, and others.

A chair had literally been placed at OAS headquarters in Washington, awaiting a Canadian occupant. But it remained vacant, in large part because of the historic Canadian urge to be seen as trans-Atlantic and free of American coat-tails. "Our overriding national preoccupation," said Allan Gotlieb in a review of diplomatic history, "has been about how to limit U.S. power over our national destiny while deriving maximum advantage from our propinquity." Membership in the other international organizations served as counterweight to American influence. Membership in the OAS would serve as an unwelcome reminder. The OAS invoked many of the same fears as free trade. It was thought that joining the organization would mean becoming more of an American nation. To be American was too raw and too violent and too racist and too unintellectual. Europe was culture and moderation and for Canada, counterbalance. One of the reasons why Canadians could sometimes love Pierre Trudeau was because he was so European and, conversely, one of the reasons they could so often loathe Brian Mulroney was because he had "American huckster" written all over him.

The OAS was seen to be thoroughly dominated by the United States. Originally established in 1890 as the Pan-American Union, it comprised thirty-one Central and South American nations. In its purpose, the OAS sought to promote peace, goodwill, development, and understanding. In fact the organization proved helpless as time and time again the CIA and U.S. marines reordered Latin American governments to suit Washington's taste. Interference by the United States in Latin America became an American pastime. In the post-war period, the region became a cold war playground. As the Soviets sought to maintain tyrants of the left in Eastern Europe, the United States sustained tyrants of the right – Batista, Trujillo, Somoza, Pinochet – in Latin America.

Ottawa had considered joining the Pan-American Union as early as the 1930s. In his first speech to the House of Commons in 1935, a young MP named Paul Martin advocated that his government, the King government, make the step – only to be told that the British didn't want it. In 1940 Franklin Roosevelt tried to persuade Mackenzie King to join the OAS, but despite the warm relationship between the two men, King was unmoved. The issue remained off the agenda until John F. Kennedy visited Ottawa in 1961. Many in the White House, having read speeches from External Affairs Minister Howard Green, believed that Canada was interested in coming in. A memo to Kennedy from Walt Rostow, a top State Department official, suggested this, adding a sarcastic slap at Green for his earlier, gratuitous advice on Cuba. "I take it they are prepared to join on grounds other than 'mediating' between the U.S. and Cuba." Diefenbaker decided against the OAS, however, and reportedly told Kennedy this at a meeting in his Ottawa office. But, displaying some of the brass for which he was famous, Kennedy, in his address to Parliament, went over Diefenbaker's head to the Canadian people. "Your country and mine are partners in North American affairs; can we not become partners in inter-American affairs? . . . To be sure it would mean an added responsibility, but yours is not a nation that shrinks from responsibility." Canadian diplomat Ed Ritchie recalled, "I shuddered when I heard him say that."[3] Diefenbaker shuddered more, particularly when the Kennedy team accidentally left behind a memo in which the president was instructed "to push them towards a decision to join the OAS."

Lester Pearson contemplated joining the OAS in the 1960s, but rejected the idea on the grounds that it could be seen as symbolic of a move toward the United States and that it increased the potential for conflict between the two countries. "They were afraid," recalled his son Geoffrey Pearson, "that they would have to vote or be seen to be voting with the Americans. And if they didn't vote with them, they'd have more problems with Washington."[4]

Pierre Trudeau's Latin American policy differed substantially from Washington's. The idea of taking a chair at the OAS table never got far. When Trudeau toured South America in 1976, he stopped in to see Castro and concluded a speech by shouting "Viva Castro! Viva Cuba!" In Trudeau circles, despite serious Cuban transgressions on human rights, there was some respect for the accomplishments of the Castro revolution: full employment, full literacy, universal health care and education. This, compared to the poverty, the squalor, and the 50 per cent illiteracy rates in countries such as Guatemala and Honduras which had remained under the U.S. umbrella. Given such Trudeauvian attitudes, OAS affiliation was out of the question.

By the late 1980s, it was easier for Mulroney to make the case for OAS membership. Joining, proponents said, was only a sign of Canada's maturity. Canadian ties with the area were deepening. Two-way trade had reached $7.5 billion. Instead of practising whisper-in-the-ear diplomacy, Canada should stand as a full player as it did in so many other multilateral forums. Joe Clark saw membership in the OAS as a furtherance of Canada's role as "an honest broker, a country of reason. . . . We possess and exercise precisely the talents which can overcome confrontation." Mulroney said it would be "fundamentally silly" to think that Canada would come under undue pressure from Washington to conform to American objectives in Latin America. He could point to Canada's voting record at the United Nations as evidence that he was not the American puppet he was accused of being. In 1988 Canada voted with the United States 63 per cent of the time, but France, West Germany, and Britain had higher totals. Critics countered, however, that on the big-ticket items, the ones that counted, Ottawa and Washington were in lock-step. On foreign policy, said Jack Granatstein who co-authored *Pirouette*, the story of foreign policy in the Trudeau years, "the Mulroney government is more in bed with the United States than any previous government we've ever had – ever." Paul Heinbecker, the thoughtful diplomat who became the top adviser to Mulroney on foreign policy, would not use such blunt terms, but he generally agreed with Granatstein's assessment. Mulroney's government, Heinbecker said, believed in co-operation, not in the type of nationalism that brought on the horrors of modern-day Yugoslavia.

The timing of the decision to join the OAS was not propitious. After so many fear-not assertions from Mulroney and Clark on the question of becoming American lap-dogs, the Panamanian crisis broke. The country's leader, Manuel Noriega, less affectionately known as Pineapple Face, had been in the employ of the CIA and had met with George Bush, who was a past CIA director. Noriega had since fallen from grace, however. His drug-running dictatorship and anti-Americanism strongly alienated Washington. Bush was looking for ways to rid himself of the wimp tag pinned on him by American conservatives and could well benefit from a show of muscle. As vice-president he had watched Reagan send in the American armada to take

Grenada, a country with the GNP of Prince Edward Island. Americans responded with wild patriotic fervour. As an excuse for the invasion, Reagan claimed that the lives of U.S. citizens on the island were in danger. Americans believed the Gipper, as they always did. Allies like Canada under Trudeau did not, though the young Tory Opposition leader of the day, Brian Mulroney, already showing his stripes, supported the invasion.

When one American marine was killed in Panama, this, along with Noriega's other offences, was reason enough for Bush to send in an invasion force of twenty thousand to bring Pineapple Face to justice. Noriega had been charged two years earlier with running drugs into the United States. Moreover, he had made a mockery of the democratic election process in his country by negating an apparent opposition victory. Bush critics liked to emphasize the word "apparent," because the CIA had helped sponsor the opposition win with $10 million in support as well as other deeds. Washington thus had to share in the blame for the mockery of democracy.

No official death toll was provided following the invasion, but estimates ranged from several hundred to two thousand dead, mainly civilians. Given that it was all for the sake of bringing one man to trial, many wondered why a small CIA team couldn't have sufficed. Ottawa was not among the wonderers. Mulroney's instant support for the invasion became one of his most egregious examples of puppet-like behaviour in the hands of the White House custodians. All OAS members except incoming Canada registered opposition to the invasion. Ottawa appeared to agree that principles of international law and non-interference in the domestic affairs of another country must be upheld, but still found ways to back Bush. Officials close to Joe Clark reported later that he would have taken a harsher stance, but Bush got on the phone to Mulroney before Clark had a chance to make his case.

In the immediate aftermath of the attack, Thatcher and Mulroney were the only world leaders to issue statements in support of Bush's aggression. Remarkably, the Canadian PM employed tougher language than the Americans themselves to rationalize the U.S. attack. Noriega was "a brute, tyrant and murderer," Mulroney said. Though he regretted that force had to be used, "the United States was justified. . . . Here you have a drug-runner and a thug running a country. . . . Here's a man who has declared war against the United States, who has assassinated American citizens and who has indicated his intention to do more."

His critics had a field-day. Mulroney had called Noriega a murderer, pronounced him guilty without so much as a hearing, they said. The prime minister had supported the Americans' violation of international law. If nations decided to invade one another whenever one of their nationals was killed or there were some charges of drug-running, they said, invasions would be taking place every week of the year. Bill Blaikie of the NDP compared the U.S. action to activities of the Soviets. "I'm sure if the situation was reversed and if in Romania a Soviet citizen was killed by the Romanian government, the Canadian government would not take the same view of a Soviet military response in Romania." Members of the OAS were outraged. "It is difficult to understand the double standard," said Marta Torres, a Guatemalan who headed the Christian Task Force on Central America. "They say they respect the law but they don't respect the United Nations charter, treaties or their own law. They've done it before with Guatemala, Chile and Grenada."

In conversations with his friend Sam Wakim, the prime minister saw the issue in stark and simple terms – it was a matter of supporting either Noriega or Bush. "What do they want me to do, Sam?" Mulroney asked his friend. "Like Noriega?" He was incredulous. How could anyone take sides against the U.S. president. It was a matter of simple logic. "How can I support Noriega, Sam? They want me to support Noriega."[5]

Canada's OAS debut was hardly auspicious. As the *Ottawa Citizen*'s John Hay put it, membership in the organization would require from Canada "exactly what the Mulroney government has lacked – the will and skill to assert an active Canadian foreign policy where it directly challenges U.S. policy."

The performance of Mulroney's government in the Arctic offered a good example, of which there were many, of its reticence in this regard. The prime minister could not get Washington to recognize Canadian sovereignty during the *Polar Sea* controversy. He was then given an opportunity to assert Canada's interest in the area when Gorbachev's Kremlin proposed measures to demilitarize the Arctic in 1987. With environmental, security, and social interests in the Arctic, Canada had much at stake. The Soviets had the largest military presence in the Arctic Circle but were prepared, as they demonstrated on the question of conventional arms in Europe, to make the largest cuts. But when Gorbachev came forward with a proposal to remove all Soviet ballistic missile submarines from the Baltic Sea, Canada baulked. Naval arms control did not interest the Americans. Washington and NATO ignored the proposal. There would be no zone of peace. Canada ran and hid.

Douglas Roche knew something about U.S. pressure. Roche, Canada's disarmament ambassador, resigned from the job in 1989. "I suppose the biggest shock I got," he said about his job upon stepping down, "was to learn the influence, the pressure that the U.S. government has on the Canadian government on the issues of disarmament and security." American influence "operates at every level and it operates in varying degrees, from subtlety and *politesse* to crude threats."

When he took the job of disarmament ambassador in 1985, Roche had Clark's backing to push for a faster pace of disarmament than was being pursued by the United States. But both men knew which way the Prime Minister's Office was leaning. If Washington was strongly against an initiative, it meant that the PMO was against it, which in turn meant that Clark and Roche had to modify their plans. Typical was the drive for a nuclear-test-ban treaty. Gorbachev declared a unilateral moratorium on nuclear testing in 1985, at the same time appealing to Washington to join him. Gorbachev maintained the moratorium past many deadlines, while continuing to issue pleas to Reagan. The pleas went ignored. In Ottawa, Roche fought for support of the moratorium and for a comprehensive test-ban treaty. The government repeatedly fudged on the moratorium, and Roche got nowhere on the treaty issue. Finally, he said, he was told by an official close to Mulroney, "When the U.S. supports it, we will support it."[6]

The Americans were slow to trust Gorbachev. Conservatives thought he was a propagandist, and the Sovietologists in the academic community were unable to shake the cold war orthodoxy that gripped them. Canada was even slower off the mark. As one of the major developments of the century took shape, Clark and Mulroney, in part victimized by bad advice from External Affairs, hung back in a cold war antechamber. They became known as the last of the cold warriors, and as startling as this description was in a country with such a long tradition of moderation, it had some merit. In 1987 after Gorbachev had been in power for two years and had initiated his *glasnost* and *perestroika* policies, Defence Minister Perrin Beatty brought forward a white paper containing such cold war vitriol that it sounded like it had been written in the 1950s. Beatty became a laughing-stock. Mulroney, according to Dalton Camp, who was then in the Privy Council Office, didn't see the paper before it hit the streets. "This was a time," recalled Camp, "when everyone was trying to offload Mulroney's agenda to limit it to free trade and Meech Lake. So the famous Beatty was just dumped on the market."[7] Paradoxically, as the cold war faded, the cold war mentality in the Canadian defence department found new life. The enemy was disappearing, but deficit-ridden Ottawa continued to spend tens of millions of dollars on an anti-tank weapon originally designed to take out Warsaw Pact forces advancing across Western Europe. A $1 billion troop surveillance system was also budgeted. The system was to protect

Canadian armed forces in Europe – forces that were being returned home.

By the time Mulroney and Clark finally visited Gorbachev in the fall of 1989, nearly every other Western leader of importance had been through to pay due recognition to Gorbachev's achievements. Gorbachev gently chided the Canadians. "Where have you been?" he asked. In fact Mulroney had planned an earlier visit to the Kremlin, but it had been cancelled during a flare-up over alleged spying by so-called Soviet diplomats in Ottawa.

The old mentality was again demonstrated when Gorbachev was taken custody in the August 1991 coup. Barbara McDougall, successor to Clark in External Affairs, drove a stake into her credibility by appearing to suggest that Ottawa was ready and willing to do business with the new Communist junta. A rising star in the Tory firmament until that moment, she never recovered.

The tardiness and foot-dragging put Canada in no position to play a lead role in bringing the Soviet Union in from the cold – a role Pearson or Trudeau would have cherished. At the summit of the G-7 in Houston, Texas, in 1990, Bush decided against sending financial aid to the Soviet Union. The reason – despite Gorbachev's ending the cold war, unilateral Soviet military cutbacks, the liberation of Eastern Europe, the release of all dissidents, the advent of *glasnost*, improved human rights, and freedom of religion and emigration – was that the Soviets were still sending money to feed the Cuban people, and were still supporting the Vietnamese government. Mulroney was unsure of whether to send aid, but when Bush's decision came down, his mind was made up. It didn't matter that Vietnam and Cuba were American problems on which Ottawa had historically different views. Mulroney would support the president and wait longer before sending major assistance to Moscow.

Clark himself later acknowledged the slowness of his government's response to the new Soviet revolution. "I'll take the

criticism," he said. "You're always going to be behind on something and we've caught up rather quickly."[8] The government
ultimately did catch up, building a good rapport with the new
Russian government and urging greater financial support from
allies to sustain the democratic changes. Next to Germany, it
led Western governments in per capita assistance to former
Soviet republics.

The closeness of the Mulroney-Bush relationship was again
manifest during the Gulf War. As with the invasion of Panama,
Mulroney was more than ready to side with the politics of the
president. The new relationship that he had fashioned on the
continent could be seen in the Gulf crisis when, for the first
time since the Korean War, a Canadian government sent troops
into combat. Since Korea, Canadian forces had served only as
peacekeepers.

In the Gulf, no challenge was put up by Ottawa to the Oval
Office interpretation of events. Bush, in talking of Saddam
Hussein, a leader whom the Americans had only recently been
supporting, compared him to Adolf Hitler. Joe Clark picked
right up on this. "Chamberlain was wrong then and we know
the consequences," said Clark, referring to the outplotted British PM's acquiescence to the Germans in the 1930s. "We cannot
be wrong again." The Hitler reference was followed by the
Canadian minister's use of hyperbole in suggesting, just as the
White House had, that Saddam Hussein would use "weapons
of mass destruction."

Friendship had obligations. Clark or Mulroney could hardly
have been expected to give voice to what some opponents of the
impending war were saying: that Saddam was many years away
from joining the club of nuclear nations; that the only country
in the world to have ever used the real weapons of mass destruction, nuclear weapons, was the United States – not once, but
twice – causing the death by incineration of 200,000 Japanese
civilians; that while Saddam had used chemical weapons
against the Kurds, it was the British, with Winston Churchill

nodding approvingly, who first used poison gas against civilians in the Arab territories they had subjugated some seventy years earlier.

Mulroney sounded more hawkish in public than he was in private. Privately, with Bush, Mulroney sided with the moderates against those who were urging immediate military action by the president. He and Clark also worked strongly to have the United States channel its activity in the Gulf through the United Nations. Many applauded the government's efforts in this regard. Others like Douglas Roche looked on in disgust as it "rolled under the Bush-Baker steamroller." Roche saw great promise in a UN Security Council resolution sponsored by Colombia which called for an Iraqi withdrawal and laid out the basis for a comprehensive Middle East peace solution. Canada's support for the resolution could have given it crucial momentum, but once the White House signalled its disapproval nothing more was heard about it from the Canadian side. When Bush decided to give up on sanctions – though there was no pressing need – and start the war, there was no objection from the prime minister.

It was further afield, in organizations having less to do with the United States, that Mulroney could show his mettle. In la Francophonie and the Commonwealth, the PM grew in stature and came to be looked to for leadership from other participants.[9] He carved out friendships, knew how to build compromises, and stood strong for progressive solutions. He demonstrated a particularly impressive ardour in the campaign against apartheid in South Africa in 1985, though the effort waned with time. In Clark, Mulroney had an effective practitioner of middle-power diplomacy who gained respect in international councils around the world. It was Clark who sometimes had the fortitude to stand up to the intransigent Israeli Prime Minister Yitzhak Shamir, and anger Washington in so doing. Canada's mere abstention from voting, as opposed to a negative vote, in the United Nations Security Council on the PLO's request to address the council was enough to draw the wrath of the incoming Bush administration. A State Department note to Bush said, "Canada's election to the Security Council requires Ottawa to think longer and harder about Middle East matters. External Affairs contacts were embarrassed over GOC abstention. . . . We expressed dismay and warned Ottawa."

But Clark failed, as did McDougall, to moderate significantly the American instincts of the prime minister. The Tories argued correctly that to disagree with the United States simply for the sake of disagreeing made no sense. But beginning with Panama, the foreign landscape was littered with examples of cases where the grounds for potential opposition were profound. With some exceptions, such as when he quite legitimately lambasted Washington for not paying its dues to the United Nations, Mulroney's American mindset held sway. Typical was a reference he made during the crisis with Native peoples at Oka. The Canadian military was sent in to take over policing. When asked for details, Mulroney told reporters they should go and get them from "the chairman of the joint chiefs of staff." That, however, would have required a trip to Washington; the Chairman of the Joint Chiefs of Staff was the American military commander. In Canada, his counterpart went by the title, Chief of Defence Staff.

As the world changed, the central planks of Canadian foreign policy remained the same. Unlike in the economic policy area, where its choices were limited by debt and dependence, in external affairs third-option possibilities abounded. The reality, however, was that the Tories saw no choice. They were committed to the American option. A line in the sand had been drawn there – in a new Nation of the Americas approach. For Mulroney, the advent of the new world order hadn't changed much. The twentieth century belonged to the United States. So would the twenty-first – and Canada had to be in position to tag along.

14

The Follies of Philistines

With the arrival of the 1990s, free trade and the new Goods and Services Tax produced a rush of cross-border activity. Together with the country's escalating divisiveness, the developments prompted speculation of future dissolution and gradual fusion with the United States. The decidedly overrated *Economist* magazine advised that Canada should get it over with – move quickly to realize its manifest destiny and fall in with the stars and stripes. Pat Buchanan, conservative commentator and future presidential candidate, published a controversial column advocating that a few Northern laurels be added to the fifty states of the union. "There is nothing wrong with Americans dreaming of a republic which, by the year 2000, encompasses the Maritime and Western provinces of Canada, the Yukon and Northwest Territories all the way to the Pole." Joel Garreau, the author of *The Nine Nations of North America*, purred mischievously in an update article discussing various break-up scenarios. He carved up Canada like a joint of beef, debating which would be the juiciest slices for Uncle Sam. Toronto almost didn't cut the mustard. Only the dwindling of the dreadfully banal WASP class, Garreau decided, made it desirable. "The only reason Toronto is no longer the dullest city on earth is that it is no longer full of anglo-Canadians."

George Bush came north, just a few months after running up the body count in Panama, to make a pronouncement, wondrous in light of the invasion, on the issue of Canada's constitutional dry-heaving. "This is not a point at which the U.S. ought to involve itself in the internal affairs of Canada," said the president. "I learned something long ago. Do not intervene in the affairs of another country." His amnesia followed publication of a work by a Quebec journalist revealing that the CIA had wiretapped Parti Québécois leader René Lévesque. A most likely time-frame for the eavesdropping was 1975-76, when Bush was CIA director and Lévesque's separatist party was winning over the province.

From the broad perspective, however, these were exceedingly good days for continental relations. "Likely the best period in Canada-U.S. relations ever," declared Gregory Marchildon, professor of Canadian studies at Johns Hopkins University. No outstanding irritants remained. Canada's acid-rain concerns had been addressed. The free trade agreement was signed, sealed, and delivered, and contrary to some dire forecasts, it as yet had visited no great cataclysm upon the northern attic. Relations on fishing banks, on defence, on the North, and on multilateral affairs were calmed. The president and the prime minister got along splendidly on a personal level and, if further bliss were occasioned, events in the east bloc were vindicating the Western powers. The cold war antagonist was forfeiting the fight, democracy was triumphant, and the new peace, so it would seem, would offer billions upon billions in defence savings to deal with debts and poverty and other exigencies.

George Bush came, as the 1990 baseball season began, to Toronto's SkyDome – the wondrous, white-whale addition to the continent's many covered stadia. Bush loved baseball. It was the American game, and he once played for Yale. His popularity in these days was as high as that of the Blue Jays, Canada's team, and he didn't mind if his presence helped boost a prime minister who had plummeted to near rock-bottom in public esteem. When given a chance, the president lauded Mulroney and the prime minister would reciprocate. It was a far cry from the day Lyndon Johnson grabbed Pearson by the shirt collar at Camp David and shouted, "You pissed on my rug!" On this visit, nobody was about to despoil hogtown's astro-turf.

It was fine symbolism: the president comes north across the free trade border to witness non-Canadians playing America's game. The fantastic success of baseball north of the border was yet another sign of the times. Major-league ball now enjoyed charter membership in English Canada's new continentalist culture. In sport, as in music, film, and books, it was a culture less conscious of borders.

In sport, Roy MacGregor, journalist and author, noted an interesting shift in allegiance. Toronto City Council voted to close nearly one hundred outdoor natural ice rinks, a breeding ground for hockey greats. The money saved would perhaps find its way to Ontario coffers to pay off some of the massive debt incurred with the new baseball colosseum. The hockey rinks cost only $400,000 to maintain but would die as Toronto set a new attendance record in baseball. Canadians had become more crazy about America's game than the Americans themselves – despite the fact that the team boasted no native Canadian talent, its uniforms were toilet-freshener blue, and it had the wimpiest name in the game – the "Jays."

Baseball had come north while hockey continued its expansion south with three-quarters of the NHL's teams based in U.S. cities. In 1992 the NHL awarded franchises to Anaheim, California, and to Miami, Florida, while Hamilton, which had built a grand arena and had been lobbying for years to get a franchise, was overlooked again. Alan Eagleson, at the centre of the hockey world for a quarter-century, left no doubt as to who was calling the shots for Canada's game. "The Americans run the league," said Eagleson, "and they're hard-nosed businessmen. They look at markets."

As baseball came to Canada, as hockey looked to southern

markets, the star-spangled bannering of the Canadian sports culture broadened with the announced plans of the Canadian Football League to expand into the United States. Teams in Portland, Oregon, and Sacramento, California, were slated to begin play in 1993 or 1994. A Grey Cup game pitting Sacramento against Portland would be possible. As CFL governors saw it, given the way the continental market was shaping up, the league would not remain viable unless it turned to the United States.

It was difficult to find a better example of a "Canadian institution" than the CFL. The CFL had decades of heritage, its own unique, Canadian style, a stretch of franchises east and west, and a classic piece of Canadiana for its annual climax – the Grey Cup game. The Grey Cup was watched annually by more Canadians than any other TV program. By the mid-1970s, the CFL was still so valued as an institution and an instrument of Canadian unity that the Trudeau government intervened to block an American football league from setting up shop in Canada. The Liberals determined that the World Football League's Toronto Northmen would cut into the CFL's market. The team was ordered to pack its bags and move out. "My government is widely prepared," said sport minister John Munro, "to do what it can to preserve the CFL as a Canadian entity and the Grey Cup game as an instrument for national unity."

In the 1970s the strategy was to prevent Americanization. By the 1990s the strategy was to court it – which the CFL was doing. No lament or legislation came from the Conservative government. To intervene would be to tamper with the market. To think in interventionist or protectionist terms like they did in the 1970s was simply not good form. It was bad baseball, and football. It was *passé*, old Canada. And besides, a strong argument could be made that, given the nature of the new economy, taking the game south was in fact the only way to save it.

The new Canadian way – wooing American influence

instead of warding it off – was seen in Michael Wilson's handling of a conflict with culture minister Marcel Masse. The issue wasn't football but book publishing. In the Tories' first term, Masse had introduced a publishing policy that, unlike the Tory continentalism of the period, set out to boost Canadian ownership in the book publishing industry by making American takeovers more difficult. But Wilson, Masse concluded, was trying to subvert the policy. He wrote to the finance minister saying there was a shift away from the policy's intent that could erode Canada's all too vulnerable culture. Wilson countered unequivocally, citing his two great motivating themes – the market and the Americans. The goals of strengthening Canadian ownership were too contentious and too costly, said Wilson in a return memorandum. Forcing foreign investors to sell off indirect acquisitions "runs counter to the government's open-for-business philosophy and could pose a continuing irritant to our relations with the United States."[1]

Being a continuing irritant to the United States was not of foremost concern to Masse, not when the health of a Canadian cultural industry was at stake. "The exemption of cultural industries from the FTA would make little sense if we abandoned the goal of strengthening Canadian ownership [in the book publishing industry]," he wrote back. "I am not prepared to ask cabinet to reconsider the goal of strengthening Canadian ownership and control." To do so "would inevitably erode the too fragile sense of social, political and cultural community which has come to exist among Canadians." In a magazine interview, Masse summed up his base problem in attempting to bolster the national culture. "If Canada succeeds in de-colonizing herself, it's a worrisome prospect for American producers."

With Wilson, whom columnist Allan Fotheringham called "deputy lapdog," and the entrenched economic philosophy of the Tory government, American producers had little to worry about. As the free trade agreement was being hatched, it was

Ronald Reagan who characterized Canada as now being a sub-
scriber to the American way. Canada and the United States
were demonstrating to all, the Gipper happily noted as his
presidency drew to a close, that "there are indeed no limits to
what people can accomplish when they are free to follow their
dreams. We're making that dream a reality. It is the American
dream."

Marcel Masse and Flora MacDonald, another culture minister, fought against the onslaught of continental culture, and in
some instances they fought hard. Their intentions were good.
In books, in film, in music, their idea was to strengthen Canadian ownership and distribution so that Canada could start
winning back control and perhaps lose its ignominious ranking
as the most foreign-dominated culture in the Western world.

A departmental policy paper entitled "Vital Links" outlined
the problem. "The Canadian marketplace is abnormal for two
reasons: the vast majority of books, films and records available
here are produced elsewhere. And the revenues generated by
their distribution largely flow out of Canada to finance production industries elsewhere." The statistics on foreign control, in
a country said by some to be too protectionist, were staggering:
90 per cent of TV drama was non-Canadian in origin; 76 per
cent of books sold in Canada were imported; 89 per cent of
earnings in the music industry in Canada went to foreign-
controlled firms; 97 per cent of Canadian movie theatre time
was taken up by foreign films.

An analysis by Paul Stothart of the accounting firm Ernst and
Young concluded that Canadian cultural companies captured
only 16 per cent of their own market, while producing 80 per
cent of the cultural works in the country. "The result of this
market structure, then, is the existence of a quasi-nation where
a child of 12 has spent 2,000 more hours watching American
television shows than attending schools. When the child does
make it to the classroom two-thirds of the textbooks are American. As the child ages some 90 per cent of the movie viewing,

70 per cent of the book reading, and 70 per cent of the music listening time will be directed toward the American product."

The Tory governors who confronted this situation tended toward the low-brow. This was not a cabinet or caucus of great cultural depth. Don Mazankowski was once a used-car dealer. Michael Wilson's idea of a good read was the Toronto stock exchange mutuals. Joe Clark, life-long politician, was no longer the unversed and awkward young man who on a tour of foreign capitals stood on the banks of the Jordan and intoned, "You have a lot of rocks here," or who inquired, when on a farm in India on the same trip, "How old are the chickens?" But he was hardly a sophisticate.

If the prime minister himself didn't border on the philistine, his MPs brought him closer to the edge. Of the National Gallery's $1.8 million purchase of the Barnett Newman painting "Voice of Fire," Tory MP Felix Holtmann said he could have done a better job himself with two cans of paint and a roller. He was not alone in this criticism. Vancouver MP Chuck Cook wondered why Tories should encourage Canadian publishing when, he claimed, only 10 per cent of Canadians read anyway. In the East, John Crosbie railed against the literati who criticized the free trade agreement. They were, he said, "a bunch of Toronto encyclopedia pedlars." Mulroney's government, despite lobbying by literacy advocates, would tax the enyclopedias and all other books at 7 per cent.

Typical of the cultural follies of the Mulroney government was the rise and fall of a powerful bill that could have revitalized the wobbly Canadian film industry. The bill dealt with the criticial area of distribution rights. American control of distribution was a primary factor in allowing American films to capture almost all of the Canadian market. The proportion of screen time of all domestic films in the Canadian market had fallen in recent years to a mere 3 per cent. To break the stranglehold, the proposed legislation would limit American control and increase the Canadian market share by an estimated thirteen percentage points. The bill began its march through the political process at the same time that the Tories were promising that cultural industries would be exempt from the free trade pact then being negotiated.

Immediately the battle lines were drawn: the cultural "pains in the ass," as they were known in the PMO, lined up against the market giants – Michael Wilson in league with the powerful Hollywood film lobby. On the Hollywood side, noted Flora MacDonald, was the big-screen veteran himself, Ronald Reagan. "This was the one Canadian issue the president understood," MacDonald said.[2]

From the start the California moguls held the trump card, and used it. Reduce our distribution rights, they said, and it will cause problems in the free trade negotiations. They'd hate, they pointed out, to see free trade founder because of something like this. The big-hitter among American lobbyists, Jack Valenti, came to Ottawa. Accompanied by three lackeys, the one-time aide to President Johnson marched into Flora MacDonald's office and proceeded to deliver a twenty-minute harangue. Canada was limiting freedom of speech, he cried. This cultural nationalism stuff was meaningless. There was nothing to Canadian culture. Whether it was Canadian or American, it didn't matter. It was all entertainment, pure and simple!

Valenti's attitude was hardly abnormal. Canadians' concern for their culture was derided by the Washington power-brokers. They didn't think there was any. Lead U.S. trade negotiator Peter Murphy said, following the signing of the free trade accord, that he thought the culture issue was "a joke." With comments that had a hint of ridicule about them, Clayton Yeutter, the head of the U.S. trade office, said there was no reason why cultural industries shouldn't be on the bargaining table. "Both of us have our cultures at stake. I'm prepared to have America's culture on the table and take the risk of having it damaged by Canadian influence after a free trade agreement." Owing to the sensitivity of this issue in Canada, the remarks outraged Mulroney. He said they constituted a display of stunning ignorance and were totally unacceptable to the Canadian government. This being a rather hefty rebuke, a Canadian reporter then dared bring up the matter at the daily briefing of journalists at the White House. Was there any reaction to the PM's words? he asked. Canada was never high on the agenda at the news briefings, and just asking the question brought on sardonic remarks and mock laughter. Reagan spokesman Marlin Fitzwater issued a long, vague reply. Mock cheers followed. "Don't ever say I haven't done my homework," added Fitzwater. The discussion ended when an American reporter asked with obvious sarcasm whether the issue had been brought up at the highest levels of power that day. To more laughter, Fitzwater said he didn't think so.

As Jack Valenti continued his harangue in Flora MacDonald's office, the minister was getting her dander up. "The man comes up to my shoulders, which gave me a lot of confidence right from the beginning," she said. MacDonald told Valenti he'd had his twenty minutes and now it was her turn. Canada, she explained, was a leap of faith that was born out of opposition to the American way, and that had existed for 120 years by standing up for itself. It wasn't about to stop now, she said. Her history lesson, including pointed references on the importance of cultural nationalism in keeping the country alive, left the undoubted impression that there would be no changes in the proposed film legislation. Valenti and crew had had enough. They stood and headed for the door muttering what a pain in the ass the lady was. As they left, an excited MacDonald aide remarked on what a great show it had been. "We should have sold tickets."

If it was a good show, it was also a meaningless one. In the end it was Valenti and crowd who got their way. MacDonald couldn't withstand the pressure from the Americans, the pressure from other countries who didn't like the bill either, and the pressure from her own government's Finance Department. The bill was rewritten and stripped of much of its power. As if this wasn't enough, the Americans collaborated on the redraft. Ottawa let the U.S. film distributors put their imprint on the new legislation so as to ensure that they would be satisfied with it. No similar contribution from the Canadian film industry was permitted.

While this was transpiring in the back rooms, a façade of Canadian credibility had to be maintained. Sensitive to the politics of the situation in Canada, the interested American parties put out public statements saying they were still opposed to the bill's amended version. With such a ruse in play, Ottawa could still argue that it was sticking it to the Americans.

The plot was foiled, however, by leaks to the media that uncloaked the skulduggery. Alain Gourd, the Culture Department's deputy minister, sized up the disaster, saying in a departmental memo that it was "very damaging to the government, in that consultations have taken place with the U.S. on key aspects of amending the proposed act without similar consultations with Canadian distributors. . . . More damaging is the perception this all creates with regard to the government's credibility and real intentions concerning the cultural exemptions under the [free trade agreement]."[3]

Not even the watered-down version of the bill saw daylight. It was introduced in 1988, but died on the order paper with the election call that year. Though dead in political Ottawa, its fate would be remembered in arts circles. At the Genie awards ceremonies in 1992, a sombre moment came when Michael Spencer, founder of The Canadian Film Development Corp., stood to receive an award and raised the matter of how Canada's caving in to American lobby pressure was crippling the film industry. Spencer cited a "cozy conversation" between Mulroney and Ronald Reagan that he said had killed the film bill.

Following the 1988 election, Marcel Masse, back in the portfolio, tried to reintroduce tough legislation but was blocked by Wilson. In the meantime his publishing policy was also being compromised. It stood in words, but in practice it was not followed.

On culture, the Mulroney government was playing a decoy game – the decoy being the free trade agreement. With bold rhetoric from the prime minister, Wilson, and others, the government stated its commitment to the country's cultural integrity and promised that cultural industries would be protected under the provisions of the free trade pact. By and large they kept that promise. But in a sideshow, well beyond the glare of publicity surrounding the trade negotiations, cultural protections were quietly being bargained away in a number of areas: publishing, film distribution, and on reduced postal rates for shipment of Canadian publications. In effect, by agreeing to remove the national protections in these areas, Ottawa was conceding to a de facto form of free trade without a formal agreement.

Following the passage of the FTA, Paul Audley, one of the Communications Department's key consultants, prepared a tax credit plan designed to stimulate Canada's cultural industries. It had the support of the minister but was ground down by Finance, said Audley – one of the reasons being that the United States wouldn't like it. But the biggest obstacle to developing a strong Canadian culture was not the Americans, Audley said. "It is our own people in Ottawa like Wilson who basically agree with the Americans."[4]

For the film and book industries, the government declined to make legislative and structural changes to help. But the ledger didn't tell a story of total gloom. The Tories did come through with large injections of cash to keep the industries alive in the short term. In the book industry, this cash solution was favoured over Masse's original Canadianization solution by many publishers. The Tories also delivered substantial financial support for art galleries in Toronto and Montreal. They brought in a public lending rights program, which compensated authors whose work was borrowed from libraries.

These few positive initiatives were overshadowed, however, if not by what happened to film and books, then certainly by the high-profile budget cuts to the CBC. These cuts became the symbol of how the Conservatives looked upon culture. Given the layers of fat in the broadcasting company, there was justification for some of the pruning. But the reasons for the cutbacks ran much deeper than the need for slimming down. This became apparent when the prime minister, stung by some critical CBC reports during the course of his rise to power, looked on contentedly at attacks on the corporation reminiscent in their vitriol of those of Spiro Agnew. In the Nixon era, Vice-President Agnew lashed out at press critics, calling them "nattering nabobs of negativism." The Tories seemed to have found their Agnew in academic John Crispo. Crispo, a standard-bearer of the right, assailed the CBC as a "lousy, left wing, Liberal-NDP-pinko network." The Tories loved it. In short order Crispo was appointed to the CBC's board of directors.

Mulroney was not terribly unhappy about taking the scalpel to the CBC, but had he listened to his party he would have finished it off altogether. At their annual conventions, the Conservatives had voted to privatize the corporation.

As the country dragged through another national unity crisis after the collapse of the Meech Lake accord in 1990, there appeared to be little sense on the part of its governors that national culture and national institutions were very much part of the glue that had kept it together. Like the CFL, the CBC had become one of the country's defining institutions. It had done so, not by operating like a standard corporation in which every move was profit driven, but by following, by and large, the rationale set out back in 1957 when television was beginning to emerge as a dominant cultural force. The rationale was stated in the report of the Royal Commission on Broadcasting of that year. "There is no doubt that we could have cheaper radio and television service if Canadian stations became outlets of American networks. However, if the less costly method is always chosen, is it possible to have a Canadian nation at all? The Canadian answer, irrespective of party or race, has been uniformly the same for nearly a century. We are prepared by measures of assistance, financial aid and a conscious stimulation to compensate for our disabilities of geography, sparse population and vast distances; and we have accepted this as a legitimate role of government in Canada."

In 1990 the CBC announced that owing to Ottawa's $108 million in budget cuts, it would have to close or severely reduce operations at eleven TV stations across the country and eliminate more than a thousand jobs. The Canada Council, the granting agency for artists, was also hit with sizeable funding reductions. Canadian book publishers were falling by the wayside. Lester and Orpen Dennys and Summerhill Press disappeared. Many long-standing theatres either closed down or ran up huge deficits.

It was not the spirit as articulated in the 1957 royal commission's report that was triumphing, but rather the market solution. The conservative creed was at its zenith in the United States under Reagan, and it could hardly be otherwise that, as with almost all things from the great empire, this conservative creed was closely echoed in Canada. The liberal commentators who had occupied centre stage for so long in Canada surrendered the limelight to right-wing stars such as Barbara Amiel, and William Thorsell. The very conservative Sun chain of newspapers took off, going continental with an outpost in Houston. *The Globe and Mail*, one of the country's national institutions, dropped its two moderate editors, veered sharply to the right, and in a measure rich in continentalist symbolism entered into a copy-sharing agreement with the *Wall Street Journal*. Completing the picture, the conservative aristocrat Conrad Black bought a large stake in Southam's, Canada's biggest newspaper chain, with the likely intention of gaining controlling interest. Conservatives were attaining dominance in Canadian print journalism.

Michael Adams, the public opinion guru who was doing a lot of crystal-ball gazing for Canadian élites, could see no end to the trend. In the era of the global economy, the market was winning, he said. Nothing would stop the push of continentalism. "This country will be ruled by market forces. People are realizing the inexorable reality of market forces."

As he departed as boss of TV Ontario, Bernard Ostry remarked on what the relentless advance of globalization in communications meant for Canada. "Even at the tables of the culturally richest nations, the mass of cheap mental junk food kills the appetite for homecooked nourishment: the chatter of cleverly bland time killers drowns out the still, sad music of humanity." The march to global uniformity had to be stopped, Ostry said. "Nature abhors homogeneity. Uniformity of culture would make human survival more chancy than ever."[5] His message was for more protection, not less. Removing the economic barriers between Canada and the United States required a redoubling of efforts to maintain a distinct culture and a better value system than that of universalized, bottom-line materialism.

In Canada the more the market triumphed, the more American values triumphed. It was an unexpected source, *The Globe and Mail*'s Thorsell, a disciplined conservative thinker, who pointed out the cultural pit into which North America had tumbled. In a masterful excoriation entitled "The decline and fall of the American cultural empire," Thorsell wrote that "we are drowning, gagging and sputtering in a morass of cultural mediocrity that is honoured as the best North America can provide." Americans, he said, were losing the ability to assess cultural meaning. Their malaise "is rooted in the rampant superficiality of their own time and place. Ruined by the deadly provincialism that attends any monopoly of power, infantilized by wealth, adolescently arrested by a simplistic ideology of individualism and blinded by narcissism, American culture drifts ever more obviously into the shoals of a bewildered mediocrity."[6]

The culture of which the editor spoke was the culture that deluged Canada. One of the more noteworthy American imports to hit the Canadian market was a board game called "The Serial Killer," complete with body bag and seventy-five toy babies. The Americanization of the Canadian culture remained "the real threat" to the country, said former governor general Jeanne Sauvé. Part and parcel of that problem, she said, was that "we lack a leader who has a clear idea what the country is."

Curiously, as the 1990s began, the government began to show modest signs of a change of mind on the arts. Even the reputed culture-killer Michael Wilson began making noises about its importance as the soul of the nation. Perrin Beatty, the young-fogey still trying to get over the Soviet threat, was an unlikely choice for culture minister, but once in the job, he announced that culture was so important to the country it could be categorized as "the CPR of the twenty-first century." Just as the national railway had knit together the country from sea to sea, a strong national culture would now do the same.

It was something that Marcel Masse and Flora MacDonald had realized in earlier years when the Wilsons and Mulroneys were unprepared to let them do something about it. The identity of nations in the new global village would no longer be determined by geography or by national economies, but by culture. The raging constitutional debate over distinct-society for Quebec had been sadly misplaced. With its own language, Quebec was secure as a culture-nation for generations to come. English Canada had the much more profound distinct-society problem with the United States. The open-border market philosophy, as even some Tories were beginning to realize, was smothering what distinction remained.

One Tory who was coming to grips with this was Peter White. A long-time friend and business associate of Conrad Black, White served as principal secretary to Mulroney for a spell before moving back to the Black table. Sharing many of

Black's conservative views, he wasn't one who would normally be associated with advocacy of big-government support for culture. But, like many analysts, given Mulroney's economic policies – which he admired – White saw economic union with the United States as now inevitable. He looked at the economic union that was shaping up in Europe and saw a rough parallel developing in North America. It was becoming an American Community, but one without, at least for English Canada, the different languages of Europe to sustain separate cultures. He explored these thoughts further when, in 1991, he co-chaired a cultural task force. With this experience behind him, White's view on the importance of national culture hardened, and, as 1992 began, he sent a memorandum to the prime minister.[7] It advised that his old friend Brian Mulroney should astonish the nation with a great burst of cultural nationalism, before it was too late. "In the final analysis," said White, "culture's the only thing that's important for Canada. Because if we are not going to protect culture, what are we protecting? Why not throw in the towel and join the United States and we'll get rich and be American?"

15

The Blurring of the Border

In 1967 Canada sold 64 per cent of its exports in the United States. In 1977 it sold 70 per cent. By 1987 the level had climbed to 76 per cent. The free trade agreement then accelerated the trend. Trade experts predicted that the percentage of exports bound for America would move well into the 80s.

The question that such reckonings and other variations on the all-eggs-in-one-basket theme invariably invoked was, Would Canada's economic integration with the United States lead to other forms of integration? Having negotiated the free trade agreement, Gordon Ritchie wrestled with this possibility. "I'm caught in a sort of Tolstoyan middle world where I see these very powerful and generally laudable economic forces developing," he said in reference to the opening of markets. "But I'd do anything I could to counter the political integration."[1]

Many shared Ritchie's concern, but not those in the places that counted – the boardrooms of the governing Tories. They appeared oblivious, leaving some to wonder if they really knew what they were getting into with free trade. From where he sat on the Liberal Senate benches, Michael Pitfield detected no long-range strategy or sense of where the Conservatives wanted to take the country. While Trudeau's vision of the Just Society sought to sustain the British North American tradition of a more caring and ordered society, Pitfield wondered what the Tories had in mind other than an American Society.[2]

With free trade, Reaganomics, and constitutional renegotiation, the Tories had set loose forces that could fundamentally alter the chemistry of the country. There were also the profound changes in the world economy. In Europe economic integration was followed by tentative political integration – a development that gave pause for thought to all those who claimed the two didn't go hand in hand.

Until the recent developments in Europe, history had offered few precedents for Canada to ponder. Back in 1876, when Toronto newspaperman George Brown failed to conclude a reciprocity pact for Canada with the United States, it was instead Hawaii that hooked up with the Americans. The paradise islands desperately needed a big, secure market for their key export, sugar. With a free trade pact with the United States, they got that and more. As part of a quickly tightening American embrace, exclusive rights to Pearl Harbour were ceded, and further restrictions on Hawaiian autonomy followed. In 1898, twenty-two years after free trade, the United States, its economic interests in control, swallowed the islands whole. Hawaii eventually became the fiftieth state.

The case was noteworthy but hardly similar to Canada's, as Hawaii may well have been annexed, free trade or no free trade. The Zollverein offered a yet more antique case study. The Zollverein was a free trade area in central Europe under Prussian auspices. Economic development within the various Germanic states had been crippled by dozens of differing tariffs, so in 1818 authorities abolished duties in the Prussian regions, creating the Zollverein. When the advantages of the new trading arrangement became apparent, other jurisdictions gradually followed suit. By late in the century, the area had become a unified Germany. History books identify the creation of the customs union as one of the chief reasons for the union.

The concept of the Zollverein was taken a great deal further with the creation of the common market of European states in 1957. At its inception few envisioned major compromises to political sovereignty of the signatories. None appeared in the first two decades, and when talk of free trade surfaced in North America, the Common Market was held up as an example to dissenting Canadian nationalists. Look at Europe, free trade advocates said. A common market with the autonomy of nations intact. It would be the same, they said, in North America.

But eventually the argument blew up in the face of every adherent. Soon, a pan-European parliament was operating in Strasbourg, and Brussels, where the EC was headquartered, was viewed as the economic capital of the continent. Member governments worked out plans for a common European-wide currency. Leaders of countries that had warred with one another through the centuries were now arguing that it made sense to integrate politically as well as economically.

By 1992 growing opposition by nationalists was threatening to derail the European unity proposal. Yet the fact that continentalism had advanced so far suggested a great deal for North America where, to begin with, Canada and the United States enjoyed greater cultural and linguistic similarities.

Though Canadians had displayed no interest in political integration with their neighbour, the same had been true of the many European countries that suddenly found themselves very far into the process. In large part, it had happened by stealth. Over time the economic dynamic of Europe had been quietly altered to the point where integration had become the advisable strategy.

The European example placed economic integrationists like Tom d'Aquino, Canada's representative of corporate interests, on softening terrain. North America was not the same as Europe, he asserted. In Europe there was greater symmetry of nation size, whereas the U.S. population was ten times that of Canada. The two continents couldn't be compared.

These contrasts, however, were the very reason critics suggested that Canada was even more vulnerable to assimilation than European nations. D'Aquino himself inadvertently suggested as much: "If it were just the case of the Netherlands or Denmark forming an economic union with Germany there would have been enormous opposition. In my view it never would have succeeded."[3]

Mel Clark, the Canadian expert on the GATT multilateral trading system, opposed the free trade agreement because of the David-Goliath imbalance. "I learned at a very early age," said Clark, "that you don't get locked in a pact on an important issue with a country that's a lot stronger than you are."[4]

In the PMO, the longer-range ramifications of policy making, the egg-head stuff as one adviser termed it, was far removed from the pressing matters of the moment. Once free trade was secure, once it was ratified in the 1988 election victory, Charlie McMillan noted that a sense of vindication took hold. Little care was given to the exceedingly difficult task of its fair and wise implementation.

"One could have made the argument," said McMillan, "that now we had to build unprecedented overseas relationships as counterbalance against the elephant-mouse thing for the political sensitivity of the country."[5] But this wasn't strongly considered, nor did the government follow up on promised adjustment programs to ease the transition for those who would suffer under free trade. The base problem, as McMillan saw it, was that Mulroney thought he'd won the election on free trade when in fact he hadn't. Only 42 per cent voted for his party in the election, a percentage considerably less than the 46 per cent who would vote in favour of the Charlottetown accord in the 1992 referendum. Instead, said the Mulroney adviser, the election was won because of the prime minister's strength in Quebec, confidence in his government's economic management, and lack of confidence in Opposition leader John Turner. Canadians were divided about the prospect of free trade. To make them enthusiastic, the government would have to work to make free trade work. Instead the chips were left to fall where they might.

In the first desultory years under free trade, nationalists and continentalists debated its impact with predictably partisan renderings. The agreement's supporters pointed to studies showing that it was making Canadian enterprises more outward looking and global, and that it was helping manufacturers reverse a long-term decline in productivity. The free trade agreement was weeding out the losers, of which there were many. Nationalists countered with a gloomy statistic: in the first three years of free trade, the country's manufacturing sector had been gouged out to the tune of 300,000 to 400,000 lost jobs, depending on whose figures one believed.

The nationalists were tying the grim statistics of the recession to the trade pact. Continentalists more accurately saw the recession in the context of a worldwide economic decline following the 1980s boom. Additionally, continentalists and almost everyone else pointed to the brutal insensitivity of the governor of the Bank of Canada, John Crow, in forcing a zero-inflation, high interest-rate policy on the nation. This increased the severity and duration of the recession. At the same time, the draconian monetary policy hiked up the value of the Canadian dollar, which badly set back exporters trying to take advantage of the new trading conditions.

The timing of the free trade agreement could hardly have been worse. "If someone had set out in 1989," said American Ambassador Edward Ney, "and said, 'What are all the things we can load on the back of this horse to sink it?' they would have had a recession and increased the dollar and did all these things that were done to free trade."[6]

According to historian Robert Bothwell, a long-time Canadian-American specialist, the country chose the wrong time to break with history. It wasn't ready. The great opportunity had been missed in 1948 when the Liberal government's free trade initiative was aborted by Mackenzie King. At that time, noted Bothwell, Canada's industries had been primed by the war. C. D. Howe felt that Canada had demonstrated during World War II that it could indeed compete on an even footing with the United States. "We missed the boat then," said Bothwell. "In the 1980s we weren't nearly as well prepared."

While the recession's effects made it difficult to disentangle the pros and cons of the trade agreement, there was one clear consequence upon which both sides agreed. This was the rapid pace of Canada's integration and harmonization with the United States. Beyond the basic provisions of the historic accord, what was tellingly registered was the psychological impact. The free trade agreement triggered a turn in the public mind, a new consciousness among Canadians that they were now members of the American economic system. While the American destiny perhaps should have been evident long before, Canada's east-west commercial mindset had lingered, the border remaining at least symbolically thick. The trade agreement changed all that, bringing on a catharsis of sorts, a green light to chase the American dream.

This wasn't the old 1960s story of the Americanization of Canada, of Canadian politicians like the great Liberal warhorse Don Jamieson going through the roof on hearing that, in his Newfoundland home, Wonder Bra had taken over Booth Fisheries. This was a wilful rush for greener Yankee pastures encouraged by a government that had torn off the country's protective layers and put out the message that now only the fittest would survive. Hundreds of companies, thousands of businesspeople, picked up stakes and moved south, looking to the United States for the better chance.

In actual tariff deductions, free trade hardly represented a radical change in the way of doing business. As the Tories kept reminding everyone, 80 per cent of trade with the United States was free to begin with, and as Larry Taylor, the economics consul at the American embassy in Ottawa, pointed out, citing economist George Stigler, "The greatest mistakes are made by confusing the margin with the norm. The FTA operates at the margin."[7] The integrational trends, he said, were well under way well before free trade.

Of greater significance than the numbers was the final crossing of the psychological divide – from thoughts of Britain and third options, to home continent. One could go back all the way to President William Howard Taft and find some apt words. Taft, an admirer of Canada, whose monstrous girth made the rocking chairs groan on his Quebec vacation-home veranda, mistakenly thought that Canada was in the mood to make the leap eight decades earlier. "Now is the accepted time," he said prematurely in 1910. "Now Canada is in the mood. She is at the parting of the ways."[8]

The eventual parting of the ways in 1988 was quickly manifest in the surge in cross-border shopping. A strong Canadian dollar (around 90 cents U.S.), combined with the hatred for the GST, likely had as much to do with this surge as lower tariffs. But in the mid-1970s, the Canadian dollar had reached $1.06 U.S. At that rate the shopping bargains below the border were even more attractive than in the 1989-91 period. By comparison, however, only a trickle of shoppers went south in Trudeau's pre-free trade days. It was un-Canadian to do so.

With free trade Canadian businesses and entrepreneurs were also heading south for the first time. The agreement altered immigration proceedings, making it easier to leave, but in the pre-free-trade era, American opportunities had also beckoned and Canadian business hadn't taken advantage. Now a new frontier had opened. Professor David Conklin and a colleague at Western University, in the middle of a five-year study of the effects of the free trade agreement, found that both business and the consumer were making a psychological shift from the Canadian to the North American market.[9]

The exodus was motivated by goods and profits, not any newborn admiration for Americans. In a Gallup poll taken in the autumn of 1990, 65 per cent of Canadians said that their lifestyle was influenced too much by the Americans. It was the highest such percentage in thirty-four years of polling. In 1956 only 27 per cent of Canadians thought that way. Opinion on the free trade agreement itself had grown increasingly negative, largely because of the recession. By almost a two-to-one margin, the agreement was opposed.

Cross-border shoppers cost Canadian retailers an estimated three to five billion dollars annually. Clothing was the big draw, accounting for about half of cross-border purchases. Three years after the introduction of free trade, same-day auto trips to the United States from Canada increased by an average of ten million a year. For the year 1991, fifty-nine million such trips took place. Tiny North Dakota got an injection of $300 million a year in business from Manitobans. Anywhere from 25 to 75 per cent of business in stores in cities like Massena, Watertown, and Syracuse in upstate New York, was coming from Canadians. Buffalo, New York, once the least likely stop on any Canadian's itinerary, became a shop-till-you-drop mecca. Montreal saw the highways out of town crammed every weekend with shoppers headed due south to a bargain mall in Plattsburgh, New York. British Columbia was losing an estimated 1,200 jobs each year due to cross-border shopping alone. In a nasty bit of symbolism, The Bay, the grand pioneer of Canadian retailing, couldn't take the losses anymore. It stopped buying merchandise from Canadian suppliers and switched to less expensive American ones. The chain could then come closer to matching the prices in U.S. stores.

Shoppers were boycotting their own country. Bankruptcies sank so many retailers that the government had to introduce tax and other measures to keep Canadians at home. But habits became set. In the new *laissez-faire* environment fostered by their government, Canadians moved where the market led them. The border became less of an obstacle to daily life. Bob Richardson, a high school teacher in Burlington, Ontario, saw the border as a sagging hammock. With the United States now more accessible, greater numbers of Canadians would come to enjoy its higher temperatures and lower taxes. "Free markets move production to places where costs are low and markets are most abundant," said Richardson. "This is at the core of market philosophy. It will happen. It even happened to our poor American brethren directly across the lakes. The surging south and west of the United States will suck the lifeblood out of free trade Ontario as surely as it has devastated the rust belt counties of New York and Michigan."

Mulroney, many suspected, didn't understand economics well enough to grasp the potential consequences of what he had set in motion. "They say Mulroney's instincts are continentalist," said Carl Beigie, a Toronto economist. "I don't know whether he has any instincts. He's a stroker. I briefed Mulroney in the leadership race. He's a stroker. He was then. He is now."[10]

When Beigie worked at the C. D. Howe Institute, he was in touch with Charlie McMillan in the PMO. "Charlie told me, 'You've got to send him some stuff to read, he's a voracious reader.' Well, Christ, he couldn't understand the C. D. Howe stuff. You'd have to send him cartoon strips."

If this prime minister was short on economic expertise he was hardly the first. Canada wasn't exactly a country where Plato's prescriptions for preparation for political office applied. Trudeau demonstrated only a cursory and erratic interest in economics, Pearson had no background in the subject, and Diefenbaker was an economics ignoramus.

Bob Rae, the harried Ontario Premier, liked to measure policies in the longer, historical perspective. He found a lot of truth in what people like Bob Richardson were saying. Dodging for a moment the thunderbolts from Bay Street, he talked as 1992 began of the figurative disappearance of the border. It was, he said, "in good measure a reason for the national angst. There are two debates about the national identity going on in this country. One is over Quebec and the Aboriginals. The other one, the underlying one which we're very reluctant to talk about, because we don't know how to deal with it, is in terms of our relationship with the United States." Canada agreeing to free trade, observed Rae, was like an eleventh person joining a choir. When you come in as number eleven "it's hard to argue that the other ten are all going to start singing like you do."[11] Rae had told an Ottawa audience that the central government's ceding of its national leadership role raised fears in him of "an erosion of the capacity of Canadians to see themselves as having something in common and a greater and greater force drawing each region . . . away from each other and towards the United States."

The blurring of the border could be seen in the activity of businesses, big and small. South of Buffalo, on the site of an old steel works, so many former Canadian companies had moved in – trucking firms, trading companies, light manufacturing concerns – that they called it Canada Row. Between the summer of 1987 and the summer of 1990, eighty-seven Canadian businesses moved to the Buffalo area. The emigration of Canadian business was most pronounced in Ontario, where much of the restructuring was taking place. The transfer of allegiance had begun before free trade. From the mid-1970s to the late 1980s, the proportion of Ontario products sold to other parts of Canada declined from 22 per cent to 15 per cent. The products were now going south. With the free trade agreement, the trend was accelerating.

Among the Canadian companies on the move was one of the oldest, a pre-Confederation giant established in 1847, Massey-Ferguson Ltd. The producer of more than $3 billion a year in farm equipment, diesel engines, and auto parts had changed its name to Varity Corp. Canadian governments had injected almost half a billion dollars into the company in the previous decade to keep it viable in Canada, but in 1991 it became Buffalo-based.

Tridon Ltd. was an industrial parts maker in southern Ontario once considered to be a prime example of the quality company that would lead Canada into the twenty-first century. Tridon moved to Nashville, Tennessee. The majority of its 550 workers were left without jobs. They were among an estimated 146,000 men and women in Ontario who lost their jobs in manufacturing industries in the first two years after free trade came into effect. Tridon's reasons for changing country were the same as most others taking the same route: cheaper land, lower taxes, lower labour costs. The president of the company, Paul Davidson, considered himself a strong Canadian. He became so ashamed about moving his Burlington operation that he refused to allow his picture to appear in *The Globe and Mail*. His friends, he said, even his dry cleaner, saw him as a traitor.

Would-be traitors could be found everywhere. According to the Canadian Federation of Independent Business, more than one-third of the 44,000 businesses in the organization made inquiries about moving to the United States. It was becoming the thing to do. In Tennessee, Tridon's Davidson would find many compatriots. In recent years Canadian companies had invested $400 million in the state and had created 8,000 jobs for Americans.

Taxes were a prime consideration. The advantage on the American side was obvious. As a percentage of national income, personal taxes in Canada – federal, provincial, and municipal – were 34 per cent higher than in the United States. The tax gap left public officials like City of Toronto planner Peter Tomlinson holding their heads in their hands. How, he wondered, could he help maintain the competitive position of the local economy when the other country enjoyed such an advantage? For a Canadian business executive making $100,000 a year, the tax difference meant, he noted, a saving of $20,000 a year by moving to the United States.[12]

Now that a more open competition with the United States had begun, Tomlinson pondered two unattractive possibilities. One, the exodus would continue, and it would drain away many of Canada's best and brightest and gradually pull down the nation. Or two, Canadian taxes would have to drop, which in turn would eventually necessitate a drop in the quality of social programs and other expensive government programs that had made Canada special and different.

For the Toronto city planner, the costs of free trade outweighed the benefits. The great advantage of the Canada-U.S. Auto Pact was that it guaranteed Canada a share of the production. He only wished that free trade negotiators could have been able to work in some of the same protections.

As had been predicted even by the promoters of free trade, many of the businesses moving south were branch plants of American multinational enterprises. They had been set up in Canada to get in behind the tariff walls. With the tariffs removed, some head offices saw no reason to maintain Canadian branches. Retrenchment became the order of the day.

In the United States the free trade story was a muted one compared to Canada. Most Americans, polls showed, thought trade was free before the signing of the deal. After the signing, most didn't know there had *been* a signing. It was a country where the level of education on foreign affairs was always suspect. Once, in responding to a multiple-choice quiz, Americans identified U Thant, then the secretary general of the United Nations, as a "submarine." That few would know about free trade was hardly astonishing.

But the trade pact was, of course, of considerable interest to American business. And, as the opening to the north widened, American business got aggressive. Companies increased advertising in Canada to lure shoppers. Some big American retailers, taking advantage of falling tariffs that made it easier to ship goods north, opened shop in Canada. State governments set up trade offices in Canada to offer businesses enticements to move down to their regions. Among the inducements were financing below market rates, footing the bill for training new employees, and special land deals.

Before free trade, New York was one of the few states to have a trade office in Canada. In the first two years after free trade, New York was joined by Illinois, North Carolina, Ohio, Michigan, and Florida. More prepared to follow. Their purpose, stripped to its essence, was to sap Canada. A survey by the Canadian Manufacturers' Association showed that nearly a quarter of their member companies had been approached by a representative of an American state. The United States, said Bob Miller of the Illinois trade office, was beginning to treat Ontario and other provinces like other states in the union.

Joel Guberman, a Toronto lawyer, specialized in emigration. His practice had taken off since free trade, even though the great majority of Canadians didn't know how the rules had changed to make it easier to move across the border. If they ever did, he said, there would be a flood. Before free trade, those who came to Guberman's office were fed up with Canadian winters, many of them older couples. After free trade a new breed, middle-aged professionals between thirty and forty-five, became the bulk of his business. Estimates suggested that the number of professionals leaving Canada roughly tripled after free trade.[13]

While Canadian students ostensibly got nothing from the free trade agreement, they, too, were looking south. In the academic year 1986-87, 15,700 Canadians studied as undergraduates and graduates at American colleges and universities. For the 1990-91 academic year, the number had grown to 18,350. Admissions officers at prestigious Canadian private schools noticed not only an increased level of interest in American universities among their students, but also, as in the case of business, a new assertive campaign by the American colleges to recruit Canadian students. "The two societies are moving together," said David Matthews, director of admissions at Upper Canada College. "The prestige factor of a number of American schools, not just Harvard and Yale, is now known up here."[14] One third of students due to graduate from Upper

Canada College applied to American universities. About half of them went.

Canadian Richard Taylor, a Nobel Prize winner in physics in 1990, gave a speech to the Royal Society of Canada in 1991 on "scattered electrons and scattered Canadians." Taylor pointed out that "you could make an enormously wonderful university out of the Canadian faculty at Harvard, Cornell, Stanford and Berkeley. . . . There's more Canadian content in the U.S. scientific establishment than on the television screen in my hotel room here in Kingston." In the last decade, four other Canadians had become Nobel laureates. Three of them, he said, did their work at American universities.

Lones Smith, a brilliant student at Carleton University, left to do a Ph.D. in economics at the University of Chicago. Upon its completion he considered jobs in Canada but opted for a posting at the Massachusetts Institute of Technology, where the academic environment, in his view, was superior. At MIT he became a junior professor of economics. Five of the seven junior professors in the department are Canadians.

Coinciding with free trade, other developments contributed to the southward trend. Globalization was being felt most noticeably right at the time that free trade came in, and the one reinforced the other. As researchers at the University of Western Ontario were finding, many companies would have been on the move with or without the free trade agreement. The recession and the GST alone had whetted the appetite to look for alternatives.

All things considered, however, the free trade agreement was the major player in this new phase of the blending of the continent. Three years after the agreement took effect, Donald Macdonald, who played such an important role in convincing the prime minister to go ahead with it, observed that "Canada isn't held together by the tariff system."[15] Yet never in the pre-free-trade era had there been anything like the amount of cross-border travel, or business relocation, or north-south integration.

"What we've done," said Macdonald, "is opened Canadian business to the marketplace." But the marketplace on the continent, as Bob Richardson suggested, was rooted below the Canada-U.S. border. It was located where the taxes were lower and the weather was better, and the gasoline that fuels the American dream was almost half the price it was north of the border.

As Canada and the United States continued their march toward inevitable economic integration, it seemed just as inevitable, as Allan Gotlieb saw it, that new forms of joint management would have to be created.[16]

16

An Explosion of Relations

It was a U.S. specialist, Stephen Blank of the Americas Society, who said Canada's role on the continent could be considered a "civilizing mission." Ronald Reagan, who thought Canada should share in his country's own divine mission, would hardly approve. But the conceit as expressed by Blank arguably bore some merit. When in 1988 George Bush spoke of the need for a kinder, gentler America, he might well have pointed to Canada as his example. With its sane gun laws, Canada had not a fraction of the violence that bloodied and chilled America's streets. With broad social programs, it cared for its needy in a more substantial way. Its culture, as nourished by government subsidies and a large, public broadcast network, the CBC, was less profit-driven and therefore less crass. Its level of racial intolerance, while sometimes suspect, never rose to the heights of its neighbour. And in its outlook on the world, Canada's middle-power status enabled a more peace-loving approach.

The Canadian tradition of big government – big as measured by American standards – contributed to the more civilized ethic. Ottawa spent considerably more as a percentage of its GDP than did Washington. Ottawa did not have Washington's fantastic bite of military spending which, although helping to keep the American economy pumped, cut deeply into social spending capacity.

But these traditions were cast aside by a government which was changing Canada from a society that offered a modest alternative to the American way to one that converged with it. What most galled the nationalists, those who deeply believed something better could be built on the northern half of the continent, was that the Tory governors relished the change. At root, their way was the American way, and if they had to preside over the demise of the Canadian dream – if such a grand description could be used for the civility, compassion, and restraint that Canada stood for – then so be it.

Seymour Martin Lipset, the dean of experts on Canadian-U.S. attitudes, had for decades set the conventional wisdom on differences between the people of the two countries. While some dissimilarities had eroded over time, Lipset remained convinced until the mid-1980s that three strong pillars upheld Canadian distinctiveness. Canadians were more "group-oriented, statist and deferential to authority."

As the decade closed, however, Lipset was changing his mind. Canada, he said, was turning into a "more classically liberal, libertarian society." The Charter of Rights and Freedoms, which gave more power to the individual to challenge the state through the courts, had been a highly significant step under Pierre Trudeau. The Charter served to lessen the tendency toward group-mindedness. Mulroney's conservative, decentralizing initiatives further carved away at the statist characteristics of the society. And the Canadian social landscape was now littered with examples of a new Canadian animosity toward élites, notably political élites.

So many of the new trends in Canada had an American look. Participatory democracy gained in comparison to representative democracy. Regional populist parties like the Reform Party in the West and the Confederation of Regions party in New Brunswick came to life. The Reform Party in particular was an

American-derivative, its anti-government style closely resembling Reagan republicanism. Talk of referenda and constituent assemblies became the order of the day in Canada. American-style lobbying came to Ottawa in the Mulroney era with astonishing speed. In 1980 about thirty lobbying groups were located in the capital. By 1990 the number had grown to four hundred. The style of the PMO itself became more American. Like the White House, the executive branch in Canada came to withhold so much of the federal decision-making power that some began calling the system "executive federalism."

So many elements of the American way were being grafted onto the parliamentary system, asserted *Globe and Mail* columnist Jeffrey Simpson, that a hybrid Canada was in the making, something halfway between a parliamentary democracy and an American system – "a philosophical muddle." John Crosbie noted the same trend. "Just look at what's happening to us in the political sphere. I mean all the changes in our political system are following the U.S. example."[1]

A World Values survey taken in 1981 and again in 1990 with unusually large opinion samplings compared Canadian and American attitudes in thirteen areas of opinion. Through the 1980s, the survey concluded, the two societies converged in eight of eleven areas – including the areas Lipset had long held up as those that set the countries apart. The survey results received confirmation from a joint study by the University of Western Ontario and the University of Alberta. William Johnstone, a sociologist at the latter institution, found that, in all of the areas people traditionally looked to for contrast between Canadians and Americans, there were "no significant differences."

As analysed by political scientist Neil Nevitte, also of the University of Alberta, the World Values study revealed a pattern of allegiances on the continent that held intriguing portents. It showed that the values of English Canadians in political and economic domains were closer to those of Americans than to those of Quebeckers. Substantiated, at least to some degree, was the idea that Canada had its priorities skewed, that the most pressing distinct-society problem was not English Canada *vis-à-vis* Quebec, but English Canada *vis-à-vis* the United States. The finding that most surprised the authors of the study came in answer to the question of whether respondents wanted the border to be erased. As many as 24 per cent of Canadians and 46 per cent of Americans were in favour. Another result pertinent to the continentalist debate showed that those favouring economic integration of the continent also supported more strongly the concept of political integration. The further the two societies moved down the road of economic union, the study suggested, the greater the possibility that forms of political union, as in Europe, would follow.

The convergence was mainly, but not only, a matter of Canadians falling into American ways. While a country one-tenth the size of its neighbour couldn't expect to have a great impact beyond its own border, the Canadian example did get some attention. In the area of health care in particular, and also in the areas of multiculturalism and bilingualism, many Americans were looking to the Canadian example. Health care became a major issue in the 1992 American election campaign. The Canadian system, decried by the Republicans as socialist, admired by many Democrats as realistic, was put under the microscope.

In the multicultural area, with Hispanics becoming a majority in Miami and parts of California, Americans were discovering that, as David Crombie put it, "you can't melting-pot them." Canada understood this long ago, said the Mulroney government's one-time multicultural minister. "And our whole bilingual program, which everybody is now down on, and our multicultural programs were very early attempts to cope with the fact that the ethnics are un-meltable. I think three policies, bilingualism, multiculturalism, and medicare, are policies which you are going to find increasingly accepted by the rest of North America." The debate, Crombie advised, should not be seen as one about what Canada is or what the United States is. "It is a debate about what North America is."[2]

The convergence of the two nations was most apparent and most open to acceleration in Western Canada. It was in the West where, without the Great Lakes and the St. Lawrence as a physical divide, the forty-ninth parallel – an arbitrary line set two hundred years earlier in response to political and military conflict – could be most readily exposed as gratuitous.

Political borderlines had been more viable in pre-globalization times. But when barriers to trade, communication, and travel began falling, nation states or regions within them began seeking natural allies. The old political borders remained, but they meant less. People increasingly wanted to manage their own affairs and their own relations. "There is a realization that nation states can't deliver the goods any more," said pollster Michael Adams. "So people don't defer to élites. They want to be in power themselves."[3] In this way, said Adams, Mulroney's devolutionary thrust, whether by accident or design, fit the sociology of the times.

The changes brought on by the revolutions in communications and technology found their broad extension in Mulroney's politics of decentralization, most particularly in free trade. In Western Canada it wasn't until the free trade agreement came into effect that the cross-border blending became fully apparent.

In the rest of the country, the market push southward was piecemeal. But in the Prairies and British Columbia, a more structured integration with northern American states proceeded. Formal transborder organizations appeared. Civic partnerships with Americans, grass-roots partnerships, and joint economic development programs were developed. A sense grew that states of the American Northwest and provinces of the Canadian prairies were natural allies.

In 1992, Jim Horsman, the deputy premier of Alberta, travelled to a bilateral meeting in Seattle, Washington, and brashly proclaimed, "I love the United States of America." He boasted of measures his government had taken to co-ordinate policies with neighbouring states such as Montana. At the same conference, British Columbia premier Michael Harcourt offered an extra-terrestrial perspective. From outer space, he said, there was no border between British Columbia and Washington. Harcourt headed an NDP government, and the NDP was the traditional nationalist party. He, too, was sold on globalization. "We have to prepare for the global economy. We cannot prepare for it by building walls around ourselves." As well as directing more business to the United States, Harcourt was leading an even more pronounced effort to expand economic ties to Japan and the Pacific Rim. Economic salvation for British Columbia lay west and south – everywhere but the direction in which the rest of the country lay.

The politicians may have been gung-ho at the Seattle conference, but they were restrained compared to the busines leaders who advocated nothing less than the abolition of the border. Larry Swanson, a Canada-U.S. trade expert at the University of Montana, felt the potential for closer ties was always there but that the border, until the passage of the free trade agreement, was too tall. Then he noticed a change. "We met in Great Falls and we met in Lethbridge, and there was so much commonality," he said of talks with Canadians to explore new ways for co-operation. "When you break down the obstacle of the border and you get together in the room, the whole thing about us and them just isn't there. You have commonality."[4]

Susan Cribbs had become director of U.S. affairs for the province of Alberta in 1983. In the first five years she found little interest in co-operation. She occasionally attended meetings with business leaders from the Dakotas and Idaho and Oregon. Economic interaction was talked about, but not much happened. The border was a big divide. But then came free trade and, despite the recession, said Cribbs, "there was almost an explosion in relations. It really dates from that – free trade."[5]

Northwestern American states had formed a group, the Western Legislative Conference, to co-ordinate trade and economic activity. It signed up Alberta and British Columbia as honorary members after free trade came into effect. A year later, it offered the two provinces full status. "They wanted to recognize us as states," said Cribbs. "That was too much. We declined."

The Legislative Conference had small ambitions compared to another new Canadian-American alliance. This one called itself the Pacific Northwest Economic Region or PNWER. It grouped Alberta and British Columbia with Montana, Idaho, Oregon, Washington, and Alaska. American-based, it had resources and clout. PNWER put out slick literature packets in which it listed the world's nine largest nations by GNP. Tenth on the list, it noted, following China, Italy, and Canada was PNWER. Annual GNP – $280 billion.

To develop north-south ties, PNWER organized task forces with representatives from each state and province in such areas as workforce training, telecommunications, forestry, and education. The Montana and Alberta governments began joint tourism advertising: "the two-nation vacation." Through joint marketing efforts, PNWER planned to make itself the world's major supplier of environmental and pollution clean-up technology.

In the Prairies, where Westerners felt long embittered toward Ottawa, the idea of this much closer alignment with the American states struck a chord. Radio hotlines buzzed with positive feedback on PNWER. On the U.S. side, proponents talked of eventually turning it into an autonomous region. To John Vincent, the speaker of the Montana Legislature, the idea made perfect sense. "It seems so natural geographically. If you take the arbitrary lines on the map off, then everything else fits. The various concerns, the emphasis on agriculture and natural resources. There are a lot of common denominators that lend themselves to an effort like this."

Complementing PNWER and the Western Legislative Conference was the Red River corridor, linking Minneapolis, St. Paul, and Winnipeg in a trade zone. The Red River organization had funding from provinces, states, both federal governments, and private sources. One of its purposes was to promote trade within the corridor, which had a population of 1.5 million. The other was to promote the region internationally. Nowhere did the word "national" fit in. "During the Reagan years we learned that Washington didn't really give a tinker's dam about us and that if we were going to have an economic future, we had to take control of it ourselves," said Jerry Nagel, the Minnesota-based director of Red River. "Collectively we can have an international presence. International trade is moving away from the purview of national governments."[6]

Boundary-hopping without any thought of Washington or Ottawa, Nagel's bilateral network forged an alliance with the region of Brittany in France. Brittany was a major food-processing centre, and Red River was hoping to become a key supplier for the business. It would receive a rich transfer of food-processing technology in return. As a binational trading zone, Red River was looking to make other international partnerships. To Nagel, who had made a long study of transborder trends, regionalization, regardless of borders, was the way of the future. Free trade was good because in his view it accelerated by several years a process that was already underway. Many American experts on the bilateral relationship shared his view. Economies would be managed more and more on a local basis. The centres in Washington and Ottawa would pull back, thereby allowing regions, cross-border in some cases, to forge stronger identities.

On the Pacific Coast, the Seattle-Vancouver corridor was also being promoted as a borderless, integrated market. Called Sea-Van for short, it was planning a cultural as well as economic partnership. Possibilities included merging the performance seasons of cultural institutions, symphonies, and dance companies in each city and creating a joint Sea-Van opera company.

Contained by the mountains on one side and the Pacific on the other, the corridor was home to people who had more in common with each other than they did with residents outside the region in either country.

A growing number of Canadians were taking their entrepreneurial skills across the B.C.-U.S. border. Near the border, the town of Blaine, Washington, saw more Canadian-owned new businesses than American. In the first half of 1992, forty-one Canadian businesses were set to cut the ribbon. An estimated eight hundred jobs for Americans would be created, another $57 million invested. Meanwhile, cross-border shopping had become a deluge. "It's too bad. I feel unpatriotic," said a Vancouverite lining up at a Blaine gas station. "I don't enjoy this." Not so, the Washington state residents. "We love it," said Blaine's town clerk, Laura Amundson. "I think they've got to wipe that border out."

There was no likelihood of any Canada-U.S. cross-border region seeking autonomy. It was easy to exaggerate the transborder links. Yet the developments were difficult to ignore. Increasing north-south trade and business flows would eventually give rise to transportation lines and producer services crossing the border that would erode the east-west infrastructure that had held Canada together. In the global economy, a nation's political space was no longer the same as its economic space. This was bringing on, in the jargon of the academics, an unbundling. Regions such as the Red River corridor developed not just national but multiple loyalties: to the region itself, to binational structures, to regions in other countries. This kind of dynamic created pressures for new systems of governance such as the EC, where supra-national and sub-national units were gaining voice.

In Canada, distress at such a dynamic was expressed not only by liberals and leftists, but also by conservatives. David McFadden, the president of the Canada-U.S. Business Association, surveyed the developments and concluded, "If we do not have a federal government that is able to give some central direction and vision, then the driving force in Canada could be a series of these relationships." Mickey Cohen, one of the architects of the Mulroney government's economic policy, sounded dubious in an article he co-authored in 1991 about whether the free trade agreement was the route to go under such circumstances. "In a country with an already weak sense of self-confidence in its overarching nationhood, the effect is to make the FTA seem to be part of a nation-weakening thrust."

As regions began to form cross-border alliances irrespective of their national governments, so too did cities. In 1992 Peter Tomlinson, the Toronto planner, attended a meeting in Racine, Wisconsin, where an organization called North American Cities International was formed to meet the challenges of disappearing economic borders. The idea was to establish close partnerships between Canadian and American cities with compatible interests and, beyond that, with cities overseas. Toronto twinned with Frankfurt, Germany, in 1990 in order to promote, among other things, its growing fashion industry in Europe. As its manufacturing base was declining, Toronto was forging an identity in North America as a continental metropolis, a gateway to the United States. Safer, cleaner, more stable, it was selling itself as a better base for multinational corporations than American cities. Tomlinson didn't like what was going on, certainly not from a Canadian perspective. "But once the border is erased economically, you have to start looking for these opportunities, even if it's radically different from what you've done in the past."[7]

Peter Karl Kresl, an American academic specializing in regionalism, was the force behind the new organization of Canadian and American cities. His study of ten cities located on both sides of the border found that free trade had generated a new level of interdependence among them. For nationalists it was another note of discouragement. Once competitive and suspicious of each other, the cities were now seeing the advantages of co-operative crossborder interaction. In most of the cities, plans for economic development were being altered to fit continental rather than national roles. "They have begun," said Kresl, "to see themselves as natural points of access or bridges in a North American context."[8]

The disadvantages of free trade, Kresl said, lay on the Canadian side. American businesses had little incentive to expand operations to Canada, but Canadian firms, seeing lower production and operating costs to the south, were finding it very attractive to move. Secondly, as Canadian firms reformed to fit the more open, continental market, they adopted the standards of the big pace-setters, the American models. The end result, said Kresl, would be such pressure for the reduction of taxes and other costs of doing business in Canada that it could well cripple the social welfare system.

Pierre Paul Proulx of the Université de Montréal, a student of north-south and east-west trade flows for two decades, feared Canada would no longer be able to resist the north-south economic pull. "We're just moving into this process where technological change and business strategy are driving things. It's technology taking over. It's business strategy and rationalization on a North American scale and it's the end of our national policy."[9]

"The end of our national policy" was as precise a way of labelling the change as any. If the national policy had been to build an east-west infrastructure to counterbalance unremitting Americanization, current events were signalling its doom. As Proulx spoke, an opportunity to retie some of the old network was disappearing. The federal government was backing away from an effort that, by dismantling internal barriers to trade among the provinces, would bring about an economic union. The union plan was part of a constitutional negotiation whose central thrust was denationalization – the devolving of more powers to the regions and the provinces, most notably Quebec, so that they could be more satisfied with their status in confederation.

In September 1991, federal proposals called for a court-enforced Canadian common market that would guarantee the free flow of goods, services, people, and capital. The federal government would give itself new powers to manage the national economy. If Ottawa was eliminating trade barriers with the United States, it thought that it had better do the same within the country. Otherwise Canadians would become more economically beholden to Americans than to each other. But while the provinces were making substantial gains in the constitutional negotiations, Ottawa was unable to gain anything in return. When some provinces baulked, Ottawa backed down on the union proposal.

The outcome flowed in part from the prime minister's abiding wish to find favour. What was important to Mulroney was the deal and the art of the deal. Trudeau took a sometimes bristlingly hard line on provincial rights and American relations because, in his view, to do otherwise would be to leave the country tied together by nothing stronger than an elastic band.

Under Mulroney, what had begun as an effort to bring Quebec into the constitutional fold, after the Trudeau-Lévesque war of 1981, became a full-scale overhaul of the Constitution during which it was open season on Ottawa. (It never occurred to the Tories that by having not agreed to Trudeau's constitutional package, many Quebeckers may have curiously achieved what they wanted – a form of sovereignty-association.)

Mulroney, first and foremost, wanted to please. To please meant to appease. In dealing with the provinces, his approach was the same as it was to the United States. He was prepared to bargain away protections that the centre in Canada had always held.

17

The EC and the AC

In his bid to keep his provinces and his big neighbour contented, Brian Mulroney's generosity was of extravagant proportion. On the domestic side, Alberta was one of the provinces upon which he looked most favourably. Trudeau had fought vigorously with Alberta, and had paid the political price. Alberta had a long list of grievances, but Trudeau's attitude had been that Ottawa had its own needs and that the central government was paramount. It represented all Canadians. He, Trudeau, was its leader, and he was not about to wear a Stetson hat.

In stark counterpose, Mulroney was prepared to try to stroke away every oil and cattleman's ache and pain. Alberta was high Tory country and it would get what it wanted. Alberta hated the National Energy Program. Mulroney dismantled the NEP. Alberta wanted the National Energy Board transferred to Calgary. Mulroney moved the NEB to Calgary. Alberta got the deregulation in transportation that it wanted. Alberta got the heavy-oil upgrader and the major military contract that it wanted. Alberta got its natural gas exports approved.

And on it went. The ailing Alberta agriculture sector needed hand-outs. Mulroney provided government largesse that topped up the silos. Alberta was gung-ho on free trade. Alberta got free trade. Alberta had a wish list in the constitutional negotiations. Alberta's wish list was catered to.

Having gone to such pains, having played Santa Claus for twelve months a year, Mulroney may well have expected some return on his investment. What he got, however, was a rearguard political rebellion that threatened to rob him of the power base that the province represented for his party. The Reform Party, hatched in Alberta, took flight, topping the provincial polls while the Conservatives fell to near Trudeauvian depths. The prime minister couldn't buy love. As many a leader of many a federation had found, the more Mulroney gave to the constituent parts, the more the constituent parts demanded. Decentralization bred fragmentation. Through the early 1990s it was becoming apparent, most noticeably when another bid at constitution-building, the Charlottetown accord, came crashing down, that regionalism in Canada was a serious and enduring condition.

The Canadian family was drawing apart at the same time that its allegiance to the United States was tightening. For its part, the United States was entering a period of relative isolation it had not known for half a century. While the United States was still the world's number-one power, while the Gulf War and U.S. intervention in Somalia demonstrated it had yet to relinquish its global policeman's role, the end of the cold war stripped the country of its prized status as leader of the free world. Its importance to Europe and other parts of the world diminished. Budget shortages and domestic crises now drew the American gaze inward. The global economy followed the same trends, and saw an increasing regionalization in Asian, European, and American zones.

The consequences left Canada, which prided itself on its internationalist tradition, facing a paradox: in the new, globalized world, it was a country increasingly isolated and bound to a shrinking and – as measured against the glories of its post-war supremacy – declining American empire.

* * *

Through 1990 and 1991, the first two years of the post cold war era, Bush's response to a fundamentally changed world order was cautious. The old engines that had driven public policy since 1945 had suddenly been rendered obsolete. But the Bush administration chose to run on them. It was business as usual. The CIA continued to spend $30 billion a year on espionage and counter-espionage. Defence spending cuts were marginal. NATO remained a priority. Though there was much talk of the new, the old world order sufficed.

The American response cued the Canadian response. At no other time had the world changed so much, but in Canada the pivotal events produced little new thinking. Not even a royal commission to study Canada's role in the new world was merited. In the post cold war era, Canada still held firmly to American coat-tails.

Mulroney vacationed at Kennebunkport, where he fished with the president on his boat, *Fidelity*, and where they talked of the possibility of the prime minister becoming head of the United Nations. They were men who saw the world through the same lens. Their friendship had grown warm through the years, and it was soothing for the unpopular Mulroney to bathe in Bush's glow. Bush spoke of the relaxed rapport he had with the Mulroney family. "He and Mila came to Maine, brought the kids, and there was no formality. There were no Marines or Mounties around. . . . We had a good, easy time. And we could argue and talk frankly. He could point out that he was irritated with us over some damn thing about lobsters." But the irritations were few. In the summer of 1990, as the two leaders made plans at Kennebunkport for responding to Iraq's takeover of Kuwait, clean air legislation was making its way to the president for final approval. Mulroney had pressed for six years for such legislation. It would reduce sulphur dioxide emissions by ten million tons between 1994 and 2005, substantially reducing the levels of filth that drifted into Central and Eastern Canada to fall as acid rain.

Even if Mulroney had wanted to, it would hardly have been a propitious time for him to throw any obstacles in the way of the president's Gulf War plans. Far from setting obstacles, Mulroney so impressed the president with his co-operation that, following the expulsion of Iraq from Kuwait, Bush chose Canada as the first stop on his post-victory parade of nations. As Bush was then widely held in high esteem, it was a fine honour for the prime minister, especially when the president thanked him for Canada's "key" contribution – two boats and a few guidance aircraft. "Americans knew from day one where Canada stood," said the president. When his turn came, Brian Mulroney spoke so glowingly of Bush's grasp of the issues, his breadth of vision, his patience, his decisiveness, and his place in the history of free men and women, that Bush squirmed in his seat.

In some respects the harmony in North America paralleled that in Western Europe. In 1991, the same year that talks began between Canada and the United States on bringing Mexico into their free-trading fold, the European powers met in Maastricht in the Netherlands where they extended their plans for European integration. The new Europe would resemble a supranational union consisting of one market and one currency tying together twelve nation states: Belgium, Denmark, France, Germany, Greece, Italy, Ireland, Luxembourg, the Netherlands, Portugal, Spain, and the United Kingdom. There would be a common foreign policy and common social and environmental policies. The common parliament, headquartered at Strasbourg, would be endowed with more powers, with member nations ceding appropriate degrees of sovereignty. European mega-projects, such as the expansion of transportation links like the GTV, France's high-speed train, would create a suitable infrastructure. "A great power is being born," said French President François Mitterrand at Maastricht, "one at least as strong commercially, industrially, and financially as the United States and Japan."

The plan required approval from each member nation, and it was soon apparent that gaining such approval would be tough. The plans for integration had been fashioned by the European political and bureaucratic élite with a minimum of public consultation. Finally, when Europeans began to wake up and understand the full meaning of what was transpiring, the nationalists made their opposition known. Denmark, surprisingly, voted against Maastricht, and in a crucial test in France the treaty passed only by a hair.

These and other setbacks seemed likely to slow but not stem the tide of integration. The European Community was the biggest trading bloc on the globe and was growing rapidly. In 1990 the EC countries accounted for 19 per cent of world imports, compared to 14 per cent for the United States, and 6 per cent for Japan. The countries of the European Free Trade Association (EFTA), which included Sweden, Finland, Austria, Iceland, and Switzerland, entered into a free trade relationship with the EC in 1991. The entire east bloc, including the former Soviet territories, lay waiting, ready to be colonized. Their ideologies had become compatible. They wanted in. Though incomplete and untested, the EC was a club of nations with potential to dwarf a North American bloc.

One message to Ottawa and Washington was that Europe was looking inward. Barriers to business and trade inside Europe were being removed at a faster pace than barriers to the outside world. A second message was that the concept of supranationalism could well be the model for other nation state groupings: such as Canada, the United States, Mexico.

With a stretch of the imagination, the Canada-U.S. free trade agreement could be seen as comparable to Europe's 1957 integration, which started it on the road to unification. The free trade accord institutionalized an economic bonding of neighbours, as in Europe, and opened the door to integration in other areas. The precedent of Canada-U.S. relations was clear – integration led to more integration. Moreover, by almost every measure – social, cultural, linguistic, economic – Canadians were closer to Americans upon embarking on free trade than the European nations were to one another. In Europe the argument for integration led logically to the plans for full monetary union. In a single market, a single currency made perfect sense. It would simplify matters enormously, decreasing the costs of doing business. Similarly, in North America monetary union was seen by some to be the next step. The BCNI's Tom d'Aquino said that with the full implementation of free trade and so much other harmonization it would only make sense to create a monetary union. Since both currencies were known as "the dollar," monetary union would not require the same psychological leap as in Europe where countries pondered their pounds, marks, and francs being turned into something that sounded like a farm animal – the ECU.

Canada was experiencing populism, power dispersal, and high-volume southward integration. Power showed signs of devolving both from the centre to the regions, and from the centre to continental authorities – the independent, binational panels, for example, that governed the free trade agreement. As nation-state governments continued to lose the power to effect change in the global economy, their publics would lose confidence in government's ability to improve their lives. The publics would be prepared to transfer loyalties. Just as the creation of an EC supra-nation would fit the global economy's changing dynamic in Europe, the creation of an American Community supra-nation could one day do the same for Canada, the United States, Mexico, and perhaps others in the Americas.

As the Canadian economy continued to fold in with the American, the likelihood was that those in the lumber industry in British Columbia, or in agriculture in Saskatchewan, or the fisheries in Atlantic Canada, would start to wonder if it would not be better, instead of going to Ottawa which was fading in power, to have representatives where the real economic power was held – in a Brussels of North America located in the United States.

The possibility of an AC of North America had caught the attention of External Affairs professionals. "If you'd asked these questions five or six years ago," said Michael Hart, the American-option enthusiast, "I'd have said, 'You're nuts. Who is this guy?' But after what's happened, these questions are now legitimate ones."[1] Allan Gotlieb imagined an overarching network of legal mechanisms and transborder tribunals to govern North America.[2] Supra-nationalism, he said, was on the way, and it would require a strong central government in Canada to exercise clout in the new system. Paul Heinbecker, a Mulroney adviser on his way to the German ambassadorship, said Canada was "perhaps becoming the world's first post-nation state."[3] The post-nation concept suggested a configuration lacking a national economy, and defined increasingly by local cultures.

The comparison of North American integration with the development of the EC was inexact in many areas. Politics were a driving imperative of the EC – the notion, as EC architect Jean Monnet had convincingly seen it, that the only way to overcome a history of wars was to form a union. Of course there was no such requirement of the Canadian-American relationship. The last war was in 1812. Specialists used the term "natural integration" to describe the Canadian-American economic development. By that they meant integration driven by business – a bottom-up, market-driven integration. In Europe, the integration process was more a government-prescribed, top-down phenomenon.

But while there were different reasons for integrating in Europe and North America, the general direction was in many ways comparable. In Europe people didn't wake up to what was happening until 1992. In Canada the Rubicon was crossed, as it had been in Europe in 1957, with the free trade election of 1988. Now the country marched quietly toward an American destiny.

*   *   *

In the three years after the free trade agreement was signed, Canadian trade predictably increased with the United States while it declined with the rest of the world. Canadian investment in Europe dropped precipitously. With the Asian bloc, no extraordinary business relationship was forthcoming. Developments offered further vindication for diplomat John Halstead's simple history lesson – the more Canada traded with the United States, the less it did business with the rest of the world.

Even so, possibilities outside North America remained. The evolution of the world into more pronounced trading zones did not signal a complete sequestering. In 1990, for example, the United States did 24 per cent of its trade with the EC, 22 per cent with Canada, and 16 per cent with Japan. There was no Fortress America or Fortress Europe. The rules of the GATT militated strongly against such an eventuality. Canada still did business in Europe, as evidenced by the strong presence there of Montreal-based Bombardier Inc., McCain Foods of New Brunswick, and Northern Telecom Ltd. Bombardier and Nortel were contributing to the construction of the Channel Tunnel linking Britain and France beneath the English Channel. Bombardier, making inroads in the rail transit sector, had six plants in Belgium, two in France, one in England, and one in Austria. McCain's held the turf as the largest producer of frozen french fries in Europe.

Unquestionably, though, for nations like Canada, which belonged to another economic zone, inward-looking Europe was becoming a harder market to penetrate. "Our main exports are resource-based and Europe has other sources for that and will have even greater sources once the former Soviet Union gets its act together," said European trade expert Sylvia Ostry. "So we have no comparative advantage left . . . and since we don't have a very big investment presence, and investment is the name of the game, I think we'll become less and less relevant."[4]

Despite the global changes, Canadian firms, concentrating on the North American market, continued to limit their own reach. Catherine Swift of the Canadian Federation of Independent Business said that "for most of our members, Europe is really the eleventh issue in the top ten."

Canada was distancing itself from Europe, not just economically, but also politically, demographically, and psychologically. The end of the cold war made Canada's ties to Europe less relevant. NATO had given Canada a European presence, and now, without the Soviet threat, Canada, like the United States, was becoming increasingly disengaged.

In the past Canada had been a country of mainly European descendants. Now its make-up was changing. Immigration from Europe dwindled; the bulk of new Canadians now came from the Asia-Pacific regions and Latin America. These newcomers had no affinity to Europe. The strong overseas counterweight to the American influence that Britain and Europe once provided was now greatly diminished.

Given Canada's weakening link with Europe, given the strength of its commitment to the United States through the free trade agreement, the country's continental future appeared fixed. Donald Macdonald had not favoured free trade with the Americans at the expense of trade with other nations. But after a few years of free trade, he worried that the Canadian opportunity in Europe had been lost. Other countries had set up interests in the new Europe before the unification measures took hold. The United States and Japan increased investment. The EFTA countries entered the free trade zone.

By the late 1980s, the conventional wisdom was that to be highly successful any major enterprise had to have a presence in each region of the triad of North America, Europe, and the Pacific Rim. Brian Mulroney had three mentors on whom he counted for advice on these trading blocs. Derek Burney was his North American specialist, Sylvia Ostry his European scholar, and Charlie McMillan his East Asian authority. These specialists could scarcely be described as nationalists, yet all were beginning to sound gloomy. Burney was convinced that free trade had been the proper course, but felt Canada needed a strong central government rebuilding the country's internal infrastructure as a counterweight to continentalism. He thought that the Tories were leaving the centre weakened. McMillan felt Canada had missed glorious opportunities in Japan and the Far East, Sylvia Ostry thought the same was happening with regard to Europe.[5]

In the Prime Minister's Office, McMillan had pushed hard to have Ottawa move to create ties with the Asians. But any increase in economic activity was modest. By 1991 he would lament, "We're a non-player in Asia, a non-player in Japan. The Americans knew that in a wide variety of areas you had to go to the Far East. The CEOs in Canada just didn't have that mind-set." Ostry didn't like the look of the future. "The notion that we could find a safe haven in North America when we have only a limited presence in the other two blocs of the triad is a very questionable notion. The original premise of FTA was that if Canada had secure access to the North American market, it would be able to be more competitive, capturing economies of scale and specialization, to move into the two other markets. But it just hasn't worked out that way. Not yet anyway."

The increasing isolation of Canada in a fast-integrating American Community raised valid questions. "Watch this process carefully for the homogenization of Europe is like an architect's model of our own future world," said the *Ottawa Citizen*. "When Canadian trade ministers talk about globalization and competitiveness they are really talking about doing to Canada what Europeans have done to themselves: that is, throw whole chunks of national sovereignty willingly into a blender for the economic benefits that accrue."

Europe, however, had social safeguards. In some measure, the

removal of economic borders signalled a triumph of free enterprise. Multinationals and business generally gained more freedom and latitude. Banks were being freed to do business
throughout the EC, customs checkpoints at borders were coming down, nations would no longer be able to use rules on
product standards to exclude products from neighbours, and
restrictions on foreign exchange transactions were being lifted.

But the idea of the EC was not to turn Europe into a free-
market parking lot. Jacques Delors, the president of the European Commission and a principal architect of the unification
movement, was a socialist. "The United States is no model for
my goal of European union," he said. "Our union must be as
efficient as the United States, but without falling into its errors.
It must be deeply rooted in social justice and the welfare state
and be firmly based on our own European traditions." The goals
of Delors were like those of Jean Monnet, who had sought to
have capital pooled to assure an equal sharing of market in each
of the EC countries. Airbus Industrie, the four-nation European
consortium for the production of civilian aircraft, was a modern example of what he had in mind. Governments sank $9
billion into Airbus, the success of which demonstrated how
business, labour, and government could work in concert in the
new Europe.

The managed system, allowing the have-nots a share,
reminded the Liberal Party's Lloyd Axworthy of the value of the
Canada-U.S. Auto Pact, which did the same. But when Canada,
he noted, entered into the free trade agreement, there were no
safeguards. "In Europe when they brought Spain and Portugal
into the common market it was a case of providing them a fund
to help bring the underdeveloped regions up to a standard, so
you don't get harmonized down. In the American system the
philosophy has been different. They believe in opening up all
roads because they are the dominant power and all roads lead to
Rome. It's what Britain did in the nineteenth century."[6]

The Maastricht Treaty included a social charter endorsed by

all EC members, except Britain, which aimed to ensure worker benefits, minimum wage and salary levels, and other social programs across the community. The measure caught the eye of Ontario Premier Bob Rae. Rae had been at Oxford University at the time England was in deep debate over joining the Common Market. As a young MP, he spent some time as a guest of the EC. The advent of free trade for Canada rang alarm bells for Rae because, in the move to economic union in North America, he saw none of the protections Europeans enjoyed. Meanwhile, the pressure to harmonize was becoming tremendous. To compete, Canada would have to continue to approach the lower American costs and standards, and Rae wondered if medicare and other social programs would be bargained away. To discourage the possibility, he wanted a commitment. "The social charter idea came from that, as well as the need to try and maintain what we have in common as Canadians."[7]

The Ontario premier added the social charter idea to the constitutional negotiations. The Conservatives hadn't given it much thought and, to no one's surprise, big business was opposed. There were already enough social protections in the Constitution, the BCNI argued. A charter would only add to the legal morass. Opposition was also strong from Alberta, which, in its romance with Reform and the American right, also frowned upon bilingualism. Despite this resistance, however, constitutional hearings found so much support for the social charter that it forged its way onto the new constitutional map.

What also impressed Rae about the EC was the capability it provided for member states to address grievances at the umbrella institutions in Brussels and Strasbourg. In this way they stood a better chance of keeping the playing field level. Canada, on the other hand, was speeding toward integration with no such formula for redressing disparities in competitive strength. The much lower American gasoline prices, for example, were drawing Ontarians across the border in droves. "The biggest help they [the United States] could give us would be to get serious about gas taxes and begin to level up rather than us having to level down all the time," said Rae. But there was no recourse to EC-type forums. His province had experienced fantastic growth in business with the United States, particularly with the Great Lakes states. During the 1980s, Rae said, Ontario's export reliance on the United States had grown from 80 per cent to 90 per cent. At the same time, the only regional body for managing the huge relationship, was the anemic Great Lakes Governors' Association. The binational panels that oversaw the free trade agreement could not attend to the dozens of questions outside their purview.

To make it a fair game, Rae wanted new forms of transborder authority. And therein lay the dilemma. To move to new umbrella structures of joint governance was to move to forms of political union.

18

Inedible Crow

"I want you to know," said Brian Mulroney, whose sense of humour could be gritty enough, "that when I took office the country's economy was teetering on the edge of the abyss. I'm proud to say that since that time we've made a valuable step forward."

The times demanded a sense of humour. The recession hit, then dragged along endlessly. Voters turned their anger toward incumbents. Regions looked to assert their own power. The shifting international economic currents created an atmosphere of angst.

For the American option to succeed, the prime minister and his party needed evidence that market economics and continental integration were working. But as Mulroney approached the end of his second mandate, the evidence, as recognized even by those who had worked closely with him, was clearly to the contrary. Unemployment rates soared, the ranks of the poor multiplied, regionalism worsened, the social contract was coming apart, the exodus to the United States continued. And while the government would have liked everyone to believe it could all be blamed on the accident of a worldwide recession, the evidence was to the contrary. Canada was the first on the continent to enter into the recession and last to get out. The government had not provided the adjustment programs to ease the pain of the transfer to free trade. It had stuck, with draconian insensitivity, to a corporate agenda – a zero-inflation, price stability commitment that sucked money from a country desperately in need of economic stimulus.

In January 1989, when free trade took effect, the unemployment rate was 7.4 per cent – a level that Canadians, by and large, had come to live with. That same year a trade official from a western province attended a federal Finance Department briefing in Ottawa. On one of the large graphs arrayed around the room, the official noticed a line crossing the unemployment numbers at 8 per cent. He asked an economist from Finance what the line meant. The economist was candid. He explained that for the government's anti-inflation program to work, they had to get unemployment moving up – beyond 8 per cent.[1]

The visiting trade official was a conservative himself. He generally agreed with Mulroney economics. Still, he was somewhat rattled by this, by the callous lengths to which the Tories were prepared to go, by the apparent indifference to the suffering of the jobless. The unemployed were but a number to these members of the ruling class. The government's strategy was to put more in the unemployment lines. It was an assignment, and as it turned out, one of the easier assignments the government ever had. With the high interest-rate policy of John Crow, the governor of the Bank of Canada, no one had to work hard to get the unemployment level above 8 per cent. Unemployment soon rose to 8, to 10, to 11-plus per cent. Inflation fell precipitously, just as the Tories had hoped, but the levelling of prices didn't stir activity among consumers. Most were unable to pay for goods even at uninflated prices. And so the economy continued to crawl, and Crow continued to squeeze almost everyone but himself. In these tight-money times, he allowed his own salary to double to $250,000.

Crow was a stranger to Canada until age thirty. He was raised in a mean end of London but educated in private schools where he honed his élitist edge. He left for Washington, where he worked for many years at the International Monetary Fund. With his American wife, he then came to Canada and took out citizenship before, in 1987, becoming the most powerful unelected official in Canada.

Succeeding Gerald Bouey, Crow brought a single-minded zealotry to the Bank of Canada. With Michael Wilson's support he launched his anti-inflation crusade. Nothing else mattered. In effect he was an inflation czar. The customary government strategy was to try to maintain a rough balance between inflation and unemployment, as they were both grievous problems. But the Mulroney government dispensed with the tradition. There was an inflation czar, but no employment czar.

The warnings came. Almost every economist, conservative as well as liberal, warned Crow that if he persisted in maintaining high interest rates and a high dollar he would drag Canada into a recession; a homemade recession that would hit early, earlier than one in the United States.

The warnings turned out to be accurate to the letter. In tandem with the recession, his high dollar policy, it was predicted, would sabotage the government's free trade policy by making it even more difficult for exporters. Crow wasn't fazed. There was also the matter of the deficit. Because of interest payments on the national debt, the deficit rose by more than a billion dollars for every percentage point in increased interest rates. Crow showed no concern.

The policies of the unelected Brit were jacking up the Canadian unemployment rate, stoking the recession, stymying free trade, and pushing up the deficit. (In 1992 the WEFA Group, a private think tank, calculated that Crow's policies had increased unemployment by 2.1 per cent, had reduced economic growth by 3.1 per cent, and had added $25 billion to the deficit.) But because Crow was not accountable to the electorate and largely unaccountable to the politicians, he could dismiss his critics with a cold sneer. The prime minister, who did not understand economics well enough to have confidence in his own view, relied principally on Michael Wilson. Wilson supported John Crow, but the chorus of anti-Crow sentiment from other economists and specialists became so deafening that Mulroney began to waver.[2] At one point, early in his second term, said his principal secretary Peter White, Mulroney was "climbing the walls" in anger at what the bank governor was doing.

It was at this point that Mulroney edged close to a decision that would have represented a decisive turn for him and perhaps for the country – a move away from his rigidly right-wing economic agenda. Mulroney instructed White to go and have a talk with Crow; the intent obviously being to signal his displeasure with what the high interest rates were doing to free trade and the economy.[3] Derek Burney, then Washington ambassador, was among those who had provided signals to the PM that a change of course should be considered.

As Mulroney was well aware, sending an emissary to the governor of the Bank of Canada was a delicate business. Tradition and the law required that the prime minister keep arm's length. Both Mulroney and White remembered the scandal that shook the country over Diefenbaker's handling of bank governor James Coyne. They were prominent young Tories at Laval University in the early 1960s when Coyne inspired the wrath of the governing party for much the same reason as John Crow – intransigence on high interest rates. While he, too, was manic about price stability, Coyne's motivations were far different from Crow's. Coyne was a dedicated Canadian nationalist who didn't hesitate to express his fears. "If we do not effectively change the trends of the past, we shall drift into an irreversible form of integration with a very much larger and more powerful neighbour," he said. "I do not believe this is what Canadians want. For it means surrendering the very idea of Canadianism, the dream of Canada which gripped the imagination of Sir John A. Macdonald, George-Étienne Cartier."[4]

Coyne's highly political statements, his interest-rate policy, and his feathering of his own nest with a cozy pension arrangement led to his being fired by Finance Minister Donald Fleming. Coyne refused to hand over his own head, however, and a public fracas ensued, highlighted by outbursts such as that of Liberal Paul Martin who, pleading that Coyne at least deserved a hearing, shouted, "Even Eichmann had his day in court!" Eventually Coyne got a hearing before the Senate Finance Committee which, dominated by Liberals, ruled that he did not engage in misconduct in office. Exonerated, the bank governor resigned gracefully and the Diefenbaker government marched red-faced into electoral embarrassment.

There was another precedent. In 1979 Prime Minister Joe Clark became exasperated over high interest rates under Gerald Bouey and dispatched an adviser, Jim Gillies, to question him. Gillies first met with Finance Minister John Crosbie. Crosbie said to him, "Look Jim, I meet Bouey every Friday morning. Come on over and put all your arguments to him as to why the policy is wrong. So Jim came over and he never had a convincing argument that Bouey couldn't dispose of. So that solved my problem with the PMO."[5]

Crosbie was annoyed by all the bashing of John Crow. "What bloody choice did he have? . . . We're lucky we've still got people willing to lend a cent to Canada. . . . When I hear the businessmen complain about the high dollar, it's all bullshit. These are excuses for exporters 'cause they're not as competitive or as sharp as the people they're dealing with."

What the public and what many economists didn't realize, Crow's defenders said, was how hamstrung he was by the debt. To meet debt payments, the Tories had to borrow from abroad, particularly from the Japanese. If interest rates were substantially lowered, the Japanese would stop buying bonds. When Dalton Camp came to work in the Privy Council Office, he had dinner with Michael Wilson. One of the first things Wilson told him was how delicate the government's debt position was with the Japanese. Crow's critics noted, however, that in 1992 the interest rate tumbled to 7 per cent, and foreign lenders, including the Japanese, remained ready and willing.

Peter White wasn't a Crow critic. Since he basically agreed with Crow's approach, he wasn't an ideal choice as an inquiring envoy. His meeting with the governor, as he recalled it, was remarkably short. "Mr. Governor," White said, "the Minister of Finance has the right to instruct you how to carry out monetary policy. What would you do if you received such an instruction?"

"I would resign."

White departed. The government did not issue any instructions to Crow. Forcing a resignation was considered too risky. Crow remained and continued to push his zero-inflation agenda with an absolutist zeal that would lead another former principal adviser to the PM, Stanley Hartt, to speak out publicly against him. In sticking with his approach, and the harsh conservatism of finance ministers Wilson and Don Mazankowski, the Mulroney government began to resemble more and more the R. B. Bennett Tories of the Dirty Thirties, who defiantly refused to stimulate the economy until the final year of their mandate, when it was too late. The 1990s didn't bring a depression, but the recession dragged on relentlessly and the government remained aloof, mired in trickle-down economics, chained to an agenda that immobilized the country.

The plight in which Canada found itself was ascribable in part to the free trade agreement. While free trade was not a direct cause of the recession, the toll the agreement had on the Canadian manufacturing sector clearly exacerbated and prolonged it. In the long term, after the shakedown, after the Canadian economy was rationalized to continental standards, the legacy of free trade would perhaps be different. But in the short term it was impossible to explain the staggering failures in Canada's manufacturing sector in the context of the recession alone. Free trade bore responsibility. No other recession-hit country was losing factory jobs at the same rate as Canada. Moreover, the plunge in this sector of the economy began well before the general recession started in the spring of 1990. In the year before the recession hit, the first year of free trade, Canadian job losses in manufacturing totalled 6 per cent. After three years of free trade, nearly 20 per cent of Canada's manufacturing jobs had vanished. Defenders of the government said that in the 1981-82 recession, manufacturing losses were just as bad – and there was no free trade agreement then. Indeed, the numbers were comparable. But the economy rose steadily out of that recession and the blue collar jobs returned. This time there was no rebound nor any sign of a rebound. Experts searched for an explanation. Among them was one explanation that the Tories did not wish to hear. It held that Canada had torn down its protective barriers when the nation was unprepared and was now getting crushed in the survival-of-the-fittest game by a neighbour ten times its size. It was just as a dashing young campaigner for the Tory leadership in 1983 had warned. With free trade "you're a dead man," Brian Mulroney said then. The elephant would roll over and "they would crank up those plants in Georgia . . . and they're going to be shutting them down up here."

Most of the empty factories lay in Ontario where free trade registered the most pain. Industries died, or they packed up and moved to the United States, or American head offices pulled out their subsidiaries. Judging by the important balance-of-trade criterion, the United States was emerging as the free trade winner. It was substantially reducing its heavily negative trade balance with Canada during this time, primarily as a result of a great surge in the export of services to Canada. As could be expected when tariff walls come down, Canada's exports to the United States grew with free trade, but not in the same proportion as American exports to Canada. The suspicion among Canadians that the country had been taken grew, and when the

Americans appeared to be ducking the free trade agreement's fair play rules, the suspicion heightened.

One purpose of the pact was to shield Canada from the vagaries of American protectionist practices. The FTA's dispute-settlement mechanism held out promise for more peace and stability in trade relations. Trade fights would continue, Ottawa said, but they would be rare.

Far from rare, the trade fights continued at a pace equal to the years before free trade. In a dispute over American duties on exports of Canadian pork, the United States tried numerous tactics to avoid the dispute settlement route as called for in the FTA. In a fight over Canadian lumber exports, the U.S. Department of Commerce imposed a preliminary countervailing duty of 15 per cent. In a conflict over the importation of Honda cars, the U.S. Customs Service ruled that the Canadian-made Hondas did not qualify for the American market. Customs decided that the make of the cars' engines violated rules-of-origin clauses stipulating that the automobiles had to have 50 per cent North American content. Ottawa was irate at all of Washington's measures, but particularly at the Honda one. The supposed violation of content rules was intriguing, said Derek Burney, because the engines were made in Ohio.

Other hostilities surfaced, leading Burney to invoke the words of former Secretary of State George Shultz. The secretary had said that good relations were like good gardens; they needed constant attention, nurturing, and careful weeding. Well, said Burney, "the trade weeds are sprouting in our shared garden and it is getting harder to see, let alone smell, the roses." FTA negotiator Gordon Ritchie went public to declare that the U.S. administration and Congress were violating the spirit and in some cases the letter of the free trade agreement. Michael Hart hadn't exactly expected smooth seas, "but what disappoints me," he said, "is that there doesn't seem to be a strong commitment to what the FTA stands for. I mean, it's not supposed to be business as usual."

But the way the United States saw the agreement, much of the trade business was, in fact, to be as usual – and not even as high-priority as usual. Memoranda to President Bush in 1989 noted that bilateral trade disputes involving U.S. antidumping and countervailing rulings against Canadian industries should not even be raised at high level talks between the president and the prime minister. "At the outset of the relationship between the Bush and Mulroney administrations, it is worth an effort to channel this type of issue into other areas," the State Department told Bush. "This would allow the summits to concentrate on major issues in our bilateral relationship or significant global issues."[6]

In a review for Bush of the free trade agreement, it was noted that the United States achieved virtually all it wanted from the agreement. The purpose of the agreement from the American perspective, the review said, was "to preserve liberalizing steps taken by the Mulroney government and prevent a return to inward looking, nationalistic policies of the 1970s, especially in investment, and banking and financial services." Canada, Bush was told, "moved decisively toward market-oriented policies when Mulroney took office in 1984."

While the United States got what it wanted from the free trade agreement, the briefing papers noted that Canada did not. In the trade negotiations, "Canada's primary objective," the State Department told Bush, "was to gain secure access (often defined as exemption from U.S. trade laws) to the U.S. market." The State Department memo goes on to say that the dispute settlement mechanism created by the FTA "leaves national [U.S.] laws in effect."

Having achieved its goals, and having seen Canada fail to gain secure access, Washington was nonetheless still ready to play hardball. In preparing to meet Mulroney, Bush was told that Canada had wrongly interpreted the FTA as it applied to steel exports. Washington had imposed steel import restraint programs in the past but had exempted Canada. Ottawa felt that the FTA's intent secured exempt status in the future. This was an important matter to the Canadians, Bush was informed, because a steel restraint program "strikes at Canada's rationale for the FTA-secure access to the U.S. market and brings political pressure on Mulroney."

Nonetheless, Bush was requested "to avoid acceding to any request by the Prime Minister" for an exemption. Under the heading "Suggested Position," the memo said: "We have made it clear to the Canadian government that under the FTA the U.S. steel industry retains all its options."

While almost everything had gone wrong with the launching of free trade, the Canadian establishment still viewed the pact as being in Canada's long-range interest. With the passing of the recession as well as the passing of John Crow, free trade would find public favour, supporters said. Significantly, no great movement had yet developed, beyond Canada's leftist nationalist core, to scrap the free trade agreement. Unlike the opposition to the NEP, where one province, Alberta, led a clamorous and effective campaign, no one province or region was showing the same kind of firebrand opposition to free trade.

The Liberal Party under John Turner had proposed to scrap the free trade agreement altogether. Now, unable to resolve a conflict between the more continentally inclined party members and the leftists, the Grits backpeddled. The party wouldn't tear up the agreement, it would renegotiate parts of it. Jean Chrétien visited Bush to inform him of the plan and was politely rebuffed. Bush informed him he had no wish to change anything. That being the case, Chrétien said he would reserve the option of abrogating the treaty and relying again on the GATT system.

Chrétien saw the trade disputes as further evidence that Mulroney's backslapping approach with U.S. presidents was not paying off. "Every time the president sneezes," he cracked, "the prime minister catches pneumonia." Chrétien's Washington visit and the statements that followed brought a riposte from Mulroney. "Mr. Chrétien is meeting with George Bush?" he asked sarcastically with eyebrows raised. "He went to Washington to see the enemy?" On a more serious note, he added: "You just look back at the anti-Americanism that has dominated the Liberal Party. It's viscerally anti-American."

Americans viewed free trade as a *fait accompli*, and the assumption of the governing class was that Canada ought to be delighted with it, despite the failure to obtain secure access. "Americans simply can't believe Canada would back out of a deal in which there are so many advantages," said Charles Doran, director of the Center for Canadian Studies at the Johns Hopkins Center in Washington. "The view is that it is strongly in the Canadian interest to be part of this common market and to have more of a guarantee than anyone else."[7]

As an American negotiator of the agreement, Bill Merkin liked the package he got for his country. But in 1992 he still considered the agreement as a plus for Canada as well. "There are a lot of industries up there that have been going through a very painful adjustment on free trade but are now coming out of it leaner and meaner."[8] The integration was unavoidable, he said. "In a lot of cases it's one company in both countries. So the huge amount of trade is there whether you like it or not. And so it made sense to solidify that trade, improve it to the extent you could and try to isolate it from disruption. I don't think that means you should ignore other parts of the world and I don't think that's what Ottawa's been doing."

The U.S. action on lumber and Honda cars gave Mulroney an opportunity to refute charges that he was Bush's toady. He had used American trade actions to lash out at Washington during the Reagan years and offset such accusations. Now he would do the same again. There was a growing sense, as election year approached, that although he had to fend off challenges from the Reform Party, Mulroney had also to be seen as less pro-American. Mulroney's new chief of staff, the astute Hugh Segal, was a red Tory who favoured this approach. Peter White

was suggesting that the PM astound the country with an outburst of cultural nationalism. Derek Burney, frequently in contact with Mulroney, urged him to undertake national projects
to rebuild the country's infrastructure.

Apart from trade matters, the Bush administration also
annoyed Mulroney with its criticism of his decision to with-
draw Canada's NATO forces from Europe. Ottawa had announced the move, feeling that with the cold war's end and
with Europe's own military strength, Canadian forces were
rather superfluous. They pumped a lot of cash into the economy of Lahr, Germany, but were serving no other purpose.
Mulroney and External Affairs Minister Barbara McDougall
now wisely looked to the United Nations for peacekeeping. On
military spending, the prime minister had nothing to apologize
to the Americans for. With Michael Wilson in the role of lead
hawk, the Tories were the only big Western government which
did not noticeably reduce defence spending and provide their
population with a peace dividend after the cold war.

The PM lashed back at Washington, citing its repeated failure
to pay its fees for the cost of United Nations operations. "We
don't believe you can be a member of the club and not pay your
dues. Otherwise, you're a deadbeat." On trade matters, the
United States was engaging in "vexatious harassment and protectionism of the worst kind. If you had told me that some
tinpot dictator in some tiny little country somewhere was
engaging in this kind of harassment, I'd say, 'So what else is
new?' But for the United States, this is most unworthy."

The trade disputes were taken up at the annual Bush-
Mulroney summit of 1992. As Mulroney spoke of his vexa-
tion, Bush looked on calmly. "I don't want to be standing
here next to a good friend of the United States of America and
a good free trader in some contentious mode," he said.
Though he promised to eliminate any feeling of harassment,
everyone knew that, with dozens of more urgent matters on
his plate, the president had no interest in these trifles. "The

president," said Edward Ney, his good friend and ambassador in Ottawa, "is not going to get into a Honda audit or a ban on the export of logs."[9] Ney, who made his views known to Bush, was hardly sympathetic to Canada's case. On the contrary, he thought that there was a near-conspiracy at work in Canada against free trade.

The Canadian media had always been anti-free trade, and remained so, Ney said. He found it curious that when the United States started a trade action against Canada all hell broke loose, but when Canada did the same against the United States there was total silence. "Somehow," Ney shouted, "it never seems to make the paper!" No wonder Canadians were angry. "If I was a Canadian and saw the media every day, I'd have said, 'Geez, they're a terrible group of people. What are they trying to do to us poor little Canadians?'"

But the opposition in Canada, Ney noted, ran deeper than the press, and it was more than random opposition. In an outburst uncharacteristic of an ambassador, he said it was a "deliberate strategic decision by a group of think tanks, others [that is, the media], and political parties to portray the FTA as a failure." Ney also charged that Derek Burney was overstepping diplomatic bounds with his aggressive behaviour in Washington. "Here's what I'm saying, and you hear what I'm saying." In his scraping voice, Ney told of press meetings Burney was holding in Washington. At these, the Canadian ambassador was actually "calling!" Ney Cried, "calling for Canadian manufacturers to come to the U.S.-Canadian governments so they can start actions." By actions he meant retaliatory trade actions against the United States. "You want to see them?" Ney said, his voice now a dramatic whisper. "I got the clippings. Right here."

Evaporating support for free trade across the country did not deter Mulroney and the Tories from pursuing its expansion. The government entered negotiations with the United States and Mexico aimed at extending the bilateral pact to a trilateral one – one that would feature three of the West's most indebted nations. The world was dividing into trading blocs, and this, cynics suggested, would be "the debtor bloc."

Although Canada's trade with Mexico was minuscule, the government wanted in on the three-way negotiations to forestall a separate U.S.-Mexico trade agreement that could divert American business away from Canada. Moreover, the United States appeared set on using a deal with Mexico as a model for future pacts with other nations in the Americas. If Canada stayed out of the negotiations, it was in danger of becoming just a spoke in the wheel with Washington as the hub. The Tories frequently boasted that Canada was the only country in the world to have a secure bilateral trade pact with the United States. It was now in the process of losing that status and had to get to the table to see what was going on.

Shortly after Bush's election in 1988, Mexico's new president, Carlos Salinas de Gortari, had come to Washington to signal his readiness to liberalize trade. In 1990 Bush launched his Enterprise for the Americas Initiative, which envisioned an Americas trade zone from Alaska to Argentina. Bush was, in effect, embracing as well as extending the concept of a North American accord as preached by his predecessor Ronald Reagan ten years earlier.

In fact, Bush sounded more bullish on the possibilities of a North American accord than Reagan. Giving Canadian nationalists their most glorious "I-told-you-so" opening in years, Bush peered into the future at the North American Free Trade Agreement (NAFTA) signing ceremony a week before Christmas in 1992, and saw the road opening to one big country.

"More than 150 years ago," he said, "Simon Bolivar, the liberator whose statue stands outside this hall, spoke about an America united in heart, subject to one law, and guided by the torch of liberty. My friends, here, in this hemisphere, we are on the way to realizing Simon Bolivar's dream, and today, with the signing of the North American Free Trade Agreement, we take another giant step toward making the dream a reality."

It was almost a century since a United States president (Teddy Roosevelt) had invoked Manifest Destiny so glaringly. For Bush it was out of character because he had shown only passing interest in continental trade and the overall direction of Canada-U.S. relations. But the much-maligned mind of the Gipper suddenly looked visionary. He had been instructed by advisers in the early 1980s to downplay his accord proposal to allow for the laughter to fade. Better to let the initiatives come from the other countries, advisers told him – believing they never would. But Canada had come forward in 1985, and then Mexico three years later. By mid-1992 a three-amigos pact was on the books. Not only was Reagan's vision in place, so too, it could be said, was the Tory vision of turning Canada into a nation of the Americas. Free trade with the United States, free trade with Mexico, membership in the Organization of American States, and a dozen other examples of continentalist overtures gave trenchant testimony to Canada's new vocation.

Myer Rashish, the undersecretary of state for economic affairs in the Reagan administration who helped Reagan develop the North American accord proposal, saw NAFTA as the final foundation stone of the accord.[10] Three priorities of the accord that Rashish fleshed out for Reagan were free trade, open investment, and a sharing of the continent's energy resources. All were in place except the energy-sharing end with Mexico; in NAFTA Mexico had refused to open its energy vault to the United States as Canada had done in the FTA. Some things were sacred. Unlike Canada, Mexico's rich energy sector would remain its own.

Shortcomings aside, the progress toward the North American accord had been remarkable given the dismissive attitude which greeted its unveiling. As in Europe, questions of sovereignty had taken a back seat to economic imperatives. "My view was that the sovereignty issue was overdone in Canada," said Rashish. "Integration was an unavoidable fact, even when Trudeau was entertaining the notion of the third option. The same stood for Mexico. So if the reality was for greater integration, then all the more reason to try to have it evolve under rules that are perceived as fair for all sides."

Even Trudeau, Rashish thought, had come around to this opinion by the time he left office in 1984. "He started off with a different set of views than he ended up with. He started living in the real world." Mulroney, on the other hand, was credited by the Americans as having fully understood the trend. His vision of "a closer, civilized, communal relationship with the U.S.," did not mean he was "a patsy," said Rashish. It meant, he said, that Mulroney had a sense of the inevitable.

NAFTA still had to travel the thorny path of ratification by the signatory nations. Many of its provisions were loosely set and others wouldn't come into full effect for fifteen years. Canada's two-way trade with Mexico was less than 1 per cent of what it was with the United States, and trade experts predicted that, in the short term, NAFTA would increase Mexican trade by only a small margin. Because the stakes were apparently so low, Canadians reacted to the signing with a predictable lack of enthusiasm. In trade terms, the significance of the agreement lay in the Mexican-American end. Mexico, it was forecast, would become the second largest trading partner of the United States, replacing Japan.

The long term ramifications for Canada were important, however. Canada was now safely in a trading bloc. Other nations of the Americas, like Chile, had shown interest in NAFTA and were likely to sign on. All was relative in these discussions because the GATT, which brought down barriers everywhere, was still in place. The Uruguay Round of the GATT talks was still stalled in early 1993, but if successful it would further liberalize trade in a broad range of areas, some of them also covered by the FTA and NAFTA.

NAFTA and its potential extension was a further signal,

however, that North America was moving, like Europe, toward continental integration. Rather than Canada being one small partner in bed with a giant, as in the free trade agreement, NAFTA served a better purpose for Canada in that it created a counterbalance. With several countries in a trade accord, Washington's influence would be more diluted than it was in just one bilateral agreement. Still, in comparison to the somewhat disproportionate strength of Germany in Europe, the U.S. dominance in its own hemisphere was overwhelming. Moreover, Canada's trade with Mexico, and any new members in future accords in the Americas, would be minute compared to its trade with the United States. The balance would hardly be altered.

NAFTA had several positive features. Canada was getting in on the ground floor of the Mexican economic revolution. There would be more potential for better economies of scale. It could potentially assist Mexico's development.

Less favourably, this was indeed the debtor bloc with the dominant member, the United States, entering, many believed, a period of decline. The pact furthered the interests of big business and multinationals without addressing the likely social consequences – a deficiency also apparent in the free trade agreement. It did little to enforce environmental and workplace rights, and the long-term effect here could well be to cut into Canadian sovereignty in these areas. The continent was being further harmonized in accordance with the value system of big business.

Another fault was noted by Gordon Ritchie and Jean Chrétien. The intent of NAFTA, as Michael Wilson stated it, was to allow "the rule of law, not power" to prevail in settling trade disputes. In the previous three years, however, the Americans had taken advantage of loopholes to try to avoid FTA arbitration. Instead of strengthening the enforcement provisions, NAFTA may well have loosened them more in certain areas.

Concerned over public opposition to NAFTA, the Tories planned a scorched-earth attack on its critics. A transcript of a

conference call among ministerial aides, obtained by
Maclean's, advised an attack on "the looney left." James Ramsay, chief of staff for Wilson, led the hardliners. Opposition to
NAFTA was being directed, he said, by the "old left-wing,
crypto-communist, anti-free trade, NDP-Liberal, con group."

In promoting NAFTA, the government relied on the same
arguments it used to sell the free trade agreement. An added
emphasis this time was the competitiveness theme. Competitiveness rivalled globalization as the economic buzzword of the
day. Opening up to the United States and to Mexico, Wilson
said, would help prepare Canadian industries to take on the
best in the world. The government carried out a $15 million
awareness campaign on the competitiveness theme. Teams of
bureaucrats fanned out across the country to 175 communities
seeking the views of Canadians on how to beat the other guy.
Confidence-boosting TV commercials told Canadians that,
with a little effort, they could kick the tar out of any opponent.
The Tories had already taken Americanization to new heights.
Adopting the ultimate American credo – the winning-is-everything ethic – was yet another stratum.

The government was in part trying to address the crisis
caused by the decline in Canada's natural-resource economy.
Traditionally, Canada's strength lay in minerals, metals, fossil
fuels, agriculture and fish, and forest products. World markets
had begged for them. But, in the 1980s, increased competition
from developing countries with cheaper labour led to tumbling
prices. New technologies also affected the market. As a proportion of Canadian exports, the contribution of natural resources
fell from 65 per cent in 1960, to 47 per cent in 1970, to 35 per
cent in 1987. Foreign interest had plunged by almost half. The
difficulty, said economist Lester Thurow, was not so much that
Canadians and Americans were doing any worse than before.
"It is that the rest of the world has gotten better, and since the
rest of the world has gotten better you and I have to change, and
we are very reluctant to do that in North America because we

have lived in the most successful part of the world for the last 100 years." The trade figures did not suggest that Canada's natural-resource industries were doomed, but that the country had to upgrade the resource products it offered – to manufacture, as the economic jargon proclaimed, more "value-added" goods and to find "niche markets" for them.

Ed Lumley, the pro-business Liberal in the Trudeau government, determined in his portfolios that it was wrong to try to shift Canada away from its traditional resource strengths. The Tories, he said, had to guard against turning Canada into something that it wasn't. Lumley had walked into Trudeau's office one day and delivered a brief monologue. "You know, Prime Minister, I might be the dumbest cabinet member you ever had," he said, "but I keep hearing about all this hi-tech stuff and how we should all be concentrating on hi-tech.

"Well, you know what? Even if I had all the money to fill every application from our hi-tech industry for assistance, all the jobs created wouldn't match the number for one auto company."[11]

As part of its competitiveness effort, the government split expenses with the BCNI to hire an American, Harvard economist Michael Porter, to tell Canadians what was wrong with their economy. For the most part, the report confirmed what its sponsors had been saying all along – that Canada had relied for too long on protectionism, natural resources, and paternalistic government policies.

The exercise, in the view of nationalists, was a sham. The combined wisdom of Wilson, the BCNI, and a Tory-favoured American economist could yield only a predictable result – a panegyric to the market solution. Porter was analyzing a country with some strikingly different traditions, but to advance and prosper in the modern world, Canada, he said, would have to follow the corporate agenda and go forth and globalize like everyone else.

*   *   *

The advocates of the free-enterprise solution on the continent had ridden a wave through the 1980s. But with the beginning of the new decade, the results began to come in and they weren't handsome. The sustained preoccupation of the media saw to it that it was the public sector that usually received the intense scrutiny. The government waste, the incompetence, the perks of officials, and the scandals were chronicled daily, and with good reason. It was rare, however, that the private governments, the big businesses, were held up to the same penetrating light and compared.

One of the country's own leading establishment figures, Hal Jackman, the chairman of National Trust and later lieutenant-governor of Ontario, had the courage to compare government and big business in a speech at the University of Windsor. Jackman made the point that in the 1980s corporate debt had grown at twice the rate of government debt. He wondered, with all its new freedom in a deregulated, low-tax environment, what big business had accomplished. "Where are the new factories, the new jobs, or the new industries in this country?" he asked. "While the business world or large parts of it was indulging in an orgy of self-gratification, our industrial plants deteriorated, the necessary retooling and restructuring to compete in global markets was neglected, research and development expenditures were postponed and concern over environmental issues ignored."

Corporate Canada's own Tom d'Aquino, when asked about the speech, said he agreed with much of what Jackman had said.[12] The same business sector that was hallowed ground for Michael Wilson, the same business sector that had long used big government as its favourite whipping boy, ran up worse debts, gave its managers salaries and perks of a magnitude unheard of in the public sector, and saw its directors engaged in scandals that made those of politicians pale by comparison.

In the United States the 1980s saw the mammoth savings and loan institutions scandal, a spree of junk-bond buy-outs in which once proud companies were flipped like nickles, a recession that later ended the career of trickle-down champion George Bush, and the creation of great accumulations of wealth that only the top 10 per cent of the population saw. The rich got richer, the poor poorer. In Canada, where Mulroney and company championed the same creed, the empires of the Reichmanns and Robert Campeau and other barons tumbled, poverty reached new proportions, deregulation saw an airline industry and others beating themselves to death by being hell-bent on competition, and the recession was worse than in America.

Walter Russell Mead, author of *Mortal Splendor: The American Empire in Transition*, made the case that this legacy of the 1980s had shown that the true believers, the Reagans and the Thatchers, were the losers. "The true believers of the economic world are like people who say that dams are unworkable – water seeks its own level, so it is useless to dam it up. They are right that water seeks its own level – and that markets seek an equilibrium – but wrong to apply these principles in a simplistic way to all the varieties of problems we find in real life. Some dams are good; they prevent floods; they conserve an important resource; they generate power." According to Gilles Paquet, one distinguished Canadian economist willing to challenge the conventional business view, the marketeers had it all upside down. Much of the growth, much of the building of Canada, was through government while, he said, "the business community demanded like mad of the state and never made a contribution." Paquet, of the University of Ottawa, had what was once considered a mainstream perspective. Through the 1980s his views didn't change, but in supporting modest protectionism he had now become a radical.

Canada, said Paquet, could be as protectionist as it always was – which was only mildly protectionist – and be as successful as ever. Japan – planned and protected – had proved this was possible. "They've done it through brains and imagination, through targeting and specialization." In the modern economy, economies of scale were no longer important. "It's specialization. You watch. The Japanese will come and produce a car only for the Canadian market and they will make it work."[13]

Japan's success, he noted, had nothing to do with low tariffs because its tariffs remained high. It had nothing to do with great amounts of foreign investment and foreign ownership, because Japan had walls to stop both. As a discreditor of American economics, Paquet observed, Japan wasn't alone. Joining it among the world's leading economies with the highest standards of living were the democratic-socialist Scandinavian countries, strongly *dirigiste* Germany, Austria, Italy, and others. The idea that Canada had to strip itself of protections and march out into the world to take on all comers, Paquet said, was foolhardy conventional wisdom that should be viewed as a vogue, a discredited vogue, and not as the basis for trying to revolutionize the way Canada worked.

Gilles Paquet was depressed over how many fellow economists had been bought off by the greed ethic. Instead of building something different in Canada, all they could talk about were classic American values – this, he noted, when America as world leader, as model for the rest, was leaving the stage.

19

The Model

"When we came to power," said Charlie McMillan, "the assumption in a whole bunch of areas was that the American model was *the* model. The problem is, we brought in free trade precisely at a time when in a lot of areas the American model was no longer *the* model."[1]

As Brian Mulroney sang the praises of the American way while campaigning to become prime minister in the summer of 1984, his timing could hardly have been more appropriate. At that moment, Reagan's America, unchallenged economically, militarily, or culturally, basked in a mood of triumph not enjoyed in decades. At the Los Angeles Olympics that summer, a great golden halo crowned the proceedings as the Americans draped themselves in medal upon medal. The east bloc boycotted these Olympics, and so the victories, coming as they did over diluted opposition, were modest triumphs, the athletic equivalent of the American conquest of Grenada. But the old actor used his magic to sprinkle his world in stardust and turn these and other advances into soaring manifestations of the American spirit.

By 1992 much had changed. The victories, which included robust economic growth and the disappearance of the Soviet threat (the Republicans, trying to take credit for the end of the cold war, said Al Gore, was like a rooster taking credit for the sunrise), ended in dark defeat. The golden halo of Olympic-year Los Angeles had been turned to a pall of soot by rioting masses who torched the city. The economic boom, which ended in bleak recession, had proved meaningless to the majority of Americans. They did not share in its dividends, nor was there any dividend from the other great supposed windfall of the 1980s – the end of the cold war.

The suggestion that the Republicans formed a government of patricians for patricians found new credibility in statistic after statistic. In the 1980s' boom years, the poorest 40 per cent of the American population had seen its income decline. There was no trickle down. Conservatives who had spent much of the decade trumpeting the glories of deregulated market economics and who found great imitators in Ottawa, perused a 1980s' legacy that saw more than 60 per cent of all the nation's gains in after-tax income go to the richest 1 per cent of the population. That 1 per cent of the American population had more total net worth than the bottom 90 per cent.

By the close of the Republican era – though reports of the United States entering into sustained decline are exaggerated – the country's pre-eminence was clearly being challenged. Two budding superpowers, Japan and a unifying Europe, are closing the economic gap, and the possibility that one of them could replace the United States at the top of the heap early in the next century is real. The American share of the world's GDP has declined 15 per cent since 1950 and will drop, experts predict, another 5 per cent through the 1990s. The national debt, resulting mainly from fantastic military overspending – "deterrence," said Bob McNamara, could have been maintained at a mere "fraction" of the cost – is crippling recovery potential. Militarily, though more dominant than ever, the Americans have lost their distinction as leaders of the free world.

Morally, the Reagan years have been exposed as a junk-bond

fraud. Culturally, genuine art was increasingly overshadowed by shallow, commercialized TV pulp. To the novelist Norman Mailer, it was the country's most depressing time. "There is a gloom commencing," he said. "It's become an ugly country. It used to have a kind of funky charm in the small towns, and now there's just the bypass and the mall. People are loutish. They used to have at least a certain respect for culture. Now the kids don't want any of it."

Rather than alleviate the many well-known American problems, the Reagan-Bush years served to exacerbate them. More than 35 million Americans lived below the poverty line. In the richest nation in the world, child poverty was the worst of any industrialized economy. The country's level of violence easily surpassed that of any other OECD country. Half of Reagan's own shining city on the hill, Washington, D.C., was a hell pit of drugs, poverty, and violence. In spite of all its money and power, the United States was unable to start to address the screaming blight in its own capital city. More people were killed in Washington in 1989 than in Israel's occupied territories or in Northern Ireland. The level of violence, 484 homicides in 1990, was worse, reports said, than in Saddam Hussein's Baghdad. At high schools metal detectors were used to screen students for handguns.

As grave as the maladies were, it was folly to read too much into them or into the lengthy economic slump of the early 1990s. For all its problems, the United States was still the world's largest economy, still a world leader in productivity, still the world leader in military might, still the world leader in advanced centres of learning, and still the magnet for those in every corner of the world whose dreams were big. If Canada had to be assimilated by another country, it could do far worse than have the United States in the role of assimilator. No less an opponent of Mulroney's Americanization than Trudeau's lieutenant Michael Pitfield closed a discussion on the integration of the continent with a tribute to the American way. "It's still a wonderful country, isn't it?" he said, dismissing reports of long-term decline. "Still prosperous and free." As the Mulroney government surrendered Canada's social contract, Pitfield ventured that maybe Canadians could find a way to become one with the United States.

His comments reflected the Canadian predicament. As much as Canadians preferred their own country, the United States was not so odious as to provoke fierce and enduring opposition. America had too much to offer that was good. An abrupt and complete convergence with the United States would not be tolerated by the majority of Canadians, but a continued, gradual slide, a quiet, steady integration, a bleeding away of Canadian nationalism, was quite possible. It had been taking place on many fronts since the signing of the free trade agreement. That formal event allowed opposition to find focus and take on a sharp edge, though not sharp enough to defeat the agreement. However, there was no such degree of opposition to the more subtle shift toward continentalism that followed.

There was the hope that Canada could cream off much of the best of the American way and leave the worst behind. But it was with telling irony that just as Americans began looking to Canada's admired national health care system for inspiration, the Mulroney Tories, in furthering their American agenda, were de-nationalizing their prized system by off-loading responsibilities for its financing to the provinces.

The American market-driven health care system spent $2,600 per person, yet left more than thirty million Americans without coverage and countless millions more with only minimal protection. Canada's socialized system spent $700 less per person, covered everyone, and was generally considered far superior. Senator Edward Kennedy, who looked longingly at the Canadian example, had been trying since the 1970s to pass similar medicare legislation. In 1989, when Bush's Republican candidate lost a Senate race in Pennsylvania to a Democrat espousing a new medicare system, even the Grand Old Party began looking north. Bush eventually backed off, but contenders for the Democratic nomination for president drew up government-sponsored plans, many along the lines of the Canadian model. Bill Clinton scored points against Bush in the election campaign by advocating a larger role for government in national health care.

In Canada the Tories had begun serious tampering with the social security system. Michael Wilson diminished the government role in medicare, as he had in culture and in other social programs, by employing a crafty, stealth offensive. On the big canvas everything was made to appear proper. In its trade agreements the government stuck to its promise: cultural and social protections were not bargained away. But in the back rooms, technical amendments to taxes and programs – details hard for the non-professional to understand – got the job done.

On medicare, Wilson made quiet cuts and froze federal transfer payments to provinces. If there was ever a subtle way of slipping something big under the door it was by this, the transfer payment route. The public yawned at the very phrase. No one wanted to know the details. Traditionally, Ottawa doled out money to the provinces to cover medicare and enforced national medicare standards by withholding cash from any province that didn't measure up. Now the federal Tories were planning to shift all the funding authority to the provinces, opting out of responsibility altogether and reserving no power for the federal government to enforce national standards. Under their plan, individual provinces strapped for cash would be in a position to start charging user fees without having to answer to Ottawa. The urge to be competitive with bordering American states would add another strong incentive for ending full coverage. The Canadian Medical Association cried that Wilson was "financially strangling medicare." Few got the message.

Before any province could get around to it, the federal government was providing its own example of how medical prices could be harmonized with those in America. With its legislation extending the protection of brand-name drugs produced by the multinationals over home-made, cheaper duplicates, a rise in Canadian prices was assured.

The Conservatives, whose election campaigns were well-funded by the multinationals, made the case that the pharmaceutical companies' plans to do more research in Canada made the legislation worthwhile. Nationalists countered that the costs to the consumer, which would total an estimated $5 billion over the next fifteen years, would hardly be compensated for by the results of more research.

The government also argued that they were only bringing Canada's system into line with the United States and other GATT countries. "In other words," a Canadian commentator wrote in summing up the Tory position, "because we've devised a better system that means less cost for the consumer, we've got to move to a system that's inferior."[2]

In the United States, Bill Clinton's enthusiasm for a better social contract for Americans is demonstrated in his eagerness to bring in a new medical insurance system. This is a president out to empower those ignored or forgotten by the ruling class in the trickle-down decade. The perceived failure of the Republican strategy, along with, more importantly, the passing of Communism, is presenting opportunities for new thinking in his country that have not existed since the 1960s.

For almost half a century, anti-Communism had bonded America politically, morally, and in good measure economically. Out of anti-Communism could come superpatriotism, the Reagan pieties that even intelligent people accepted, and a strong fear of liberalism. With Communism's disappearance can come the reverse – the possibility of a broadening of the American mind beyond conservative orthodoxy. Opening up gradually in the 1990s is a chamber of American politics long held shut by the presence of the Communist demon: the left side of the political spectrum. In the 1990s the pressure from the thought police is waning. No longer will anyone to the left of Ted Kennedy have their credibility erased simply by the incantation of the phrase, "soft on Communism."

The Republican decade witnessed a remarkable triumph of the old 1950s American chauvinism. Those who didn't abide the chauvinism were stamped incorrect and unpatriotic. Attention spans, so shortened from decades of TV conditioning, were catered to with the basest inanity. Reagan's jingoistic juggernaut gathered such momentum that George Bush could make the pledge of allegiance to the American flag a foremost issue in the presidential campaign of 1988. The trend led *Time* magazine to assert in 1992 that the American right had enjoyed "a complete, almost unopposed success" in labelling as left wing anything which "in a saner polity would be seen as ideologically neutral." The choice in America had narrowed to less than half a political spectrum – a choice between moderately right Democrats and pure right Republicans.

But if it was accurate, as some argued, that the long decades of Communism had the effect of moving the American polity to the right, the disappearance of Communism could well shift that polity back toward the moderate centre. The United States could come into closer alignment with a traditionally more centre-left Canada.

Clinton is open-minded enough to understand the possibilities that the post cold-war era offers. The tragedy of George Bush lay in his failure to grasp the opportunity that history presented to him. The United States spent roughly $200 billion annually, more than half of its defence and intelligence budget, to meet the Soviet threat. As that threat disappeared, Bush was suddenly given manna from heaven, billions upon billions of dollars to heal his crumbling domestic infrastructure – the inner cities, schools, the health system. Caution advised against too radical a transfer of resources. A 50 per cent cut in defence spending, as advocated by some Democrats, would bring mass unemployment in the defence industry. Bush, his mind locked in times past, wouldn't tolerate 5 per cent, much less 50 per cent. He continued to post gigantic military budgets, with recommended cuts of 4 per cent – a pittance in the context of the great sea change that had occurred. And even though virtually every LeCarré spy novel was now old hat, Bush kept the $30 billion CIA budget intact. It was the continuance of history. It was cold war spending without the cold war, and it opened the door for Bill Clinton and the Democratic Party.

But from Bush's northern flank, the applause kept coming, right up until the president's last days in office. The president spent his last weekend at Camp David, and it was fitting that he invited Brian Mulroney and his family to spend it with him. The Canadian prime minister came in from Palm Beach, Florida, where he was vacationing. His daughter came from college at Harvard in Massachusetts, and a son from the secondary school he attends, Hotchkiss, in Connecticut.

Bush had been bombing Iraq in his last days in office, because even though it had been bombed silly in the Gulf War, and even though it was on its knees, weak and defenceless, it was violating some United Nations resolutions of no great consequence. To no one's surprise, Mulroney was gung-ho in his support of the new attacks on Baghdad – actions that were forcing the hand of an incoming president and that, as even Bush's defence secretary acknowledged, could have easily been pushed back to another time. Mulroney had supported almost every American military adventure in the Bush years, and he wasn't about to change now. Saying no to the White House for Mulroney was tough. Saying no to the White House when one of his close friends was in the Oval Office was near impossible. For all intents and purposes, independence on Canadian foreign policy had been surrendered. While the unprecedented intimacy with Bush gave Mulroney potentially more input on the great multilateral questions of the day than any other PM, it was, in fact, input primarily of the cheerleading variety. Great relations with a president are not difficult to attain if the head of state seeking such relations offers agreement with almost everything the president says.

The prime minister shared some poignant moments with his friend at Camp David and praised Bush as a visionary. The signal sent to the incoming Democratic persident by a Canadian prime minister so tight with an outgoing Republican that he spent his last weekend with him could not have been propitious. Though Mulroney said he expected to have great relations with Clinton, he was hardly laying the most favourable of foundations. While some saw similarities between the new president and the prime minister, Mulroney was too far to the right of Clinton for there to be much compatibility.

The new president cannot be categorized as a liberal. His youth and enlightenment are infused with an establishment savvy and conservatism that serve to limit his daring. He is a new-generation president, the first president to be born after the end of World War II. But the chances of a new-generation fever sweeping the United States were narrowed when, for his two key cabinet posts of Treasury and State, Clinton chose aging establishment figures, Lloyd Bentsen in his seventies, and Warren Christopher in his sixties. A conservative Democrat was appointed to run the CIA, and ruling class veterans took control of other senior portfolios; though in the social policy area, liberals were given more space. The new president has yet to show willingness to address a large part of his country's crippling crime and violence problem – the catastrophic American infatuation with handguns. On the economy, signs of a turnaround have robbed him of the sense of urgency necessary for a domestic mandate for radical change.

Nevertheless, Bill Clinton's progressiveness stands out in contrast to what has come before, and it is a progressiveness that could serve Canada's interests well. Clinton is the most well-informed American president in modern history. He is steeped in knowledge of the economy and of social issues, and is secure enough in that knowledge to make decisions on his own. His economic thinking has been developed with the assistance of Robert Reich, a Clinton friend since school days who taught at Harvard and who has been appointed Clinton's secretary of labor. Author of *The Work of Nations*, Reich is a leader among American economists in his understanding of the globalization phenomenon.[3] He is one of only a small number who publicly advocate counter-measures to globalization. To bring some order to the cowboy capitalism in international markets, he wants a curtailment of the power of transnational corporations by means of a new type of GATT organization – a general agreement on direct investment setting out rules by which nations could bid for investments.

Reich recognizes the rapidity with which ever-diminishing tariffs and the technological and communications revolutions are stripping national governments of their economic power. The effect of globalization on home economies has been to create great fissures in traditional employment patterns that, in turn, create a need for greater government activism. Clinton understands the phenomenon. Much like his boyhood idol, John Kennedy, Clinton believes deeply in government, in the power of the public sector to do good. He has less reverence for the idea of the primacy of the market, and his eagerness to end trickle-down economics could serve to lessen the influence of corporations over the public policy agenda. His trade policy shows signs of being more sensitive to national interests.

Unlike Reagan, Clinton has no great continental vision. He brings to office no preconceived notions on Canada. The lack of a past affiliation is important because history has shown that presidents who have sought intimate relations with Canada were those who came to office knowing the country. Taft, who vacationed frequently in Quebec, pushed for free trade. Franklin Roosevelt, who had a cottage in New Brunswick, sewed seeds of integration with Mackenzie King. On the other hand, presidents like Richard Nixon, who had no interest in Canada nor any background connection, allowed for more distance in the relationship.

Without a prescribed continental agenda, with a more leery eye on globalization, and with more liberal, nationalist impulses, Clinton could well oversee a revival of a modest nationalism that would slow the advances of continentalism and serve Canada's national interests.

But so much of the conservative agenda has been put in place during the 1980s that to attempt a reversal would be, as Marc Lalonde noted, like "trying to unscramble the eggs."[4] The new north-south trade flows have been sealed in treaties, which Clinton is not intent on undoing. Integration has been given an unprecedented spur, and while a liberal resurgence on both sides of the border could slow it, the further folding of Canada into the United States likely awaits only the appearance of the next Bay-Street dominated government to come along.

20

From the Just Society to the American Society

Canada's embassy in Washington, a new structure of concrete, glass, and big empty spaces with the occasional splash of post-modern adornment, is white, brilliantly white in the sun, and is in the pick of embassy locations. It is situated on Pennsylvania Avenue between the White House and the gargantuan Congress building, from where, on a clear day, the elected representatives might see a beating, a car-hijack, or a routine handgun skirmish.

The embassy was a popular spot in the Bush years, one to which senators and congressmen and the president himself came as guests of Ambassador Derek Burney. The only awkward moment came when these members of the ruling class were confronted with their destitute opposites, the permanent underclass, in front of the embassy. A sewer grate is located there, and on cold days the poor huddle on it, seeking comfort from the one fine thing about sewer grates – the rush of warm air they emit.

The embassy grate served as a reminder to the Canadian ambassador and diplomats of where they were. One day in 1992, as the grate below him filled to near capacity, and the sun beamed through the glass walls of Burney's white, hi-tech office, the ambassador explained that the grate people were one reason why he'd never felt more distinct as a Canadian than during the three years he had spent in Washington. "I think part of the reason they have people sleeping on sewer grates is that they don't have a decent health-care system. I think it's a travesty for this country not to have a health-care system."

He went on. "I think we are a kinder, gentler America, and I'd like to keep it that way. I think we're closer to our environment, we have a better sense of community. . . . I don't think we have to let our infrastructure go to rot in the cities the way the Americans have. I think we are a better society racially."[1]

This same Burney had spent much of the 1980s pushing Canada into the gut of the American economic system. A forceful advocate of the right-wing agenda, he had interrupted a PMO meeting years earlier, shouting, "Jesus Christ! I'm the only real conservative in here!"

No contradiction struck him now as he sang the praises of Canada's differences. Pursuing a continentalist agenda didn't mean becoming more like the Americans. "Jesus, continentalist? I'm sorry, it isn't a negative." It was only, he said, geographic logic. One of his diplomats, citing the irrelevance of the British link, was more concise. "Canadians are big-sky people," he said, "and it's about time they faced up to it."

Burney was troubled, however, by something that was also giving pause to many of the architects of Canada's turn toward America. Continentalism was fine so long as you bolstered your own end, so long as there was a nation-building thrust at home to maintain the integrity of the country. That wasn't happening in Canada. What was absent was a policy of "national development," Burney said. "Transportation, training, culture, communications, something! This government has to have an agenda!" But instead they were "haggling over constitutional clauses which Canadians don't give a damn about."

Burney's criticism of his friend Mulroney was mild compared to that of other central figures who had championed free trade.

By 1992 it wasn't only "the looney left, the crypto-commie con group," as some Tories would have it, who were expressing doubts about the pledge of allegiance to the United States. It was high Tories themselves and the authors of free trade. Like Burney, they remained supportive of the free trade agreement itself. But, at the same time, they believed that the policy had to be counterbalanced by national affirmation at home. Instead, Mulroney and Wilson had crowned free trade with great doses of deregulation and privatization and a stripping of national institutions: a selling off of the family silverware.

Allan Gotlieb was now arguing that what was important for Canada were "powers of control, and control of the economic levers. A national policy. A national power." Peter White was pushing cultural nationalism. Donald Macdonald was distressed that the government had swung so far to the right that it had ignored his recommendations for social legislation to help those crushed by the free trade bulldozer. There was no social deal to match the commercial deal. Charlie McMillan was worried that the government had put all Canada's eggs in one basket. And Gordon Ritchie simply hadn't bargained for the day when Mulroney and Wilson would turn the country over to the agenda of continental corporations.

After negotiating the free trade agreement, Ritchie had hooked up with an unlikely figure, Mitchell Sharp. The second-option man and the third-option man were close partners in an Ottawa consulting firm. Ritchie, a large figure with thinning light hair and pinkish complexion, had a studious demeanour and it so contrasted with his old trade-team leader, the volcanic Reisman, that an American official referred to them as Buddha and the Beast. Sharp was now in his eighties, but strong of body and steady of mind. He had worked as deputy to C. D. Howe in the 1950s and respected him, never subscribing to the fashionable image of the man as one who sold out in Canada. There was no similarity between Howe and Mulroney, Sharp said. Compared to Mulroney, C. D. Howe was a Canadian nationalist.

The degree to which the Tories were trying to alter the country astonished Sharp. He had negotiated a West Coast fishing treaty for Mulroney in the PM's first term and found him "a very curious fellow, just so anxious to please." Why then, the old Grit wondered, had he tried to turn a great country upside down. "You know," Sharp said slowly, "I don't like to speak ill of anyone, but...." He stood in Ritchie's office as rain and darkness descended on Ottawa. "Yes, yes," he chuckled, "it's the second option."[2] In 1972, when he wrote the three options paper for Pierre Trudeau, he hadn't been able to find one supporter for the American option. Now it was the only game in town. Sharp shook his head and moved away, leaving behind his colleague, the free trade negotiator.

Ritchie, whose intellect is formidable, still liked the pact he had negotiated, but the indignation in his voice grew as he listed what he didn't like. Free trade was not supposed to mean the triumph of the market and corporate power on the continent. It was not supposed to come with the "parallel dismantling of government institutions," and the turning over of powers to the provinces. If Ottawa left the country to the north-south flows of the market, Ritchie reasoned, there would soon be no country. The trouble, he said, was that Wilson and Mulroney didn't understand the need for a national policy.

Conservative governors held that, in times of great debt, nationalism could not be afforded. Canada-firsters countered that nationalism didn't cost money: that legislation protecting national institutions didn't cost money; that bills giving wider access to the Canadian market for Canadian films, music, and books didn't cost money; that an investment policy to protect resources didn't cost money. Culture buffs lamented that if culture was to be the nation's CPR of the twenty-first century and bind the nation together, why couldn't culture get one fraction of the support that agriculture got?

While the Tories put the case with some persuasion that debt, the decline of the resource economy, and the new global economy required a move away from the old, protectionist Canada, compromise approaches had been possible. One was advocated by MP Paul Martin in his unsuccessful campaign for the Liberal leadership. What the country needed, said Martin, was "nationalism without walls." The catch phrase suggested an equal balance of the two goals of keeping up with the fury of globalization while strengthening the Canadian fabric at home.

But Mulroney was preoccupied with the problem of a distinct society for Quebec and unconcerned about English Canada's distinct-society problem with the United States. He was consumed by day-to-day politics, not by the big picture. As unpopularity engulfed him, he gradually became isolated, more reliant on close friends whom he could trust. These friends lacked a sophisticated understanding of the country in the context of its history and the shifting world dynamic. "He was trying to juggle very conflicting and very difficult choices, and he didn't get much help," said Charlie McMillan. "The bureaucracy didn't know how to cope with the conflicting policy instruments and the Privy Council was useless. So it was left to individuals, friends he had trusted, to carry the ball, which is not the best of things."

In pursuing, with his friends, policies of no-nationalism, no-walls, Mulroney moved a long way toward making the country a creature of the provinces and of the United States. The government was living up to conservative historian Donald Creighton's worst fears. "Continentalism is merely the upper millstone," wrote Creighton in 1971. "The lower millstone, parochialism or provincialism is its complement; and it is the attrition by these two powerful forces that has ground down the solid fabric of Canadian nationalism."[3] His soulmate, the eminent senator-philosopher Eugene Forsey, had been appalled when Joe Clark unveiled his vision of Canada as a community of communities. "If the province worshippers have their way, there will be no real Canada, just a boneless wonder. They would make us again a group of colonies, American colonies this time, with a life 'poor, nasty, brutish and short.'"

Canada's integration with the United States had proceeded on a path of inevitability. And if it was inevitable, the Conservatives could well say they were only recognizing that fact and getting on with it. If assimilation was the historic inevitability, however, Canadians would probably have preferred the slowest route possible, not the fast track. It was still well within the power of the government either to slow down the pace of amalgamation or to accelerate it with the many instruments of nation-building – Crown corporations, investment screening agencies, national institutions, east-west transportation systems, cultural agencies, resource policy, and others. The option was whether to sustain the elements of nationalism and build on them or to dismantle them.

In dismantling them, Canada was made over in America's image during the Mulroney years in ways that made past chapters of Americanization pale by comparison. To count just some of the ways was to understand how the government had changed the country. The free trade agreement broke with history in sealing Canada's bond with America. Trade declined with the rest of the world. Investment was further continentalized through the abolition of the Foreign Investment Review Agency. Canada's energy resources were opened to continental bidders with the tearing down of the National Energy Program. Tax reform was fashioned on the American model. Banking was continentalized. Crown corporations were sold off to the private market in record number. Support for national institutions, the broadcast system, and the rail system, was cut back. National science, economic, and security institutes were killed off. As the U.S. deregulation bug swept Ottawa, corporations were coddled. Government support of Canadian culture dwindled. Ottawa buckled under American pressure on the issue of film distribution. It buckled under pressure on the issue of drug patents. As once demanded by American Ambassador Paul

Robinson, social spending was reduced. Universality, one of Canada's major distinguishing features, was ended. A more hawkish American-style foreign policy was instituted. Canada joined the Organization of American States. Canadian businesses headed south in record number. Cross-border economic zones containing American states and Canadian provinces were developed. In the small-government tradition of the Republican party, Ottawa underwent unprecedented decentralization. Mulroney established the closest relations ever between a president and prime minister.

Nationalism, which suffered its most shattering defeat in the Mulroney years, is not the ideal. Unbridled nationalism, to be sure, is history's war siren. But Canada and the United States are hardly neighbours who are about to take up arms. On some far off day, when nation states are set to join in one beneficent world government, Canada can take its place. But that day is a long way off, and until that time Canada has values and differences worth protecting. Dog-eat-dog capitalism is not one of them.

A new Canadian government will likely take power almost five years after free trade's implementation. By then many Canadian companies will have retooled and rebuilt to meet continental standards. Going back would cause disruption for them, and disruption in Canada-U.S. relations. If the Liberals were to win the election, one side of the party would probably argue that abrogating the pact would be the single most important declaration of sovereignty Canada could make. It would argue that Americans would still buy Canada's products as they had – in fantastic volume – for 120 years before free trade, and that the continuing GATT process would ensure access to American and world markets. Life would go on, just as it did after the failure of another agreement whose defeat was supposed to be fatal to Canada – the Charlottetown accord. The other side of the party would make the case that abrogation would be inward-looking, protectionist, and disruptive. Under enormous pressure from Bay Street which would proclaim, like Paul Reichmann, that Canada would go under unless it followed the American way, the Liberals, unsuccessful in a bid to amend the agreement, would likely keep it intact.

Many in the Liberal Party have succumbed to the new wisdom of the 1980s – that protectionism is poison. "Protectionism" had become the new bad word, the new bogeyman. It was the candidate successor to "pinko." Anyone in Canada who wanted to insulate against the ravages of the marketplace was deemed myopic, leftist. Canada was the most foreign-penetrated and foreign-owned advanced industrial nation. Canada was the most decentralized federation in the world, except for Switzerland. It was one of the world's most open trading nations. These realities mocked the use of the word "protectionist" in the Canadian context.

But it was easy to get caught up in the rhetoric, and Canada from 1984 to 1992 was caught up in the British-American cant. Canada saw the world largely through the prism of the two countries that had always dominated it. And so the British-American rhetoric of the 1980s – the market and the anti-protectionist and the trade-means-everything cant – became the Canadian cant.

Author-philosopher John Ralston Saul used the metaphor of a guerilla force against the armies of an empire to describe the wrong turn taken by Canada. The small nations were the guerilla forces and global competitiveness was a ruse of the big nations to lure them out onto the open field of battle. Therein lay Canada's folly. "Only a fool comes out to fight on the empire's terms," said Ralston Saul. Others, like the Japanese, were not interested in trying out old-fashioned theories of unregulated competition. "They believe Americans are declining into a 19th century *laissez-faire* economy which needs a downward competitive spiral in order to succeed. . . . They think we are fools for being sucked into an outdated ideology of instability."[4]

*   *   *

As 1993 began there were signs that the years of neoconservatism on the continent are drawing to a close. The election of Democrats in Washington and, if polls hold true to form, Liberals in Ottawa, holds promise of a restoration of a measure of regulation and nationalism on each side of the border. Canadians, like Americans, want their tattered social contract redrawn.

Other forces are at work. For each measure of economic integration in the global village, there is an equal measure of political disintegration as ethnic nationalism sweeps the former east bloc. Europe is taking a long hard look at its economic union plan. If the plan fails it could have repercussions elsewhere.

Canadians have rejected a new Constitution. On one hand, the failure of the Charlottetown accord could eventually widen the cracks in the federation and enhance the prospect of yet further north-south bonding. But on the other hand, its defeat was a victory for nationalism. The agreement would have secured an unprecedented decentralization of the country – a victory for Joe Clark's community of communities vision. It would have been another boost to the continental market and a further reduction of central authority already so weakened in the Mulroney years.

The message of the great constitutional debate – one which, polls told the government, Canadians never wanted – was that Canada did not wish to make a radical break with tradition; that there were things in the country – a country the United Nations had rated the best in the world in which to live – that were worth preserving. These things included compassionate government, the social contract, and the traditional distance from the American way.

These lessons were not apparent to a government that had swung so far to the economic right of the Canadian mainstream that it had become a stranger to its own support base. When Jean Chrétien stood in the House of Commons and told the prime minister that "it is very nice to be on the side of the wealthy multinationals, but we have to care about the little people of Canada," the best Mulroney could do was to respond: "That was not what he was saying when he was on the board of directors of the Toronto-Dominion Bank."

In the same month, December 1992, after bringing in his stay-the-course mini-budget, one which reduced foreign aid by 20 per cent while maintaining military spending on cold war weaponry, Mulroney journeyed to Boston to speak to the John F. Kennedy School of Government at Harvard. He sought to defend his American policy by attacking those who confuse co-operation with subservience. He felt it necessary to highlight areas where Canada had disagreed with the United States, going so far as to note Ottawa's differences compared to Washington's environmental stance at the Earth Summit in Rio – a summit where virtually every participant had taken exception to Bush's approach.

To be sure, co-operation, as the prime minister said, did not necessarily mean subservience. But his foreign-policy coziness with Washington represented only part of his American option, a strategy of convergence which sought to move Canada into the American embrace in ways economic and philosophical, moral, and cultural. Far more than co-operation with a friend, it was an importation of and a commitment to the American way.

In the final analysis, Mulroney and his disciples had failed to understand a central Canadian paradox: that while the maximization of prosperity arguably required intimate economic relations with the United States, the survival of Canada required distance. The challenge of leadership was to balance the two scales.

Nationalists had to recognize that previous attempts at creating a third option for Canada had failed. Continentalists had to recognize that the second option, the American option, meant continued assimilation. Hope for the country lay in striking a balance between the two options in a "nationalism without walls." Canada needed a strong central government, strong national institutions, a rebuilt east-west infrastructure – elements that glued the country together. It had to somehow perform the magic of protecting what it had without being protectionist. While there were world currents from which it would be foolish and in any case impossible to hide, Canada needed a leader who could sometimes say no to the corporate agenda.

The cold war's end freed Canada from decades-old obligations and opened roads which could perhaps lead to a loosening of the continental grip. Far more likely, however, given the newly-secured continental harmonization and the border-eroding ravages of globalization, was a continued flight of the country into the American destiny. Regardless of what happened in Quebec, the prospect that the children of baby boomers would live their lives with the U.S.-Canadian border intact was slight. The Mulroney years were not just a temporary aberration in which a course was steered that could be readily altered; they were years in which the course had been firmly set by landmark treaties. These treaties, endorsed by Bay Street, would be enormously difficult to escape. Political parties needed Bay Street, and Bay Street was not interested in nationalism but in profits – and profits increasingly lay beyond the border.

Through Canadian history, the march of integration and continentalism had never been reversed. It had been contained, checked, but only until the next irresistible rush forward. The rushes had taken Canada to an 80 per cent economic dependency on the United States and a cultural engulfment of equally egregious magnitude. Among the side effects of this had been the breeding of border-boy politicians whose mindsets were but American attenuations, and who, in the years from 1984 to 1992, closed down the Canadian dream of building something unique and better. They were the years when, instead of attempting to contain the American influence, Canada avidly sought out that influence. They were the years when national policy was abandoned, when the goal of the Just Society was forsaken in favour of that of the American Society.

The broad sweep of changes, as explained by John Crosbie, had to be seen in the context of a Canada without other choices. They had to be seen in the context of an eventual economic union with the United States that was as inevitable as night follows day. This union, Crosbie knew, could well go beyond the economic. "We may have gone a lot further [toward amalgamation] than we realize." He sensed no great yearning among average Canadians for political union. "But you don't know. This thing may bubble along below the surface. Then it just happens."[5]

Whatever the case, John Crosbie was sure of one thing. The head of the Crosbie clan, Chesley, would be smiling down from the heavens at all the progress made. Asked how his father, the annexationist, would assess the Mulroney years, son John paused for a second's reflection. "I think," he said, the big, unread free trade volume peering from the shelf behind him, "that my father would have thought his policies were the right approach."

Notes

1.

1. From Burt memorandum, September 21, 1984. Obtained through application under U.S. freedom of information laws.
2. Author interview with Carroll Brown, who headed the Canada desk at the State Department.
3. Author interview with Tyrus Cobb, who served on the National Security Council.
4. Article by Lou Cannon of the *Washington Post*. Reprinted in the *Ottawa Citizen*, April 28, 1991.
5. Author interview with Ed Ritchie for *The Presidents and the Prime Ministers* (Toronto: Doubleday, 1982).
6. Description of scene at NSC meeting is primarily from author interview with Tyrus Cobb.

2.

1. Author interviews with Tyrus Cobb and Carroll Brown and with External Affairs official. The Prime Minister's Office declined to release a summary transcript of the prime minister's intervention.
2. Author interview with Myer Rashish, undersecretary of state for economic affairs in the Reagan administration. Rashish helped Reagan develop the accord proposal.

3. The Manifest Destiny doctrine as defined in 1844 by John O'Sullivan, editor of the *Democratic Review*.
4. Author interview with Joe Joeckel.
5. Author interview with Tyrus Cobb.

3.

1. John Sawatsky, *Mulroney: The Politics of Ambition* (Toronto: Macfarlane, Walter and Ross, 1991). This excellent account of Mulroney's rise to power is a particularly valuable source for the period Mulroney spent as head of the Iron Ore Company of Canada.
2. This anecdote has long made the rounds, most recently in Sawatsky's biography.
3. Author interviews with J. Duncan Edmonds.
4. Author interview with Sam Wakim.
5. Sawatsky, *Mulroney: The Politics of Ambition. Op. cit.*
6. Robert Bothwell and William Kilbourn, *C. D. Howe: A Biography* (Toronto: McClelland & Stewart, 1979).
7. Author interviews with J. Duncan Edmonds.
8. From State Department memorandum written by Richard Burt, September 21, 1984, and from statements in other memoranda during the same period. Memoranda obtained under the U.S. freedom of information laws. Also from interview with Richard Burt.
9. Author interviews with Ken Taylor.
10. Mulroney quotes are from transcript of Mulroney conversation in 1976 with *The Globe and Mail*.
11. From conversation with former Mulroney press aide, Michel Gratton.

4.

1. Author interview with Charlotte Gobeil for Martin, *The Presidents and the Prime Ministers. Op. cit.*
2. Author interview with Mitchell Sharp.
3. Author interview with John Halstead.

4. The summer student anecdote appears as recalled by John Black-wood in interview with the author.

5. Author interview with John Halstead.

5.

1. George Grant, *Lament for a Nation* (Toronto: McClelland & Stewart, 1965).

2. Bruce Hutchison, *The Struggle for the Border* (Don Mills: Longman Canada, 1955).

3. Memorandum to Lyndon Johnson from McGeorge Bundy, May 1, 1964.

4. Peter C. Newman, *The Distemper of Our Times* (Toronto: McClelland & Stewart, 1968).

5. Stephen Clarkson, *Canada and the Reagan Challenge* (Toronto: James Lorimer, 1982).

6. The American diplomat who wrote the Maginot Line memorandum requested anonymity.

7. Author interview with Marc Lalonde.

8. Author interview with Michael Pitfield.

9. *Ibid.*

6.

1. Scenes from Thunder Bay recounted by author who was reporting on the leadership campaign for *The Globe and Mail*.

2. Author interview with J. Duncan Edmonds.

3. Author interiew with John Crosbie.

4. Author interview with Michael Hart.

5. All quotes from Derek Burney in this chapter are from author interview in 1992 when, as ambassador to Washington, he reflected on his career.

6. Author interview with Michael Hart.

7. Author interview with Ed Lumley.

8. Author interview with Gerry Regan.

9. Author interview with Lloyd Axworthy.

7.

1. Description of PMO scene from interview with Derek Burney.
2. All Mel Clark quotes from author interview.
3. Author interview with Tyrus Cobb.
4. Memos and briefing papers quoted were obtained, after 18 months' wait, under U.S. freedom of information laws. Portions of some memoranda were excised for national security reasons.
5. Author interview with Charlie McMillan.
6. All Jim Kelleher quotes from author interview.
7. Author interview with Douglas Roche.
8. Author interview with David Crombie.
9. Author interview with Flora MacDonald.
10. Author interview with David Crombie.

8.

1. Author interview with Ken Taylor.
2. Author interview with John Blackwood.
3. Author interview with Charlie McMillan.
4. Author interview with Ed Lumley.
5. Author interview with Donald Macdonald.
6. Moffett's thesis is on file in Canadian libraries.
7. The historical perspective in these pages is primarily from the Joanne Goodman Lectures of 1988 by Jack Granatstein. The lectures were titled, "How Britain's Weakness Forced Canada into the Arms of the United States."
8. Author interview with Peter White.
9. Memoranda obtained through U.S. freedom of information laws.
10. Author interview with Bill Merkin.
11. Author interview with Tyrus Cobb.
12. Author interview with Joe Joeckel.
13. Michael Gratton, *So What Are the Boys Saying?* (Toronto: McGraw-Hill Ryerson, 1987).
14. *Ibid.*

9.

1. Author interview with Jim Kelleher.
2. Author interview with William Harris.
3. From profile in *Saturday Night* magazine, March 1986, by Rod McQueen.
4. Author interview with J. Duncan Edmonds.
5. Author interview with Jim Gillies.
6. Author interview with Ed Lumley.
7. Many of the main thoughts in the document were prepared by the deputy minister of finance, Mickey Cohen, in the months preceding Mulroney's election.
8. Author interview with Flora MacDonald. Ms. MacDonald remains convinced that the pension ruckus was a key determinant in moving the Mulroney team, which frequently moved along on ad hoc basis, to embrace free trade.
9. All quotes from d'Aquino in this chapter are from author interviews.
10. Author interview with Dalton Camp.
11. From G. Bruce Doern and Brian W. Tomlin, *Faith and Fear* (Toronto: Stoddart Publishing, 1991).
12. Author interviews with Mel Clark.
13. Author interview with John Halstead.
14. Author interview with J. Duncan Edmonds.

10.

1. All Derek Burney quotes from author interview.
2. Author interview with John Crosbie.
3. Author interview with Myer Rashish.
4. Author interview with Charlie McMillan.
5. Author interview with Frank Carlucci.
6. Author interview with Tyrus Cobb.
7. Author interview with Carroll Brown.
8. Author interview with Tyrus Cobb.

11.

1. Author interview with Joel Garreau.
2. George Sanderson and Frank Macdonald, *Marshall McLuhan: The Man and His Message* (Golden, Colorado: Fulcrum, 1989).
3. Author interview with Gordon Ritchie.
4. Author interview with Stephen Blank.
5. All Tom d'Aquino quotes from author interview.
6. A detailed account of how U.S. pressure was brought to bear on the Canadian government to change its legislation governing drug patents can be found in Linda McQuaig's *The Quick and the Dead* (Toronto: Viking, 1991).
7. Author interview with Jim Kelleher.
8. Reisman anecdote as described by Bill Merkin in author interview. Baker anecdote which follows also as related by Merkin.
9. Author interview with Sinclair Stevens.

12.

1. Author interview with Edward Ney.
2. The *Ottawa Citizen*, October 29, 1992, p. 11.
3. Author interview with Jim Gillies.
4. Author interview with Charlie McMillan.
5. Author interview with Marc Lalonde.
6. Author interview with David McFadden.
7. Daniel Drache and Meric Gertler, *The New Era of Global Competition* (Montreal and Kingston: McGill-Queen's University Press, 1991).
8. Mel Hurtig, The Ware Lecture, June 28, 1992, Calgary.
9. Author interview with Derek Burney.
10. Martin, *The Presidents and the Prime Ministers. Op. cit.*
11. Author interview with Lloyd Axworthy.
12. David Halberstam, *The Best and the Brightest* (New York: Random House, 1972).
13. As told by Lloyd Axworthy in author interview.
14. Author interview with John Crosbie.

13.

1. All briefing papers and memoranda cited in this chapter were obtained under U.S. freedom of information laws. The documents covered the weeks prior to President Bush's visit to Canada in February, 1989.
2. The American source for this story and the one following on Mulroney's advice to Bush on Mitterrand requested anonymity.
3. Martin, *The Presidents and the Prime Ministers. Op. cit.*
4. Author interview with Geoffrey Pearson.
5. Author interview with Sam Wakim.
6. Author interview with Doug Roche.
7. Author interview with Dalton Camp.
8. Interview by Hugh Winsor in *The Globe and Mail*, November 17, 1990.
9. Author interview with Paul Heinbecker.

14.

1. A detailed account of the Wilson-Masse dispute written by Val Ross was carried in *The Globe and Mail*, January 9, 1992.
2. The MacDonald encounter with Valenti as told by MacDonald in an interview with the author.
3. Film bill story is from author interviews and an account by Stephen Godfrey in *The Globe and Mail*, March 28, 1992.
4. Author interview with Paul Audley.
5. The *Ottawa Citizen*, November 25, 1991. An article by Bernard Ostry.
6. William Thorsell, *The Globe and Mail*, November 25, 1991.
7. Author interview with Peter White.

15.

1. Author interview with Gordon Ritchie.
2. Author interview with Michael Pitfield, whose analysis heavily stressed the view that Mulroney's Conservatives were a government driven more by a rush for political favour than any ideological agenda.

3. D'Aquino made this statement in a recorded interview with the author. In a later conversation he suggested that the implication was not as it sounded.
4. Author interview with Mel Clark.
5. Author interview with Charlie McMillan.
6. Author interview with Edward Ney.
7. Author interview with Larry Taylor.
8. Martin, *The Presidents and the Prime Ministers. Op. cit.*
9. Author interview with David Conklin.
10. Author interview with Carl Beigie.
11. Author interview with Bob Rae.
12. Author interview with Peter Tomlinson.
13. Author interview with Joel Guberman.
14. Author interview with David Matthews.
15. Author interview with Donald Macdonald.

16.

1. Author interview with John Crosbie.
2. Author interview with David Crombie.
3. Author interview with Michael Adams.
4. Author interview with Larry Swanson.
5. Author interview with Susan Cribbs.
6. Author interview with Jerry Nagel.
7. Author interview with Peter Tomlinson.
8. Author interview with Peter Karl Kresl.
9. Author interview with Pierre Paul Proulx.

17.

1. Author interview with Michael Hart.
2. Author interview with Allan Gotlieb.
3. Author interview with Paul Heinbecker.
4. Author interview with Sylvia Ostry.
5. Author interviews with McMillan, Ostry, and Burney.
6. Author interview with Lloyd Axworthy.
7. Author interview with Bob Rae.

18.

1. The source who took part in the meeting requested that he remain anonymous.
2. Even Peter Cook, *The Globe and Mail*'s respected business columnist whose views were determinedly right wing, criticized Crow for going too far.
3. Author interview with Peter White.
4. Peter C. Newman, *Renegade in Power: The Diefenbaker Years* (Toronto: McClelland & Stewart, 1963).
5. Author interviews with Jim Gillies and John Crosbie.
6. Memoranda and briefing papers cited here were obtained through U.S. freedom of information laws. The briefing memoranda from the State Department to the president do not have a single name attached. They are from the work of Canada specialists at the State Department, as monitored by the secretary and his deputies.
7. Author interview with Charles Doran.
8. Author interview with Bill Merkin.
9. Author interview with Edward Ney.
10. Author interview with Myer Rashish.
11. Author interview with Ed Lumley.
12. Author interview with Tom d'Aquino.
13. Author interview with Gilles Paquet.

19.

1. Author interview with Charlie McMillan.
2. Allan Fotheringham, the *Ottawa Sun*, December 15, 1992.
3. Reich's thinking on how the global economy is withering away nation state borders is explained in his book, *The Work of Nations* (New York: Alfred A. Knopf, 1991).
4. Author interview with Marc Lalonde.

20.

1. Author interview with Derek Burney.
2. Author interview with Mitchell Sharp.

3. Charles Taylor, *Radical Tories* (Toronto: Goodread Biographies, 1982).

4. John Ralston Saul, *Report on Business* magazine, *The Globe and Mail*, October 1992.

5. Author interview with John Crosbie.

Acknowledgements

The idea for *Pledge of Allegiance* sprang from my previous volume on Canada-U.S. relations, *The Presidents and the Prime Ministers*, which covered the relationship between the countries' leaders from 1867 to 1982. Brian Mulroney's ties to the presidents and other Americans struck me as deserving of book treatment because the United States has been a larger part of this government's thinking than of any other in our history.

I am grateful to all those who agreed to be interviewed and gave of their time. The majority agreed to "on the record" interviews, which was most helpful, and I am particularly thankful to those who have worked side by side with the prime minister and close to the president for being as candid as they were. Much of the book's content is the result of firsthand interviewing. I have also made use of memoranda, principally from the State Department, obtained under U.S. freedom of information laws. Researchers or authors who wish to use this procedure are in for a long wait. For relatively straightforward requests for this book, responses took a year and a half. Many are still outstanding. A decade earlier, on work for *The Presidents and the Prime Ministers*, the backlog was only a couple of months.

In the early stages of preparation I benefited nicely from research work done by Jim Rossiter, a bright young journalist from Newfoundland whose future is far more promising than that of his province. I am greatly indebted to Doug Gibson and Dinah Forbes at McClelland &

Stewart. They rightly advised patience when I was pushing to get the book out earlier. Our patience was rewarded in several ways, not the least of which was the arrival of State Department memoranda in time for the later publication date. Dinah Forbes gave excellent advice on early drafts of the manuscript, and there can't be many editors in the business who have a more exacting eye than Alex Schultz, who edited the final draft.

I am also thankful to those who read parts of the manuscript in advance and offered much-needed constructive criticism.

Index

Please remember that this is a library book,
and that it belongs only temporarily to each
person who uses it. Be considerate. Do
not write in this, or any, library book.